Contesting Europe's Eastern Rim

PEFC/16-33-111
CATG-PEFC-052
www.pefc.org

MULTILINGUAL MATTERS
Series Editor: John Edwards, *St. Francis Xavier University, Canada*

Multilingual Matters series publishes books on bilingualism, bilingual education, immersion education, second language learning, language policy, multiculturalism. The editor is particularly interested in 'macro' level studies of language policies, language maintenance, language shift, language revival and language planning. Books in the series discuss the relationship between language in a broad sense and larger cultural issues, particularly identity related ones.

Full details of all the books in this series and of all our other publications can be found on http://www.multilingual-matters.com, or by writing to Multilingual Matters, St Nicholas House, 31–34 High Street, Bristol BS1 2AW, UK.

MULTILINGUAL MATTERS
Series Editor: John Edwards, *St. Francis Xavier University, Canada*

Contesting Europe's Eastern Rim
Cultural Identities in Public Discourse

Edited by
Ljiljana Šarić, Andreas Musolff,
Stefan Manz and Ingrid Hudabiunigg

MULTILINGUAL MATTERS
Bristol • Buffalo • Toronto

Library of Congress Cataloging in Publication Data
Contesting Europe's Eastern Rim : Cultural Identities in Public
Discourse / Edited by Ljiljana Saric . . . [et al.].
Multilingual Matters: 143.
Includes bibliographical references.
1. Discourse analysis—Political aspects.   2. Nationalism.   3. Identity
(Psychology)   4. Ethnicity.   5. Europe, Eastern—Politics and
government—1989–   I. Saric, Ljiljana.
P302.77.C67 2010
401'.410947–dc22 2010041363

British Library Cataloguing in Publication Data
A catalogue entry for this book is available from the British Library.

ISBN-13: 978-1-84769-324-2 (hbk)

Multilingual Matters
UK: St Nicholas House, 31-34 High Street, Bristol BS1 2AW, UK.
USA: UTP, 2250 Military Road, Tonawanda, NY 14150, USA.
Canada: UTP, 5201 Dufferin Street, North York, Ontario M3H 5T8, Canada.

Copyright © 2010 Ljiljana Šarić, Andreas Musolff, Stefan Manz, Ingrid Hudabiunigg
and the authors of individual chapters.

All rights reserved. No part of this work may be reproduced in any form or by any
means without permission in writing from the publisher.

The policy of Multilingual Matters/Channel View Publications is to use papers that
are natural, renewable and recyclable products, made from wood grown in
sustainable forests. In the manufacturing process of our books, and to further support
our policy, preference is given to printers that have FSC and PEFC Chain of Custody
certification. The FSC and/or PEFC logos will appear on those books where full
certification has been granted to the printer concerned.

Typeset by Integra Software Services Pvt. Ltd, Pondicherry, India.
Printed and bound in Great Britain by the MPG Books Group Ltd

Contents

Contributors vii
Acknowledgements x
Introduction xi
Ljiljana Šarić, Stefan Manz, Andreas Musolff and Ingrid Hudabiunigg

Part I
1 Expellees, Counterfactualism and Potatoes. Enlargement and Cross-National Debates in German-Polish Relations
   Stefan Manz 1
2 The Role of Metaphor in Shaping Cultural Stereotypes: A Case Study of French Public Discourse on European Union Enlargement
   Steffen Buch and Uta Helfrich 16
3 Metaphors in German and Lithuanian Discourse Concerning the Expansion of the European Union
   Sandra Petraškaitė-Pabst 33

Part II
4 Domestic and Foreign Media Images of the Balkans
   Ljiljana Šarić 51
5 Naming Strategies and Neighboring Nations in the Croatian Media
   Dubravka Kuna and Branko Kuna 73
6 Mujahiddin in Our Midst: Bosnian Croats after the Wars of Succession
   Daphne Winland 90
7 Construction of Serbian and Montenegrin Identities through Layout and Photographs of Leading Politicians in Official Newspapers
   Tatjana Radanović Felberg 107
8 Krekism and the Construction of Slovenian National Identity: Newspaper Commentaries on Slovenia's European Union Integration
   Andreja Vezovnik 125
9 The Linguistic Image of the Balkans in the Polish Press in Discourse on European Union Expansion
   Paweł Bąk 143

10 The Eternal Outsider? Scenarios of Turkey's Ambitions to Join
    the European Union in the German Press
    Andreas Musolff 157

Part III

11 Contested Identities: Miroslav Krleža's Two Europes versus
    the Notion of Europe's Edge
    Ingrid Hudabiunigg 173
12 Masculinity and the New Sensibility: Reading a Contemporary
    Montenegrin Novel
    Biljana Jovanović Lauvstad 188
13 The Rhetoric of Present Absence: Representing Jewishness
    in Post-Totalitarian Poland
    Knut Andreas Grimstad 203

Conclusion
Ljiljana Šarić 218

Contributors

Paweł Bąk, PhD, is a German studies specialist and research associate at the German Studies Institute of the University of Rzeszów (Poland). His research areas include translation (especially translation of stylistic phenomena), the use of metaphors (metaphors in literary texts, print media and everyday communication), euphemisms and rhetoric. He is the author of *Die Metapher in der Übersetzung. Studien zum Transfer der Aphorismen von Stanisław Jerzy Lec und der Gedichte von Wisława Szymborska* (2007).

Steffen Thomas Buch is a research assistant in Romance linguistics at Göttingen University (Germany). He received his MA in 2005 in Spanish philology, English linguistics and history of arts. His PhD project is on Spanish press discourse concerning EU enlargement. He has published on bullfighting as a metaphorical source domain and is the coeditor of a book on self-reflexivity. His research fields include metaphor, visual and textual structure analysis, discourse linguistics, corpus linguistics, translation and dubbing.

Knut Andreas Grimstad is Associate Professor of Polish and Deputy Head at the Department of Literature, Area Studies and European Languages, University of Oslo. He has published extensively on Russian literature as well as on Polish Baroque literature, Polish Modernism and contemporary Polish poetry. Together with Ursula Phillips, he is the coeditor of *Gender and Sexuality in Ethical Context: Ten Essays on Polish Prose* (2005); he has also translated plays by Witold Gombrowicz. Among his main interests are popular culture and Jewish-Polish relations in independent Poland from 1918 to 1939.

Uta Helfrich is Professor of Romance Linguistics at Göttingen University (Germany). She won the Prix Strasbourg (1995) for her doctoral dissertation *Neologismen auf dem Prüfstand. Ein Modell zur Ermittlung der Akzeptanz französischer Neologismen*. She has published on language variation and norms, media discourse, language and identity, language change, cognitive semantics and syntax.

Ingrid Hudabiunigg is Professor Emerita of German as a Foreign Language and European Studies at the Technical University of Chemnitz (Germany). She spent a year at the University of California (UCSD) as a Fulbright scholar, a year as an Andrew Mellon scholar in Washington,

DC (NFLC) and 4 years at Charles University in Prague as an assistant professor for the DAAD.

Biljana Jovanović Lauvstad, MA, works on local development and multicultural issues in Oslo. She has also been a part-time instructor in West Balkan literature at the University of Oslo. Her main areas of interest are West Balkan literature, Norwegian and Norse literature.

Branko Kuna is Assistant Professor at the Department of Croatian Language and Literature at the Faculty of Arts in Osijek, Croatia. He teaches standard Croatian and pragmatics. He has written over 40 articles on syntax, word-formation and pragmatics, and edited a volume on *Syntactic Categories* (2007). He also worked as a journalist on Croatian radio and Radio Deutsche Welle.

Dubravka Kuna is an EFL teacher at the Faculty of Arts in Osijek, Croatia, and a doctoral student in linguistics. Her main areas of interest are lexicology and pragmatics.

Stefan Manz is Senior Lecturer and Director of German Studies at Aston University, Birmingham, and a Fellow of the Royal Historical Society. His research covers aspects of migration, interculturality and transnationality. Publications include: *Migranten und Internierte. Deutsche in Glasgow, 1864–1918* (Stuttgart, 2003), *Discourses of Intercultural Identity in Britain, Germany and Eastern Europe* (Clevedon, 2004; coeditor) and *Migration and Transfer from Germany to Britain, 1660–1914* (Munich, 2007; coeditor).

Andreas Musolff is Professor of Intercultural Communication Studies at the University of East Anglia, UK. He is the author of *Metaphor, Nation and the Holocaust* (2010) and *Metaphor and Political Discourse. Analogical Reasoning in Debates about Europe* (2004), and coeditor of *Attitudes towards Europe. Language in the Unification Process* (2001) and *Discourses of Intercultural Identity in Britain, Germany and Eastern Europe* (2004). He has published numerous articles on current public discourse in Germany and Britain, as well as on the history of political thought and discourse in Germany.

Sandra Petraškaitė-Pabst studied German as a foreign language at Vilnius Pedagogical University and completed her doctoral studies in Germanic linguistics at the University of Mannheim. Her dissertation was titled *Metaphor Use in Political Discourse. On EU Enlargement in German and Lithuanian Discourses*. She has held teaching assignments at the University of Mannheim and at the Pedagogical University of Ludwigsburg.

Tatjana Radanović Felberg is Associate Professor at the Department of Interpreting Studies at the Faculty of Education and International Studies at Oslo University College. Her areas of interest include political discourse analysis, social semiotics, media analysis, metaphor theory and interpreting in the public sector.

Ljiljana Šarić is Professor of Bosnian/Croatian/Serbian at the University of Oslo. Between 2008 and 2010 she was the lead researcher in the project *Media Constructions of the Images of the Self and the Other: The Case of Former Yugoslav Countries*. She has been participating in international projects dealing with discourse studies and semantics. She has authored, coauthored and edited several books and numerous articles on discourse analysis (specifically, discursive construction of cultural identity), cognitive linguistics and South Slavic languages, literatures and cultures. She is the coeditor of *Discourses of Intercultural Identity in Britain, Germany and Eastern Europe* (2004).

Andreja Vezovnik, PhD, is a researcher at the Center for Social Psychology and an instructor at the University of Ljubljana's Faculty of Social Sciences in the Department of Media Studies. Her area of interest mainly involves discourse theory and media and political discourse analysis. Her main focus is on the national identification process in Slovenia, theories of discourse, subjectivation and political representation. She also investigates the construction of family relations, social exclusion and food consumption practices in communist and post-communist Yugoslavia.

Daphne Winland is Associate Professor of Anthropology at York University. Her research interests are in nationalism, diaspora, memory and the cultural politics of representation. Her current research investigates contemporary Croatians' struggles to reinvent themselves in the changing political, social and cultural landscape of post-communist Eastern Europe. She has published articles and book chapters on the Mennonites, Hmong refugees and transnational politics among Croats in Croatia and abroad, and how Bosnian Croats are making sense of their changing position in postwar Bosnia. Her book *'We Are Now a Nation': Croats between 'Home' and 'Homeland'* (University of Toronto Press, 2007) reflects the findings of her Croatian research.

Acknowledgements

A few contributions to this volume emerged from a collaborative Norwegian-German study in the project *Media Constructions of Images of the Self and the Other: The Case of the Former Yugoslav Countries*. The editors appreciatively acknowledge the funding of the NFR and the DAAD (DAADppp support scheme) that supported the project and thus the research underlying some chapters of this volume (contributions by Šarić, Hudabiunigg and Felberg) by providing travel funds. We are also grateful to the University of Oslo and the Department of Literature, Area Studies, and European Languages (ILOS) for providing funds for the workshop *Cultural Borders and Reformulations of Cultural Identities in Europe* (Oslo, June 2007), at which the outline of this book was discussed, as well as funds for preparing the final manuscript of this volume.

Many thanks also go to Wiebke Wittschen and Donald F. Reindl for their various assistance related to the finalization of the manuscript, and to the Multilingual Matters team for their support in the realization of this book.

We would like to thank the following copyright holders: David Rooney, for permission to reprint his drawing in Chapter 3, the newspapers *Pobjeda* and *Politika*, for permission to print the images in Chapter 7, Polish jews.org for permission to reprint image 13.1 in Chapter 13, and Poland-Israel for permission to reprint image 13.2 in Chapter 13.

Introduction
Contested Cultural Identities in Public Discourse

Ljiljana Šarić, Stefan Manz, Andreas Musolff and Ingrid Hudabiunigg

Europe's eastern rim has been in constant flux ever since the watershed year of 1989. Autocratic regimes have been replaced with stable democracies, and planned economies have given way to a free-market system comprising most of the former communist countries of Central and Eastern Europe. Whereas most of these nations swiftly embarked on a course toward EU accession, the countries of the former Yugoslavia plunged into ethnic and religious infighting that left the region paralyzed for years and has left a problematic legacy until today. Further east, Turkey's long-held ambitions to join the EU received yet another setback when it was sidelined during the 2004/2007 round of enlargement. These political and economic transformations have triggered fundamental redefinitions of cultural identity. Nations and social groups have had to reposition themselves and their relationship to others within newly emerging political landscapes. Although the enlarged EU has created a new closeness between neighbors that were formerly separated by impenetrable physical and ideological barriers, at the same time it has excluded others that feel like outsiders being left behind. The break-up of the former Yugoslavia has necessitated reformulations of statehood and international relations in the Balkans.

We chose to call the area for this endeavor 'Europe's eastern rim'. With this metaphorical expression, we tried to avoid the widely used terms *Mitteleuropa*, *Central Europe* and *Eastern Europe* because each of these seems to imply different political and ideological conceptions for the countries from the Baltic Sea to the Mediterranean.

Mitteleuropa is a historically loaded term that focuses on the eastern part of Europe from an Austrian and German perspective, with explicit or implicit hegemonic intentions. The term *Central Europe*, invented in the revolutions of 1848, designates a Central European federation without Prussian or Russian domination. It reemerged in the 1980s as a kind of spiritual home for many intellectuals. However, as Maria Todorova and other Balkan experts have shown, this term is also divisive. It does not include the regions of the Balkans, but pushes them further east toward present-day Russia. Eastern Europe, in turn, clearly suggests Russian and Soviet hegemony. Furthermore, in a purely geographical sense, Eastern

Europe extends to the Ural Mountains and includes countries outside our scope.

We, on the other hand, explicitly wanted to include the area of the former Yugoslavia, most of which, as of 2009, does not have European Union membership. In this macro-region with its overwhelming diversity of ethnic, linguistic and religious groups, one can study, as though under a magnifying glass, how the still virulent backward movement of ethnocentric xenophobia has led to internecine conflicts and ethnic cleansing. Nonetheless, in each of these newly established countries, one can also observe that media and literature are making key contributions in the interchange of ideas toward a modern and tolerant form of civil society.

Public discourse has been the main platform for negotiating transformations of cultural identity, both self-referentially and in relation to others. The aim of this book is to analyze some central themes of cultural identity construction and its transformation in public discourse. It develops the ideas of an international group of researchers on discourse analysis, initially discussed at various symposia and research projects organized by the editors (Manz *et al.*, 2004). Our main concern in this book is discursive modes of identity construction (deconstruction, reconstruction, reformulation and invention) in the light of recent political changes in Europe, European Union enlargement and EU policy regarding southeast Europe. We focus on national and cross-national rhetorical strategies related to issues of transition within Europe.

Our book examines issues surrounding the discursive creation of cultural identity and combines theory-oriented and empirical approaches. The analyses of specific national discourses also address general methodological questions concerning rhetorical strategies and national and cross-national characteristics that play a role in the discursive presentation of identity construction. The contributions to this volume provide a multinational and multilingual perspective on discourse analysis and discursive identity formation, focusing on how issues of identity formation arise in several European languages, particularly among less-studied languages such as Slovenian, Lithuanian, Polish and Bosnian/Croatian/Serbian.

Three closely connected issues surrounding the linguistic means of identity construction and reconstruction constitute the chief topics of this volume: (1) the relationships between 'insiders' and 'outsiders' in the ongoing process of EU enlargement, (2) the perception of southeast Europe and its various nationalities as 'good guys' and 'bad guys' and (3) European insiderness and outsiderness in literary representations. These topics naturally arise from the larger historical and political framework. Since the early 1990s, actual and potential enlargement has been a key issue in debates surrounding the EU. The former East Germany made an entry through the 'back door' during the German unification process in 1990. Five years later, Austria, Sweden and Finland followed. Except for the negative Swedish referendum on the introduction of the euro, these accessions have been integrated relatively smoothly and hardly triggered any of the contested discourse surrounding the most recent round of eastern and Mediterranean enlargement. Considering the different nature and, not least of all, the sheer size of this last enlargement, this hardly came as a surprise. In 2004, Estonia, Lithuania, Latvia, Poland, the Czech Republic, Slovakia, Slovenia, Hungary, Cyprus and Malta joined the EU. After Romania's and Bulgaria's subsequent accession in 2007, the EU now consists of 27 member states. The enlargement process inevitably led to the exclusion of other countries. A number of candidates, including most of the Yugoslav successor states and Turkey, have been put on a waiting list.

The first part of this volume examines the discursive means by which the opposition between old and new outsiders and insiders has been created in the EU: rhetorical figures, metaphors, metonymies, symbols and conceptual blending. These semantic features are not accidental to the discourses about identity; rather, they provide the conceptual and linguistic tools for the construction, reconstruction or (re-)invention of national and cultural identities. The theoretical structure for such an approach is provided by cognitive semantics – that is, a theoretical framework comprising Conceptual Metaphor Theory (Kövecses, 2005; Lakoff & Johnson, 1980), Conceptual Blending Theory (Fauconnier & Turner, 2003) and Discourse Metaphor Analysis (Charteris-Black, 2004; Semino, 2008; Zinken, 2007). These approaches have been discussed variously as complementary and competing (Grady *et al.*, 1999; Zinken & Musolff, 2009); here, we assume their overall compatibility due to a set of shared assumptions. These include (a) an acknowledgement of the fundamental importance of metaphors for our conceptualization of and argumentation about the physical, psychological and sociopolitical world that we experience; (b) the insight that linguistic meanings cannot be analyzed as isolated entities but only as parts of integration networks, which allow us to merge and superimpose conceptual domains and spaces so as to achieve ever more complex semantic constructions; (c) the insight that these constructions are not just ephemeral, but can become entrenched in the semantic systems of languages; and (d) an acknowledgement that such entrenched meaning complexes can be used as lexical and grammatical material for further innovative uses that lead to specific pragmatic effects and thus practical political effects as well. The notion of states or other political entities as *containers*, for instance, taps into a fundamental schema of bodily and psychological conceptualization – the Self as a bounded and self-contained entity – and thus relates to universal and, possibly, transhistorical structural principles of embodied thought, as highlighted by Conceptual Metaphor Theory and Embodiment Theory (Gibbs, 2005; Lakoff & Johnson, 1999). However, in order to capture its actual communicative and cognitive effects, this notion needs to be studied in its varying discourse contexts. Several of the contributions to this volume show that the *container* metaphor with its *inside–outside* distinction has served not just to represent but indeed to redefine the relationships of individual nation states with the conglomerate entity of the European Union and its boundaries vis-à-vis other such conglomerate entities – for example, Eastern Europe, the Balkans and so on.

It is here that Critical Discourse Analysis (CDA) becomes methodologically essential for our studies, because it focuses on studying the linguistic manifestations of power relationships and social identity construction (Fairclough, 1995; Hodge & Kress, 1993; Wodak & Chilton, 2005; Wodak *et al.*, 1999). Employing a mix of pragmatic, semantic, stylistic and sociolinguistic methods, CDA studies all levels of expressing and also managing sociopolitical perception and action in texts and their media environments. Language use is thus conceptualized not so much as a mere representation of a pre-existing 'objective' reality, but as a tool to influence and shape the social environment itself, including both individual and collective identities.

Grammatical and lexical choices are of key importance in CDA: deictic or indexical expressions, such as personal pronouns and adverbs, serve to establish the deictic center; that is, the specific position from which a piece of discourse is being created that helps addressees position themselves in relation to what is presented in a text (Chilton, 2004). With lexical choices, discourse producers define the border between 'us' and 'them'. Lexical choices happen to be among the most important elements of strategies of positive self-presentation and negative other-presentation (Van Dijk, 2006). Lexical choices are also crucial means in legitimization and delegitimization strategies (Cap, 2008; Chilton, 2004). Of equal importance in discourse study are forms of implicit meanings in a text or utterance that are not overtly expressed, such as implications, presuppositions and allusions (Van Dijk, 2002). Discourse analysis concentrates on language means in creating discursive reality. However, this analysis is simultaneously a cognitive and social analysis that highlights the way we think about social reality and the social role of discourses.

The emphasis on lexical and grammatical choices and on the argumentative and discursive function of metaphors and other conceptual integration phenomena, such as metonymies and symbols, in identity construction has important consequences for the analyses in this book. Although the existence of relatively static, general and possibly universal conceptual integration networks is not denied, the main focus is on the variation, historicity and contested status of such concepts across regional, national and subnational boundaries. International political debates at times of momentous political upheaval, such as that experienced by the countries on Europe's eastern rim since the 1990s, exhibit a maximum of discursive change and variation (and they demand a matching communicative flexibility from their participants). Hence, the respective national Self's national/international Others, for instance, is continuously being redefined and threatens to render older entrenched symbols, metaphors and associated commonplace assumptions obsolete. Such previous metaphors and symbols do not, however, disappear from political discourse altogether; rather, they remain as competitors to the dominant key concepts and arguments, ready to be recycled whenever the occasion demands. Therefore, none of the following analyses of identity debates claims to capture *the* concept/image/attitude of a nation or an intranational or international grouping in the sense of a fixed, static consensus, but only the heterogeneous ensemble of competing notions and visions. These contested concepts are not the outcomes of automatic, unconscious mappings, but rather the products of highly conscious and sophisticated rhetoric that combines linguistic, iconic and other media-specific communication techniques to achieve effects in specific target-audiences. Ideally, such effects should be also demonstrable by way of quantitative analyses (Buch & Helfrich, this volume; Charteris-Black, 2004; Deignan, 2005; De Landtsheer, 2009; Musolff, 2004).

Although further work is needed in this field, the mainly qualitative studies presented here aim to provide a framework of leading perspectives for the formulation of testable hypotheses about changes in the relative weight of concepts and trends in discourses about Europe's eastern rim. These include the following research questions: How are European transitions presented nationally and cross-nationally? Does the metaphorical inventory change with the changing images of insider–outsider relationships? How are strategies of constructing identities and perceived cultural differences among the new EU member states related to each other? What happens to shared European metaphors in national discourses, and how are different discourse types (regional, national and supranational) interrelated? The focus is on strategies in conceiving national/cultural belonging and exclusion, perpetuating entrenched cultural images and contrasts, creating new images and reconstructing/deconstructing value systems.

Some contributions to this book explore these issues by devoting particular attention to the countries of the former Yugoslavia and Turkey. Nation-building was a painful process throughout the 1990s, after Slovenia, Croatia, Macedonia and Bosnia-Herzegovina declared independence from Yugoslavia. Within a microcosm of ethnic and religious diversity, this sparked protracted warfare and ethnic cleansing, which was halted only after international intervention in Bosnia in 1995, Kosovo in 1999 and Macedonia in 2001. Kosovo's declaration of independence in February 2008 was largely seen as the last step in the dissolution of the former Yugoslavia. Slovenia was the only former Yugoslav country to be included in the 2004 enlargement. Croatia's accession was blocked by former President Tuđman's autocratic leadership, Croatia's troublesome cooperation with the International Criminal Tribunal for the former Yugoslavia (ICTY) and continued human rights abuses against the country's Serbian minority. Since 2000 the situation has improved, and membership negotiations with the EU started in 2005. Macedonia gained candidate status in 2005, but no formal membership negotiations have commenced as yet. The same is true for Bosnia-Herzegovina, which signed a Stabilization and Association Agreement with the EU in June 2008. This can be seen as a first step toward accession. Serbian and Montenegrin accession are contested both within the two countries and within the EU, and will be preceded by lengthy negotiations (Cini, 2007, chapter 26; Smith, 2005).

These political developments are the context for most of the case histories in the second part of the volume. It continues the analysis of insiderness versus outsiderness, focusing on the neglected topic of southeast Europe as presented in public discourse both in the region and abroad. Because analytical treatment of discourse relating to southeast Europe is new, this section is given special prominence. Since the 1990s, the Balkan region has been the subject of extensive media coverage, with its concomitant images of regions, peoples, cultures and histories. For the most part, however, presentations have alternated between traditional stereotypes and simplified representations. Stereotypical images have been widely spread via the writings of diverse Balkan experts based on their experience as journalists, politicians or travelers, but even via scholarship dealing with this region (Fleming, 2000). This is observable in the titles of some books alone: for example, *Der Balkan. Das Pulverfaß Europas* (The Balkans: The Powder Keg of Europe; Herm, 1993), *Pulverfass Balkan. Mythos oder Realität* (The Balkan Powder Keg: Myth or Reality; Angelova & Veichtlbauer, 2001) and *Balkan Ghosts: A Journey Through History* (Kaplan, 1993). Part of nonspecialist and scholarly writing has renewed old stereotypes, and part has tried to relativize these stereotypes. However, even these writers, in choosing eye-catching titles that suggest an image of the Balkans as a wild, unstable and dangerous place, contributed to spreading simplified images. Stereotypical images that emerged in foreign discourses helped formulate opinions among the general public, including policymakers. Controversy has surrounded not only foreign portrayals of southeast Europe, but also the region's own self-definitions. Simplified images of nations and their culture have been borrowed in domestic discourses and partly internalized. During and after the wars in the Balkans, self-definition underwent various phases and transformations. Following violent upheavals, it was constructed anew or reconstructed once again. Today, identities in southeast Europe alternate between externally ascribed and self-declared characterizations.

On the one hand, all southeast European countries have made claims of European centrality and primacy in various discourses (e.g. 'Serbia in the very heart of Europe',[1] 'Croatia in the heart of Europe'; Ježić, 1996); on the other hand, they have partly internalized images imposed from outside. Bakić-Hayden and Hayden (1992: 3) argue that Orientalist rhetoric (i.e. terms with negative connotations employed in describing the Balkans and frequently used by outsiders) is 'often used even by those who are disparaged by them'. Trying to depart from the images that could call into question their 'Europeanness', southeast Europeans have tried to identify and characterize the Other among their neighbors. They have frequently used the same rhetorical strategies in creating stereotypes as some foreign discourses – characterized as discriminatory – have done. Fleming (2000) points toward the liminality of the Balkans, and how its location between multiple domains may have been a reason for its past ambivalent discursive descriptions. The author recognizes a need for extensive analyses to explain the complex relation of self-perceptions and the ways this region has been conceptualized from outside (Fleming, 2000: 1232). Several contributions in this book are a step in this direction.

The text material examined in the second part of the volume derives from various media text corpora, from within and outside of the region, that thematize the varying concepts of the Balkans and southeast Europe. Comparing the view of South Slavic countries from within and without, this section seeks to outline the recent dominant models of perception, reception and representation of the Self and the Other. An important identity concept here is contained in the term *Balkan*, which has played a central role in foreign media portrayals of the region and in the region's own self-definition (Bakić-Hayden, 1995; Bakić-Hayden & Hayden, 1992; Brown & Theodossopoulos, 2004; Jansen, 2002; Lindstrom, 2003; Lindstrom & Razsa, 2004; Šarić; Vezovnik, this volume; Todorova, 1997). In connection with the thesis of two Europes, coined by the Croatian writer Miroslav Krleža, whose seminal work is discussed in Hudabiunigg (this volume), the concept of the Balkans offers a boundary and consolidation of identity (Krleža, 1989, 1990; Škvorc, 2001). The metaphors and cultural constructs that create a dichotomy between 'Europe' and the Balkans raise the following questions: What does this dichotomy mean in different media contexts? What is the significance of the metaphorical borders between 'Europe' and the Balkans (e.g. an intended dividing line between East and West)? What other metaphorical concepts are placed in opposition to the Balkans? The discourse examined is thematically related to the events that have been important for the political development of the Balkans (e.g. debates surrounding EU expansion, Slovenia's holding the EU presidency in 2008 and the independence of Kosovo and Montenegro).

The contributions in the first and second parts shed light on the models of formulating images of the Self and the Other in the selected corpora, as well as the transformations that have been influenced by political and social processes. The individual chapters are mostly oriented toward the analysis of media texts, which are interpreted as expressions of current political debates and indicators of social and cultural changes. Media discourse is not only about texts: It also comprises pictorial representations, such as headlines and photographs, that interact with text and context features. Several chapters link the discourse-analytical approach to social science findings on public opinion and sociocultural stereotypes, as well as to changes in popular interpretations of national and regional histories. The selected texts are the result of interactions between political and cultural agents at a particular point in time. The main focus of these analyses is the implications and effects of rhetorical strategies used in their respective contexts: What can one learn from their use about the intended readers/listeners, and about the entire society in which they are created and received? Can these conceptual and rhetorical strategies serve as a means of manipulating opinions? In which sense can they be said to be effective or ineffective? Can they promote peace, conflict, hatred and tolerance?

Stefan Manz investigates the immediate effect of Poland's EU accession on German-Polish relations. By analyzing a set of cross-national debates and friction points, he demonstrates that accession did not necessarily improve bilateral relations. Instead, the new closeness reinforced negative perceptions and long-held mutual suspicions. The two case studies discussed in detail are the discourse surrounding postwar expellees from former German territories and the question of the EU voting structure. Both discourses show that bilateral relations are increasingly negotiated at the EU level.

Steffen Buch and Uta Helfrich concentrate on three newspapers (*Le Figaro, Le Monde* and *Libération*) to highlight metaphorical strategies employed by the French press to prepare the public for accession. France and, to a certain extent, Germany are constructed as legitimate, dominant and high-status EU-group members by being identified as LEADERS and MOTORS. Hierarchies are also conveyed through the SCHOOL and FAMILY concepts, which assess the ability of newcomers to integrate and assume their ostensibly rightful place within the EU framework.

Similar conceptualizations can be detected in the Lithuanian and German discourses, as Sandra Petraškaitė-Pabst shows in her comparative analysis. Through metaphors such as LOCOMOTIVE, ENGINE and ADVOCATE, Germany is seen to assume a leading role in the enlargement process, whereas the SCHOOL concept is also widely used within Lithuanian discourse in order to convey that the country has to catch up after 50 years of Soviet rule. A different set of culture-specific metaphors referring to Lithuanian fairy tales, customs and history is employed to increase the emotional identification of the Lithuanian public with distant, eurocratic Brussels.

Most of the chapters in the second part of the book focus on the former Yugoslav countries. Up to 1991, various South Slavic and other nations lived in a common state, Yugoslavia. In the official ideological framework and rhetoric, they were considered 'brothers' and 'fraternal nations'. Still, times have greatly changed since Yugoslavia's violent demise in the early 1990s: Slovenia joined the EU in 2004, thus institutionally acquiring a markedly different position than the other countries. Slovenia's EU accession and its holding the EU presidency in 2008 initiated lively discussions in public discourse outside Slovenia, in which Slovenia's identity has been redefined and its image presented to the rest of Europe (see Šarić; Vezovnik, this volume). Hyder Patterson (2003) examines Slovenian discourses in the late 1980s and early 1990s aimed at reestablishing Slovenian identity links to Central Europe and differentiating it from the Balkans. Mihelj et al. (2009) analyze Slovenian news programs from the late 1980s and the early 1990s and demonstrate how the semantic scope of deictic expressions shifted, and the role that shift played in dissociating the Slovenians from their Yugoslav 'brothers'. Redefinitions of cultural identity have also taken place in other former Yugoslav countries since the 1990s. Two important social events have given these discussions a decisive impulse: violent conflicts in the 1990s in which ethnic groups belonging to warring sides (Croats vs. Serbs and Bosniaks, Serbs vs. Bosniaks and Croats in armed conflicts in Croatia and Bosnia, Serbs. vs. Albanians in Kosovo, Albanians vs. Macedonians in Macedonia, etc.) tried to legitimize their own actions and delegitimize actions of the Other (see Kolstø, 2009, for a study of identity formation and media discourse during the Yugoslav conflicts). The second event in the postconflict period is public discussions related to the EU accession prospects of the former Yugoslav countries, in which various ethnic and political groups have been seeking to reestablish their Europeanness, which has been seen as strongly questioned or denied in some foreign discourses during and immediately after the wars of Yugoslav secession. In recent years, all of the former Yugoslav countries have been seeking to define and redefine themselves in relation to their immediate neighbors, and to the EU.

Most chapters in the second part of this book follow the discursive identity formulation practices of the former Yugoslav countries in their own and foreign public spaces. Ljiljana Šarić examines how identity patterns ascribed to post-Yugoslav societies from outside and inside relate to metaphorical geography and the term *the Balkans*. In a corpus of German-language, Croatian and Serbian media texts from 2008, various attitudes to metaphorical geography are identified. Whereas in the German-language media contexts *the Balkans* is mostly a neutral geographical label, a dual tendency can be traced in the Croatian media: A critique of the usage of *the Balkans* as a negative identity label is frequently accompanied by discursive practices in which unwanted societal phenomena are labeled as *Balkan*. In Serbian media, Balkan-related terms are much less contested, and more frequently used in instant self-identifications.

Dubravka Kuna and Branko Kuna focus on how Croats see their neighbors: Bosniaks, Serbs, Slovenians and Montenegrins. In a corpus of Croatian media texts from 2007, they follow various naming strategies for the neighboring South Slavic nations (specifically, conscious and deliberate name conversions), and examine the linguistic structure of name modifications. Unofficial names such as discriminatory expressions from populist discourse are contextually determined and linked to social circumstances. In naming the Other, not only an interplay of prejudices and stereotypes about both the Self and the Other plays a role, but also text genres, personal convictions and political standpoints. This analysis shows that the wars of Yugoslav secession, and other past and present conflicts, are still present in media discourse.

Daphne Winland's chapter follows political rhetoric in contemporary Bosnia and the continual contesting of the grounds of identity evidenced in the clash of competing narratives in the service of political aims. Departing from the thesis that inflammatory rhetoric about Islam serves to promote local, regional or national interests, she examines how discourses that have emerged with the 'War on Terror' affect local populations in Bosnia. The chapter's focus is on Bosnian Croats in particular and how they see their future as a constituent nation in Bosnia. It investigates how anti-Muslim sentiments are strategically deployed by elites in the service of different ambitions and interests, and how they are framed ideologically, culturally and historically to suit local contexts. The analysis calls attention to the need to consider factors generated in localized contexts.

Tatjana Radanović Felberg's chapter presents an example of identity negotiations between the Serbian and Montenegrin governments during the NATO bombing of the Federal Republic of Yugoslavia in 1999. Focusing her analysis on the front pages of two newspapers (Serbian *Politika* and Montenegrin *Pobjeda*) that supported the respective national governments and presidents, she considers a range of semiotic features, and a variety of their functions in building political identities. It is observed that the visual dimension of front pages relates to the different ideological positions. *Politika* supported Milošević's government, seeking to construct Milošević's identity as a strong leader and defender of the nation vis-à-vis world powers such as the United States and NATO, whereas *Pobjeda* tried to maintain an image of Đukanović as a pro-Western leader in which Montenegro was aligned with Europe.

Andreja Vezovnik's contribution to this book concentrates on the period from January 2001 to December 2003 in Slovenia, the time of the most intense public discussions on joining the European Union. She analyzes the historical and intertextual links between Slovenian national identity (re-)construction as a 'European' country after the break-up of the former Yugoslavia and the nineteenth century of 'Krekism', which formulated a Slovenian identity within the context of the Austro-Hungarian Empire. Whereas some metaphors and symbols of Krekist discourse (the nation as *mother*, and the ideal of the *diligent, hard-working and God-fearing farmer*) have been resurrected, other aspects of traditional Slovenian self-perception have become problematic in the process of joining the EU; for example, fears of being overpowered by foreign influence and being relegated to second-rank or even 'servant' status of a supranational authority.

Paweł Bąk looks at metaphors in the Polish press that comment on the EU accession of various 'Balkan' countries, ranging from Bulgaria and Romania to Croatia, Serbia and Montenegro. In comparison with Western (mainly German) conceptualizations of these countries, his corpus data show, on the one hand, a roughly similar array of metaphors, including CONTAINER, ROAD-MOVEMENT, HOME and FAMILY. On the other hand, however, the emphasis in publications is focused on *integration* models, which allow for an active role of the new accession countries (rather than making them the objects of EU *expansion*).

The final chapter in this part focuses on a country outside the former Yugoslav scope: Turkey. Turkey started EU entry talks in 2005 along with Croatia, and its EU prospects have frequently been discussed in the same context with the prospects of the former Yugoslav countries. Andreas Musolff studies the conceptualization of the potential accession state of Turkey in the German press. He distinguishes three metaphorical models or scenarios that are used to portray Turkey's current relationship to Europe: (1) Turkey as an outsider with little chance of ever getting access into the EU *house/family/club*, (2) that of Turkey's *progress toward* and future *inclusion in the EU* and (3) a *collision/conflict* scenario. In terms of the quantitative distribution in the German press corpus, the pessimistic scenarios (1) and (2) outweigh the optimistic scenario (3) – a finding that ties in with social science research on public attitudes toward Turkey and to Turkish migrants in Germany.

To complement the analyses of political and media discourse in the preceding parts, the contributions in the third part concentrate on literary texts that thematize contested national and cultural identities. This part uses literary hermeneutics to investigate literature as a point of intersection for various strands of historical and current discourses that underlie and inform the changing images of Europe in political and media discussions. The case studies reveal the emergence of a multiplicity of perspectives on national identities as self/other or as insider/outsider because literature shows a special interest in reconstructing and reexamining 'otherness' (Hammond, 2004; Longinović, 1995; Škvorc, 2001). The respective analyses focus on new ways of understanding national and ethnic identities in contemporary Polish literature, traditionalism versus modernism in the construction of a new identity in Montenegrin society and contesting the border between East and West in the work of one of the most significant Croatian authors of the twentieth century.

Ingrid Hudabiunigg's chapter focuses on the notion of two Europes, which Croatian writer Miroslav Krleža established in essays and political speeches. In these, the author challenges the widespread opinion by Western media that the center has always been located in the west of the continent, whereas East-Central Europe, and especially the Balkans, are at the uncivilized periphery. Krleža claims that presenting Europe with only one center goes hand in hand with the political and economic domination and exploitation of Western powers over the countries of the East. With this form of deconstruction, Krleža can be seen as a forerunner to Pierre Bourdieu and his theory of the 'linguistic market', linking political dimensions of conflicts to particular world visions in a dialectic relationship. The author argues instead for a common Europe with two poles, by which the achievements of great philosophers, writers and artists in East-Central Europe would be justifiably appreciated.

A picture of cultural change in post-Yugoslavia is drawn by Biljana Jovanović Lauvstad in her review of Balša Brković's best-seller *Privatna Galerija* (Private Gallery). In contrast to the predominant heroic literature (*epika*) of Montenegro depicting the bravery and patriotism of male heroes, *Privatna Galerija* is written in the first-person singular from the perspective of a young man rebelling against the patriarchal-heroic codex of masculinity. The protagonist's private life and his intimate relationships with several women are extensively focused on. Lauvstad looks at the self-presentation of the main character and the articulation of 'the new sensibility' in postmodern gender relations applying critical feminist reading.

Knut Andreas Grimstad's chapter gives a survey of Polish public discourse (novels, stories, essays and TV productions) on Jews after the fall of communism. He analyses several distinct rhetorical-discursive devices for the Polish-Jewish cultural legacy, including images of a multicultural past in Polish-Jewish small-town communities, the Holocaust and the mass expulsions of 'Zionists' in 1968 and a critique of xenophobic and nationalist tendencies in post-communist Poland. As a literary response to the antidemocratic trends in post-totalitarian Poland, writers such as Szewc, Rymkiewicz, Lubkiewicz-Urbanonowicz and Krall, according to Grimstad, contribute to a deconstruction of Jewish as well as other minority-related enemy images and may be understood as the very basis for a literary project of modernization.

What emerges from the analysis of various discourses considered in this book is not a static or homogeneous picture of the 'family of

European nations' but rather a dynamic and open-ended continuum of discourses that seek to redefine and reassess the 'family resemblances' among its different members (and groups of members), including the hitherto ostracized eastern 'branch of the family'.

Note

1. See Dobrodošli u Srbiju 'Welcome to Serbia', at: http://www.serbiatouristguide.com/live/?languageId=4. Accessed 15 August 2009.

References

Angelova, P. and Veichtlbauer, J. (2001) *Pulverfaß Balkan. Mythos oder Realität*. St Ingbert: Rörig Universitätsverlag.

Bakić-Hayden, M. (1995) Nesting orientalism: The case of former Yugoslavia. *Slavic Review* 54 (4), 917–931.

Bakić-Hayden, M. and Hayden, R.M. (1992) Orientalist variations on the theme "Balkans:" Symbolic geography in recent Yugoslav cultural politics. *Slavic Review* 51 (1), 1–15.

Brown, K. and Theodossopoulos, D. (2004) Other's others: Talking about stereotypes and constructions of otherness in Southeast Europe. *History and Anthropology* 15 (1), 3–14.

Cap, P. (2008) Towards the proximization model of the analysis of legitimization in political discourse. *Journal of Pragmatics* 40 (1), 17–41.

Charteris-Black, J. (2004) *Corpus Approaches to Critical Metaphor Analysis*. Basingstoke: Palgrave-Macmillan.

Chilton, P. (2004) *Analysing Political Discourse. Theory and Practice*. London: Routledge.

Cini, M. (2007) *European Union Politics*. Oxford: Oxford University Press.

De Landtsheer, C. (2009) Collecting political meaning from the count of metaphor. In A. Musolff and J. Zinken (eds) *Metaphor and Discourse* (pp. 59–78). Basingstoke: Palgrave-Macmillan.

Deignan, A. (2005) *Metaphor and Corpus Linguistics*. Amsterdam/Philadelphia: Benjamins.

Fairclough, N. (1995) *Critical Discourse Analysis. The Critical Study of Language*. London: Longman.

Fauconnier, G. and Turner, M. (2002) *The Way We Think: Conceptual Blending and the Mind's Hidden Complexities*. New York: Basic Books.

Fleming, K.E. (2000) Orientalism, the Balkans, and Balkan historiography. *The American Historical Review* 105 (4), 1218–1233.

Gibbs, R.W. Jr. (2005) *Embodiment and Cognitive Science*. Cambridge: Cambridge University Press.

Grady, J., Oakley T. and Coulson, S. (1999) Blending and metaphor. In R.W. Gibbs and G. Steen (eds) *Metaphor in Cognitive Linguistics* (pp. 101–124). Amsterdam: Benjamins.

Hammond, A. (ed.) (2004) *The Balkans and the West: Constructing the European Other, 1945–2003*. Aldershot: Ashgate.

Herm, G. (1993) *Der Balkan. Das Pulverfaß Europas*. Düsseldorf: Econ.

Hodge, R. and Kress, G. (1993) *Language as Ideology*. London: Routledge.

Hyder Patterson, P. (2003) On the edge of reason: The boundaries of Balkanism in Slovenian, Austrian, and Italian discourse. *Slavic Review* 62 (1), 110–141.

Jansen, S. (2002) Svakodnevni orijentalizam: doživljaj "Balkana"/"Evrope" u Beogradu i Zagrebu. *Filozofija i društvo: Journal of the Belgrade Institute for Social Research and Philosophy* 18, 33–72.

Ježić, M. (ed.) (1996) *Hrvatska u srcu Europe: sredozemni i srednjoeuropski kulturni krajolici Hrvatske*. Zagreb: Hrvatska paneuropska unija.

Kaplan, R.D. (1993) *Balkan Ghosts: A Journey through History*. New York: St. Martin's Press.

Kolstø, P. (2009) *Media Discourse and the Yugoslav Conflicts. Representations of Self and Other*. Aldershot: Ashgate.

Kövecses, Z. (2005) *Metaphor in Culture: Universality and Variation*. Cambridge/New York: Cambridge University Press.

Krleža, M. (1989) *Krokodilina ili razgovor o istini*. Sarajevo: NIŠRO Oslobođenje.

Krleža, M. (1990) *Deset krvavih godina*. Sarajevo: Veselin Masleša.

Lakoff, G. and Johnson, M. (1980) *Metaphors We Live By*. Chicago: University of Chicago Press.

Lakoff, G. and Johnson, M. (1999) *Philosophy in the Flesh. The Embodied Mind and Its Challenge to Western Thought*. New York: Basic Books.

Lindstrom, N. (2003) Between Europe and the Balkans: Mapping Slovenia and Croatia's "return to Europe" in the 1990s. *Dialectical Anthropology* 27 (3–4), 313–329.

Lindstrom, N. and Razsa, M. (2004) Balkan is beautiful: Balkanism in the political discourse of Tuđman's Croatia. *East European Politics and Societies* 18 (4), 628–650.

Longinović, T.Z. (1995) East within the west: Bosnian cultural identity in the works of Ivo Andrić. In W.S. Vucinich (ed.) *Ivo Andrić Revisited: The Bridge Still Stands* (pp. 123–138). Berkeley: University of California International and Area Studies Digital Collection 92.

Manz, S., Musolff, A., Long, J. and Šarić, Lj. (eds) (2004) *Discourses of Intercultural Identity in Britain, Germany and Eastern Europe*. Special Issue: *Journal of Multilingual and Multicultural Development* 25 (5 & 6), 437–452.

Mihelj, S., Bajt, V. and Pankov, M. (2009) Reorganizing the identification matrix: Televisual construction of collective identities in the early phase of Yugoslav disintegration. In P. Kolstø (ed.) *Media Discourse and the Yugoslav Conflicts. Representations of Self and Other* (pp. 39–59). Aldershot: Ashgate.

Musolff, A. (2004) *Metaphor and Political Discourse. Analogical Reasoning in Debates about Europe*. Basingstoke: Palgrave-Macmillan.

Semino, E. (2008) *Metaphor in Discourse*. Cambridge: Cambridge University Press.

Škvorc, B. (2001) Srednja Europa i Balkan u Krležinim romanima: Problematika tekstualnih i izvantekstualnih književnih interakcija. *Republika* 57 (7–8), 56–77.

Smith, K.E. (2005) Enlargement and European order. In C. Hill and M. Smith (eds) *International Relations and the European Union* (pp. 270–291). Oxford: Oxford University Press.

Todorova, M. (1997) *Imagining the Balkans*. Oxford: Oxford University Press.

Van Dijk, T. (2002) Critical discourse studies: A sociocognitive approach. In R. Wodak and M. Meyer (eds) *Methods of Critical Discourse Analysis* (pp. 95–120). London: Sage.

Van Dijk, T. (2006) Discourse and manipulation. *Discourse & Society* 17 (2), 359–383.

Wodak, R., de Cillia, R., Reisigl, M. and Liebhart, K. (eds) (1999) *The Discursive Construction of National Identity.* Edinburgh: Edinburgh University Press.

Wodak, R. and Chilton, P. (eds) (2005) *A New Agenda in (Critical) Discourse Analysis. Theory, Methodology and Interdisciplinarity.* Amsterdam/Philadelphia: Benjamins.

Zinken, J. (2007) Discourse metaphors: The link between figurative language and habitual analogies. *Cognitive Linguistics* 18 (3): 445–466.

Zinken, J. and Musolff, A. (2009) A discourse-centred perspective on metaphorical meaning and understanding. In A Musolff and J. Zinken (eds) *Metaphor and Discourse* (pp. 1–10). Basingstoke: Palgrave-Macmillan.

Chapter 1
Expellees, Counterfactualism and Potatoes. Enlargement and Cross-National Debates in German-Polish Relations

Stefan Manz

Introduction

Eastern enlargement of the EU has triggered not only renegotiations of European identity but also of bilateral relationships. Constructions of Cold War dichotomies between East and West need to be reconsidered as former 'enemies' now find themselves under a single umbrella that aims at political, economic, military and cultural integration. If we accept the assessment of the former EU commissioner for enlargement, Günter Verheugen, that 'German-Polish dialogue is the core of European unification' (Verheugen, 2004: 8), eastern enlargement could not have had a less promising start. The new closeness between the two nations appeared to have reinforced rather than dissolved long-held mutual suspicions and negative perceptions. Polish and German observers agreed in the immediate post-enlargement period that the relationship between the two countries had hit its lowest point since 1989. Because bilateral issues now have to be increasingly negotiated at the EU level, the belligerent past and strained present relationship between Germany and Poland even cast a shadow over Poland's first European appearance as a full-fledged EU member state. EU leaders and officials unanimously felt the country to be the new 'awkward partner' (Grabbe, 2004) – a role traditionally held by the United Kingdom (George, 1998) – that fought battles of the past instead of concentrating on a common future.

This chapter takes a closer look at the period between the run-up to 1 May 2004, when Poland and nine other countries joined the European Union, and October 2007, when national-conservative Prime Minister Jarosław Kaczyński was replaced by a more conciliatory successor, Donald Tusk. Analyzing the cross-national friction points and debates that unfolded during this period allows us to assess the extent to which bilateral relationships are increasingly negotiated at the EU level. This chapter is mainly based on German broadsheet articles (especially

Spiegel/Spiegel online, Süddeutsche Zeitung/sueddeutsche.de, Tageszeitung and *Die Zeit/zeit.de*) and aims to ascertain the effect of enlargement and 'Europeanization' (Zaborowski, 2004: 5–26) on the triangular Poland–Germany–EU relationship.

Historical Burdens

A historical outline is crucial for understanding current debates and the pervading European dimension of this relationship. Although few Central European countries were exempt from German military aggression over the centuries, it was Poland that arguably suffered most under its larger neighbor. Three partitions in the second half of the eighteenth century eliminated the Polish state from the map of Europe, dividing the country between Russia, Austria and Prussia. Throughout the nineteenth century, Prussia pursued a policy of forced Germanization in occupied western Poland, trying to push back the Polish language and Catholicism through administrative measures and mass expulsions. Bismarck reinforced these *Kulturkampf* measures after German unification in 1871, and ethnic cohesion became a cornerstone of national identity construction in the newly founded German Empire. An influential expatriate community of Polish aristocrats and artists (e.g. Adam Mickiewicz and Frédéric Chopin), mainly based in Paris, upheld notions of independence and assertiveness that remain reference points for the nation today (Urban, 2004: 17–24). Independence in 1918 was achieved not least of all through US president Woodrow Wilson's support. Long-lasting notions of the United States as a guardian of Polish security interests can be traced back to the Treaty of Versailles. Germany's invasion of Poland in September 1939 resulted in immeasurable destruction and triggered a global conflagration. It was followed by a postwar settlement that allocated a quarter of German territory to Poland and resulted in the expulsion of 7.5 million ethnic Germans. It also resulted in a border dispute over the Oder–Neisse line, which remained unresolved throughout the Cold War and continues to cast its shadow over the bilateral relationship today (Bingen, 2005; Lebioda, 2000; Müller, 2004; Urban, 2004; Zaborowski, 2004: 1–2).

The end of communism presented an opportunity to normalize relations and create a 'win-win' situation for both countries. Germany could cast off its precarious position as a *Frontstaat* (front-line state) against the east by supporting Polish integration into western economic and political structures. Poland, on the other hand, could now realize its 'return to Europe'. The era of communism was interpreted as a historical aberration, having separated the country from its 'natural' sociopolitical and economic environment (Zaborowski, 2004: 124–126). It was accepted that 'the way to Europe leads through Germany' (Holesch, 2007: 23), and Germany willingly took on the role of Poland's advocate in the EU. For the first time in 200 years, both countries' interests seemed to converge, and a *Werte- und Interessensgemeinschaft* (community of values and interests) (Hudabiunigg, 2004: 160) could be proclaimed by foreign minister Krzysztof Skubiszewski. Tangible progress was made in this direction. The treaty on 'Good Neighborly Relations and Amicable Cooperation', signed in 1991, confirmed intentions on both sides that historical burdens should be overcome and that German foreign policy would prioritize Polish EU accession. Activities launched in the wake of the treaty included a German-Polish youth association and a bilateral government commission for regional and cross-border cooperation. Together with France, the 'Weimar Triangle' was launched, which has provided for regular meetings among the three heads of state. The idea was to extend the Paris–Berlin 'Axis', which had arguably been the driving force of European integration since the 1950s (Bingen, 2005; Holesch, 2007: 26–40). The symbolic message was to accept Poland as an equal partner, to signify that Franco-German postwar reconciliation was also a realistic option for the Polish-German relationship and that Polish western integration should be solidified. These activities aimed to remove Polish fears of the unified Germany and to level out the apparent asymmetrical relationship in both political and economic terms. The 1990s have aptly been labeled a 'golden era' (Bingen, 2005: 13) for Polish-German relations.

What followed in the ensuing years was the realization that problematic issues between the countries ran too deep to be overcome by mere enthusiasm and *Versöhnungskitsch* (reconciliation kitsch) (*Tageszeitung*, 5 August 1994). As one researcher put it, 'the positive signs and accompanying rhetoric do not disguise that the condition of the German-Polish relationship as a whole is not so bright and agreeable' (Wood, 2002: 97). A new working relationship had to be established, and it was now accepted that this could not be detached from its European dimension. One example is an interview with Polish president Kwaśniewski on the eve of accession, in which he admitted that the 'frontlines' between Poland and both the EU and Germany had hardened: 'If we were now able to come to a German-Polish agreement on the question of the constitution and thereby help Europe, our relationship would gain a new quality' (*Spiegel* 3/2004).

Lech and Jarosław Kaczyński, Germany and Europe

Along with nine other countries on the EU's eastern and southern rim, Poland joined the European Union on 1 May 2004. By then the country had undergone a political, economic and social transformation process alongside pre-accession strategies set out by the Copenhagen criteria. Those that had hailed the accession date in almost teleological terms as Poland's 'return to Europe' could be nothing but disappointed by the development to come. First impressions were, however, favorable. President Kwaśniewski's pro-European stance was in line with that of the newly appointed Prime Minister Marek Belka. Both were ready for compromises regarding the EU budget for 2007–2013 and the constitution. Poland's mediating role during the Orange Revolution in Ukraine and a generally pro-European population added to the positive picture. Below the surface, however, skepticism had been building up. The marathon of conformation to EU structures had exhausted the country, and the pro-European consensus within the parties and political landscape had only proved its stability as long as it had been a condition for accession. It now gave way to opinion-makers who were more Atlanticist and less concerned with nurturing the Weimar Triangle, good-neighborly relations with Germany, or indeed the EU (Holesch, 2007: 99–100, 105–106). This surfaced for the first time during the parliamentary election campaign in autumn 2005 and was spearheaded by the twin brothers Lech and Jarosław Kaczyński and their newly founded Law and Justice Party (PiS). Lech Kaczyński, the presidential candidate, found Germany and Russia to be the 'greatest danger' for Poland. He boasted that he did not entertain any contacts whatsoever with German politicians and that the only thing he knew in Germany was 'the spittoon in the gents' room' at the Frankfurt Airport (*Tagesspiegel Online*, 2 December 2005). When Federal President Horst Köhler offered to see him during his visit to Warsaw in September 2005, he did not reply (*Tageszeitung*, 7 October 2005). Germanophobia alone did not win him the elections, but it was part of his national-conservative worldview that struck a chord with the electorate.

The Kaczyński twins had grown up with narratives of Nazi crimes; both of their parents had been decorated resistance activists during the occupation period. In the 1980s, the brothers had been major players in the Solidarity movement, but they fell out with its leader Lech Wałęsa after his rise to power as president. Their political resurrection started around 2000 with appointments to justice minister (Jarosław) and mayor of Warsaw (Lech) and, shortly afterwards, their founding the Law and Justice Party (PiS). Lech Kaczyński was elected president in October 2005. Jarosław Kaczyński took over as prime minister in July 2006, forming a coalition with the national-clerical 'League of Polish Families' and the agrarian 'Self-Defense of the Republic of Poland' (Holesch, 2007: 109–113; *Spiegel* 29/2006; *Zeit*, 16 August 2007). The double leadership was proclaimed to be the birth of the 'Fourth Republic' and a rebirth of honor, patriotism and strength at the international level.

The first bilateral row was triggered by a German newspaper and had an immediate detrimental effect on the Weimar Triangle. In June 2006, the left-wing Berlin-based *Tageszeitung* published a satirical text about Lech Kaczyński under the title *Polens neue Kartoffel* (Poland's New Potato), ridiculing his obsessive Germanophobia, political ambitions and private life

(*Tageszeitung*, 26 June 2006; 29 June 2007). The text was translated by the Polish foreign office and appeared under the section 'The Foreign Press on Poland' alongside serious articles and analyses. Foreign minister Anna Fotyga commented, 'Such an accumulation of repulsiveness reminds one of the language of the [Nazi newspaper] *Stürmer*' (*Süddeutsche Zeitung Online*, 5 July 2006). Jarosław Kaczyński seconded that insulting a head of state was a crime. Fotyga demanded an apology from the German authorities for this 'unprecedented attack on a head of state', but was told by a spokesman that the German government does not, as a rule, comment on press articles about foreign politicians (*Süddeutsche Zeitung Online*, 5 July 2006). The left-liberal Polish press agreed that a prime minister ought to deal with more important things than trivial articles in small newspapers. Lech Kaczyński was reportedly enraged about the matter and, without a compelling reason, cancelled the imminent Weimar Triangle meeting with Jacques Chirac and Angela Merkel (*Süddeutsche Zeitung Online*, 10 July 2006, 12 July 2006).

This episode foreshadowed a pattern that was to be repeated over the following years. Poland's 'path to Europe' does indeed lead through Germany, and bilateral frictions have the potential to encumber the country's relations with the EU. In a confrontational article entitled 'Europe – Still Divided', Lech Kaczyński expressed his disagreement with the framework of the proposed constitution, which would aim at deepening European divisions. It would only serve to solidify Germany's dominant position within the EU, whereas smaller countries like Poland would be discriminated against. Rather than stressing the achievements of integration and cross-national connections, he constructed a contested German-Polish dichotomy as a smaller version of Europe's divisions at large (Kaczyński, 2006). The effects of this view are examined in the following section by concentrating on the discourse surrounding two contentious themes: the problem of postwar expellees and property claims and, second, the EU voting structure.

The Presence of the Past: Expellees, Territorial Claims and Reparations

Patterns of remembering World War II within German public discourse have always been carefully observed by the international community. The latest debate, if reported selectively as has been the case in Poland, does indeed lend itself to the interpretation that major revisionist tendencies are at work in present-day Germany. The debate was triggered in 2002 by Jörg Friedrich's book on the bombing of Hamburg and other cities, in which he focused on ordinary Germans as victims of allied wartime bombings. In the same vein, an anonymous woman published her recollections of rape at the hands of Red Army soldiers after the capture of Berlin (Anonyma, 2003; Friedrich, 2002). A major cornerstone of the 'discourse of victimhood' has been the theme of ethnic Germans' expulsion from territories that are now part of Poland and the Czech Republic. Works concentrating on their suffering have included a documentation by popular historian Guido Knopp, a three-part TV series entitled *Die Flucht* (The Flight) and Günter Grass' novel *Im Krebsgang* (Crabwalk), in which the Nobel laureate reconstructs the sinking of the refugee ship *Wilhelm Gustloff* by the Red Army (Aust & Burgdorff, 2003). The traditional perpetrator–victim dichotomy was further undermined by research into Poles' participation in the killing of Jews during World War II (Gross, 2001). For the Polish right, these activities were proof that Germans were eager to rewrite history by deflecting some of their own guilt onto other groups, including Poles, which hitherto had made their status as victims part of their collective identity.

The most contentious object of debate, however, was (and still is) the planning of the *Zentrum gegen Vertreibungen* (Center against Expulsions). It was initiated in 2000 by a trust that aims to serve international understanding and the banishment of expulsion and genocide as political instruments. Its chairpersons were the president of the Association of Expellees, the CDU parliamentarian Erika Steinbach and the former SPD general secretary, Peter Glotz. Supporters included moderate voices such as Cardinal Karl Lehmann or Jewish intellectuals such as Ralph Giordano and Imre Kertész – a fact that was ignored by the Polish press. The initiative triggered a wave of vehement protest in Poland. According to Sejm parliamentarian Jan Maria Rokita, for example, this was yet another attempt by the Germans to redefine their historical self-definition as victims, being in line with the 'political selfishness' that the Schröder administration had displayed at the EU level (Urban, 2005: 34–35). Erika Steinbach was singled out as the embodiment of German revisionism. For author Pawel Huelle, she was 'proof that the Germans are still evil... If the evil Germans did not exist already, one would have to invent them' (*Spiegel* 25/2007). The conservative Polish press jumped at the opportunity. The weekly magazine *Wprost*, for example, carried a photomontage of Erika Steinbach in a Nazi uniform riding on Gerhard Schröder's back on a 2003 cover page. The picture was entitled 'The German Trojan Horse' (*Spiegel* 25/2007).

Although other Polish commentators used more moderate tones, there was widespread political and public consensus that the Center against Expulsions was not desirable. A suggestion by SPD parliamentarian Markus Meckel and two Polish German experts, Adam Krzemiński and Adam Michnik, to establish a joint Center for the Documentation of Expulsions based in Wrocław/Breslau was interpreted as a German attempt to impose historical distortions upon Poland. Even a veteran of Polish-German reconciliation, former foreign minister Władysław Bartoszewski maintained that the center would only serve the 'wrong notion that, apart from the Jews, it was especially the Germans that were the victims of the Second World War' (Urban, 2005: 34–35). To counterbalance the notion, Poland would have to build a center that depicted suppression at the hands of Germans from the late eighteenth century through 1945. In order to calm the political waves, Chancellor Gerhard Schröder joined the chorus of critical voices, and Foreign Minister Joschka Fischer stated that 'the Association of Expellees is not fit to be a museum director' (Urban, 2005: 34–35). From the Polish perspective, however, these conciliatory remarks were devalued by the fact that the German federal government has consistently provided generous financial support to the Association of Expellees.

At this point, it became clear that the project had only served to deepen Polish-German misunderstanding, and the escape route sought from the stalemate was to Europeanize the debate. In 2003, the two presidents at the time, Johannes Rau and Aleksander Kwaśniewski, made a start in the joint Gdańsk Declaration. It was made clear that flight and expulsion were generally part of Europe's history and identity and that therefore its documentation should be a European affair. Although every nation had the natural right to mourn, this grief should not be instrumentalized in day-to-day politics to divide the continent anew. Kwaśniewski and Rau called for an honest European dialogue in which respected spokesmen of society should formulate recommendations on how this documentation should be conducted. The short declaration of 320 words referred to 'Europe' or 'European' seven times, versus mentioning Poland and Germany only twice (Rau & Kwaśniewski, 2003).

What followed was a declaration of intent by the culture secretaries of Germany, Poland, the Czech Republic, Slovakia and Hungary to create a European Network for the documentation of 'forced migrations and expulsions in the twentieth century'. The German culture secretary Christina Weiss did not conceal that this was meant to counter the ill-fated Center against Expulsions. The project got off to a bad start, however, due to differing intentions by the participating states. Poland preferred the theme of expulsion to be integrated into the larger framework of victims of totalitarianism, whereas the Czech representatives seemed to sabotage the project altogether. Slovakia and Hungary more or less ignored it (Bonner Erklärung, 2004; Holesch, 2007: 96, 121; Meckel, 2007; Urban, 2005: 35ff.). In addition, the German grand coalition government, elected in autumn 2005, has been unable to agree upon the exact nature of remembrance and so far has only come up with the noncommittal phrase that a 'visible symbol' for expulsion should be created. One suggestion was to give the 2005 exhibition *Flucht, Vertreibung, Integration* (Flight, Expulsion, Integration) a permanent home in Berlin. More controversially, Erika Steinbach's exhibition on *Erzwungene Wege* (Forced Pathways) was shown in Berlin in summer 2006 and gave ample opportunity for Polish criticism. Headway could only be made after Donald Tusk's election as Polish prime minister. His government will not participate in a German documentation center against expulsions either, but has given up its categorical resistance. The German and Polish governments have also decided to revive the idea of the European Network with a general secretariat in Warsaw (Birkenkämper, 2008; Meckel, 2007; *Süddeutsche Zeitung Online*, 5 February 2008; *Zeit*, 31 October 2007, 19 March 2008).

Another point of friction that was eventually negotiated at the European level was the question of real property claims against Poland. Throughout the 1990s, nationalist circles in Poland had been suspicious of Germany's role as its 'advocate' in the EU. As *Polityka* commented, 'Germany supports the accession of Poland to the EU because it will allow them to win a war without a shot. They will come back for their property, and they will enclose the Poles in reservations' (cited in Lebioda, 2000: 177). In 2000, expellee associations from the former German provinces of Silesia and East Prussia founded the *Preußische Treuhand*, a private trust organization on a shareholding basis. Its aim is to give legal support to expellees' lawsuits for the return of confiscated real estate left behind in Poland. The *Preußische Treuhand* draws its legitimacy from the fact that successive German governments have failed to renounce these claims at the state level. The legal situation is as yet unclear. Poland passed a law in 1997 that allowed the commutation of lease into property rights because it feared German demands after its EU accession. The Association of Expellees, on the other hand, asked the German federal government to make the real-estate issue part of the EU-accession criteria for Poland – a demand refuted by the Schröder administration. The hard-line course of the *Preußische Treuhand* found no widespread support in the German public. Even most expellee organizations distanced themselves from the demands, claiming that this line would lead to dangerous confusions in the Polish-German relationship. A legal expert report, commissioned jointly by the two governments, did not clarify the situation (Urban, 2005: 38). In December 2006, the *Preußische Treuhand* used the legal confusion, as well as the fact that Poland was now situated within the legal EU framework, to submit a lawsuit representing 23 parties to the European Court of Justice. Although this incident was largely ignored in Germany because of its irrelevance and absence of any prospect of success, it was widely reported in Poland, nurturing fears of expropriation. Jarosław Kaczyński accused the German elites of passivity, allowing the country to develop 'in a direction that in the past had ended in a great European tragedy' (*Spiegel* 25/2007).[1]

German reparation claims were instigated by a fringe group that continues to be vehemently rejected by the public and in politics. In Poland, on the other hand, claims against Germany were part of mainstream politics. They entered the press, as well as policymaking at an official level, and must be seen as an (over-)reaction against the activities of the *Preußische Treuhand*. Like the *Preußische Treuhand*, they were based on legal vagueness. In 1953, the Peoples' Republic of Poland declared the Federal Republic of Germany's postwar reparations to be sufficient and renounced any further reparations. Fifty years later, national-conservative circles questioned the lawfulness of the renunciation because Poland was not a sovereign state in 1953. In September 2004, they had a resolution accepted by the Sejm that maintained that Poland had not received any compensation for the immeasurable destruction and that the government should take pertinent steps against the German government. It was calculated that Poland had lost 40% of its national assets, including two-thirds of its manufacturing plants. Commissioned by Lech Kaczyński, then mayor of Warsaw, a report on wartime damages to the capital was compiled, which listed the sum of $45.3 billion in current real-estate value. The liberal Belka administration did its best to repudiate such demands, pointing out that Germany had, indeed, paid reparations before 1953 and that those regions vacated by ethnic Germans after 1945 also had to be regarded as reparations. The liberal press condemned the claims because of their negative impact on the German-Polish reconciliation process, whereas the national-conservative press supported them as a 'necessary defensive war' (Urban, 2005: 38). In an opinion poll, 64% of Poles were in favor of financial claims against Germany (Holesch, 2007: 99–104; Urban, 2005: 38). It is those forces that came to power in November 2005 in the form of the Law and Justice Party, spearheaded by the Kaczyński twins. The past had proved to still be an open chapter in Polish-German relations and now it was also to have an aggravating impact on Poland's position within the EU.

'The Square Root Is Worth Dying For' – EU Voting and Power Equilibrium

The previous section dealt with an example in which bilateral issues were negotiated at the European level; the following section highlights an example in which a European issue is dominated by bilaterality. From the very start, Poland made it clear that it would not enter the EU as a junior partner. Jacques Chirac's ill-placed remark in 2003 that Poland ought to 'shut up' in connection with the Iraq crisis is still widely cited by the Polish press and only helps to reinforce the belief that preserving its sovereignty should be the main aim of Polish membership (Gießmann, 2008: 56). The country's asymmetric relationship with Germany has led policymakers to hold the belief that Germany's powers at the EU level needed to be contained, whereas Poland's powers needed to be extended in order to approach an equilibrium. This attitude had already led to major EU-Polish tensions during the constitution summit in Brussels in

December 2003 (Hudabiunigg, 2004: 168), which aimed to renegotiate the Nice accord of 2000. The Polish motto 'Nice or Death' alluded to the fact that the system of 'qualified majority voting' in the EU Council of Ministers worked in favor of Poland, whereas Germany was underrepresented. Defending the accord was therefore the main aim, and the summit failed to reform the voting structure due to disagreements (Gaisbauer, 2008).

A closer look at the discussions surrounding the constitution summit in Brussels in June 2007 can now serve to highlight similar patterns. The European constitutional treaty had envisaged council decisions requiring a 'double majority'. They had to be agreed by 55% of the member states, representing 65% of the EU population. The Polish suggestion was to modify the second criterion. Instead of taking the total population numbers, it should be their square roots determining the number of votes within the qualified majority voting system. The smaller countries would have gained (e.g. Latvia 1.7%; Austria, Lithuania, Bulgaria 1.5%), whereas the larger countries would have lost in voting power (e.g. UK 4%; France 4.2%; Germany 7.4%). Poland itself would have lost 1.5% but, in relative terms vis-à-vis the larger countries would have gained considerably. The Polish government was not deterred by the fact that, except for a half-hearted stance by the Czech Republic, no other EU country was ready to support the suggestion. Indeed, Prime Minster Jarosław Kaczyński asserted that 'the square root is worth dying for' and that he was ready 'to pick a fight' during the summit (*Süddeutsche Zeitung Online*, 11 June 2007, 20 June 2007; Gaisbauer, 2008: 69–77).

When it came to explaining the rationale behind the reweighting exercise, Polish policymakers were open about the fact that their foremost aim was a containment of Poland's western neighbor at the EU level. Again, historical arguments wrapped into language resembling wartime discourse were brought forward. Foreign Secretary Anna Fotyga demanded that there should not be a 'German hegemony', and according to Lech Kaczyński the EU status quo was 'almost as if Germany dictates the EU' (*Spiegel*, 25/2007). The foreign ministry's advisor on Polish-German cooperation Mariusz Muszyński claimed that in the first half of 2007 the German council presidency 'uses most of its energy for increasing its power position within the EU instead of dealing with the real problems...The Germans have to get used to the fact that we are an EU member with full rights' (*Spiegel*, 25/2007). Even the liberal newspaper *Gazeta Wyborcza* ran a headline 'Kaczyński Rules Out Capitulation' when Jarosław Kaczyński threatened to veto the constitutional treaty if his suggestion was not accepted (*Spiegel*, 25/2007).

It was when Warsaw used counterfactual arguments in order to justify its position on voting that it was met with downright incomprehension by all other EU states. In an interview with a Polish radio station,

Jarosław Kaczyński claimed that increased EU votes should compensate the country for its wartime losses: 'We only claim what was taken from us... If Poland had not lived through the years 1939 to 1945 it would now be a country with a population of sixty-six million' (*Spiegel Online*, 21 June 2007). Poland should not have considerably fewer votes at the EU level than Germany. 'It was the Germans that brought unimaginable damages and terrible suffering to Poland – incomprehensible crimes – and the Poles like the Germans, whereas the Germans do not like the Poles' (*Spiegel Online*, 21 June 2007).[2] The interview was picked up by the *Financial Times* and subsequently widely circulated in the European media. It added to Poland's isolation in the context of the Brussels summit in June 2007. The German-Polish relationship had proved to be a major stumbling block toward a European accord in a crucial policy area. Warsaw's starting point for the negotiations had been its fixation with containing the perceived German hegemony. The Polish government was caught in its own notions of historical counterfactualism and did not manage, as Luxembourg's prime minister Jean Claude Juncker remarked, 'to just make the leap into the present. You will not become happy if you only look into the rearview mirror. You lose your direction' (*Spiegel Online*, 21 June 2007). As long as the German-Polish relationship remains contested in such terms, it will have a detrimental effect on EU integration.

Conclusion and Outlook

Enlargement transformed the Polish-German border from an external to an internal EU border. It is only natural that this process triggered renegotiations of relationships at both the bilateral and European levels. However, the new closeness under the EU umbrella was not immediately conducive to a Polish-German understanding. Indeed, in some instances it exacerbated pre-existing frictions between the two countries, replacing the proclaimed common European *Werte- und Interessensgemeinschaft* (community of values and interests) with a confrontational *Konfliktgemeinschaft* (community of conflict) (Olschowsky, 2005: 31; cf. also Hofmann & Krzemiński, 2007: 205). This deterioration could be demonstrated through a closer analysis of the discourse surrounding postwar expellees and the EU voting structure. These two themes were chosen as case studies, but they are far from being the only contested areas. Further areas of friction have included German fears of being 'swamped' by cheap Polish labor after accession (Freudenstein & Tewes, 2001), or the question of German cultural artifacts (*Kulturgüter*) held by Poland. The Nazi regime had transported a large number of artifacts to what was to become Polish territory under the 1945 Potsdam settlement. Successive German governments have asked for their return, with former chancellor Gerhard

Schröder arguing that they were part of European heritage, rather than an exclusively German or Polish heritage (Wood, 2002: 106).

In retrospect, it would be tempting to dismiss the enlargement period as an unfortunate isolated episode, prompted by a conservative Polish government that prioritized national interest over European consensus and bilateral understanding. When Donald Tusk and his liberal Civic Platform won the parliamentary elections in October 2007, international reactions were overwhelmingly positive. Political commentators spoke of a new chapter and asked whether this was Poland's 'second return to Europe' (Świeboda, 2007). Federal Chancellor Angela Merkel quickly expressed her firm belief in a Polish-German *détente* and close cooperation at the EU level (*Süddeutsche Zeitung*, 22 October 2007; *Zeit*, 25 October 2007). Since then, relations have indeed improved, but now political actors must avoid the trap of the 1990s – namely, employing flowery rhetoric to gloss over obvious fault lines. The area of security possibly contains the most substantial differences and will remain contested in the years to come. Germany finds its security interests best guaranteed by working toward a common European defense strategy and strengthening pertinent structures. Poland, on the other hand, remains skeptical and prefers to rely on its transatlantic security links. Transatlanticists fear that stronger EU cooperation might offset NATO policies (Gießmann, 2008: 47–48).

These differences came to the fore during the outbreak of the Iraq war in 2003 and are now contested in connection with the installation of a missile defense shield on Polish soil. A connected theme is the relationship with Russia. For Germany, Russia is an important partner, whereas Poland sees its much larger neighbor as a threat that can best be contained through deterrence by the United States. It was especially during the Schröder chancellorship that Russia and the politicization of energy supply cast its shadow over the Polish-German relationship. When Gerhard Schröder and Russian president Vladimir Putin negotiated new gas supplies from Russia to Germany via a pipeline through the Baltic Sea (and not through Polish territory), Defense Secretary Radoslaw Sikorski argued historically: 'That is the Molotow-Ribbentrop tradition. That was the twentieth century. We do not want this to happen again' (*Spiegel* 25/2007). It is the fault line of international security that, at present, is possibly the biggest challenge to Polish-German and Polish-EU relations and needs to be addressed head-on by policymakers. A serious Europeanization of policies – as has developed in the Franco-German case – would not just require a common interest in reconciliation between the two nations but also 'an ability to compromise and redefine their interests vis-à-vis each other. So far, the developments in Polish-German relations indicate that such an evolution remains a distant prospect' (Zaborowski, 2004: 179).

The other major hurdle toward a normalization of relations is the presence of the past. The chapter has offered ample evidence that historical burdens continue to affect public discourse and, indeed, policy-making. The latest episode could be witnessed during the European football championship in June 2008. In the run-up to the Germany versus Poland match, the Polish tabloid *Fakt* (which happens to be owned by Germany's Axel Springer publishing house) showed a photomontage with Polish manager Leo Beenhakker about to behead German captain Michael Ballack. The picture was entitled 'Leo, repeat Grunwald', referring to the place where a Polish-Lithuanian army had been victorious against the Teutonic Order in 1410. A day later, the tabloid *Super Express* depicted Beenhakker holding the blood-dripping heads of Ballack and the German manager Joachim Löw. The montage bore the title 'Leo, bring us their heads' (Schenk, 2001; *Süddeutsche Zeitung Online*, 5 June 2008). So far, there is no evidence that enlargement has been a trigger for a swift improvement of bilateral relations. The evidence presented in this chapter instead points to a long path toward normalization (Bender, 2005, 2007).

Notes

1. In a parliamentary debate about the issue, Jarosław Kaczyński describes an alleged German plot (*układ*): 'In Poland there was and still is a front to defend German interests. One has to say very clearly that this front consists of active members of the German secret service, including former Stasi (East German secret police) members. This is a very large group that lives on German money and pretends to be independent scholars or independent journalists – a large number of useful idiots with the attitude of beggars' (*Spiegel* 25/2007).
2. In the same vein, Britain and France were accused of abandoning Poland in 1939 and for a second time after 1945, allowing the country to fall to communism. Those countries would therefore have an obligation to support demands for disproportionately strong voting power (*Süddeutsche Zeitung Online*, 13 June 2007, 21 June 2007).

References

Anonyma (2003) *Eine Frau in Berlin. Tagebuch-Aufzeichnungen vom 20. April bis 22. Juni 1945*. Frankfurt: Eichborn.
Aust, S. and Burgdorff, S. (eds) (2003) *Die Flucht. Über die Vertreibung der Deutschen aus dem Osten*. Stuttgart/Munich: Deutsche Verlags-Anstalt.
Bender, P. (2005) Normalisierung wäre schon viel. *Aus Politik und Zeitgeschichte* 5 (6), 3–8.
Bender, P. (2007) Neues Polen? Deutsch-Polnische Empfindlichkeiten. *Blätter für deutsche und internationale Politik* 12, 1494–1496.
Bingen, D. (2005) Die deutsch-polnischen Beziehungen nach 1945. *Aus Politik und Zeitgeschichte* 5 (6), 9–17.
Birkenkämper, A. and Holesch, A. (2008) *Von Kaczńyski zu Tusk. Eine deutsch-polnische Tragödie?* Bonn: Bouvier.

Bonner Erklärung "Europäisches Netzwerk: Zwangsmigationen und Vertreibungen im 20. Jahrhundert" (2004) – Online Document: http://library.fes.de/library/netzquelle/zwangsmigration/48bonnererkl.html. Accessed 15 May 2009.

Freudenstein, R. and Tewes, H. (2001) *Die EU-Osterweiterung und der deutsche Arbeitsmarkt. Testfall für die deutsch-polnische Interessengemeinschaft*, working paper, Konrad-Adenauer-Stiftung e. V.

Friedrich, J. (2002) *Der Brand. Deutschland im Bombenkrieg 1940–1945*. Munich: Propyläen Verlag.

Gaisbauer, H.P. (2008) Polens Vorstellungen zur künftigen Gestalt der EU und dem Grad polnisch-deutscher Kooperation. In T. Jäger and D.W. Dylla (eds) *Deutschland und Polen. Die europäische und internationale Politik* (pp. 57–80). Wiesbaden: VS Verlag für Sozialwissenschaften.

George, S. (1998) *An Awkward Partner. Britain in the European Community*. Oxford: Oxford University Press.

Gießmann, H.J. (2008) Mehr Zwietracht als Eintracht? Deutschland, Polen und die europäische Sicherheit. In T. Jäger and D.W. Dylla (eds) *Deutschland und Polen. Die europäische und internationale Politik* (pp. 35–56). Wiesbaden: VS Verlag für Sozialwissenschaften.

Grabbe, H. (2004) Poland. The EU's new awkward partner, *Centre for European Reform Bulletin* 34 – Online document: http://www.cer.org.uk/articles/34_grabbe.html. Accessed 15 May 2009.

Gross, J.T. (2001) *Neighbors. The Destruction of the Jewish Community in Jedwabne, Poland*. Princeton, NJ: Princeton University Press.

Hofmann, G. and Krzemiński, A. (2007) *Schuld & Sühne & Stolz & Vorurteil. Polen und Deutsche*. Berlin/Warsaw: Edition Foto Tapeta.

Holesch, A. (2007) *Verpasster Neuanfang? Deutschland, Polen und die EU*. Bonn: Bouvier.

Hudabiunigg, I. (2004) Drinnen und draußen. Polen und die Konstruktion einer europäischen Identität in der deutschen Publizistik der Jahre 1998–2003. In Z. Bilut-Homplewicz and Z. Tęcza (eds) *Sprache leben und lieben. Festschrift für Zdzisław Wawrzyniak* (pp. 159–176). Frankfurt: Peter Lang.

Kaczyński, L. (2006) Europe – Still divided. In K. Michalski (ed.) *What Holds Europe Together?* (pp. 131–136). New York: Central European University Press.

Lebioda, T. (2000) Poland, "die Vertriebenen", and the road to integration with the European Union. In K. Cordell (ed.) *Poland and the European Union* (pp. 166–181). London/New York: Routledge.

Meckel, M. (2007) Symbole und Netzwerke. *Dialog* 79, 64–66.

Müller, M.G. (2004) The joint Polish-German commission for the revision of school textbooks and Polish views of German history, *German History* 22 (3), 433–447.

Olschowsky, B. (2005) Die Gegenwart des Vergangenen. *Aus Politik und Zeitgeschichte* 5 (6), 27–32.

Rau, J. and Kwaśniewski, A. (2003) Danziger Erklärung – Online Document: http://www.bundespraesident.de/-,2.93344/Bundespraesident-Johannes-Rau-.htm?global.printview=2. Accessed 21 May 2009.

Schenk, F.B. (2001) Tannenberg/Grunwald. In E. François and H. Schulze (eds) *Deutsche Erinnerungsorte* (pp. 438–454). Munich: Beck.

Świeboda, P. (2007) Poland's second return to Europe? European Council on Foreign Relations, *Policy Brief* – Online Document: http://ecfr.3cdn.net/01803 d4e3cb9b9a50b_ldm6b5y15.pdf. Accessed 21 May 2009.

Urban, T. (2004) *Der Verlust. Die Vertreibung der Deutschen und Polen im 20. Jahrhundert.* Munich: Beck.

Urban, T. (2005) Historische Belastungen der Integration Polens in die EU. *Aus Politik und Zeitgeschichte* 5 (6), 32–39.

Verheugen, G. (2004) Die Zukunft heißt Europa, *Osteuropa* 4, 3–13.

Wood, S. (2002) Apprehensive partners. Germany, Poland and EU enlargement. *German Politics* 11 (1), 97–124.

Zaborowski, M. (2004) *Germany, Poland and Europe. Conflict, Co-operation and Europeanisation.* Manchester/New York: Manchester University Press.

Chapter 2
The Role of Metaphor in Shaping Cultural Stereotypes: A Case Study of French Public Discourse on European Union Enlargement

Steffen Buch and Uta Helfrich

Introduction

France has played a very important role in the process of European integration, with Jean Monnet, Robert Schuman and Valéry Giscard d'Estaing as some of Europe's most prominent political figures. In this tradition, its commitment to enlargement can be seen as a struggle for a historical endeavor bound for success.[1] Politicians have always had to rely on the media's willingness to act as a mediator between politics and the public. This mutual reliance between political discourse and press discourse clearly manifests itself in the case of the European enlargement project. Regardless of their political position, the three French daily newspapers considered in this study all try to prepare the public for this enlargement by means of continuous reporting. It is therefore of interest to analyze the linguistic means the newspapers employ to outline the various group identities and the possible conflicting attitudes involved in the extension process.

Following Lakoff and Johnson (2003), the use of metaphor is of crucial importance for the study of such attitudes, given the fact that its analysis serves in the deduction of underlying base concepts. Conceptualizations are often employed for biased evaluation in the form of seemingly unquestionable prejudices and stereotypes. Analyzing their linguistic expressions makes it possible to trace the way they create cultural identities.

Press Discourse

Press discourse is considered to represent public opinion best through the use of easily accessible image strategies such as metaphors, metonymies, similes and other anchors around which information is organized. These devices are 'grounded in social space and they are driven by shared knowledge and a sense of common identity' (O'Keeffe, 2006: 155).

They not only reflect attitudes but also contribute to shaping attitudes. It is this kind of social categorizing based on commonly shared beliefs about nationality, ethnicity or religion that is often used to label Others, not only in everyday life, but also in public discourse.

The authors of press articles profit from the inventory of discursive means available in collective knowledge to make their portrayal acceptable to their readers. The more they rely on background information or commonly shared beliefs, the better they will be able to comment on the respective topic without explicitly having to provide information about specific aspects.

From a cognitive approach, all newspaper texts show indications of persuasive and ideological language use in the sense of 'belief systems or social representations' (van Dijk, 2001: 12) in the form of conceptual mappings and frames. It is in these specific realizations of cognitive models (i.e. metonymies and metaphors) that we find recurrent elements that can be taken as (proto-)typical of a determined discourse.

Quantitative Analysis

This study is based on information on the fifth enlargement of the European Union as provided by the three most relevant French national newspapers – *Le Figaro* (conservative), *Le Monde* (leftist-liberal) and *Libération* (leftist-liberal) – from January to June 2004. Our database included 4074 entries derived from a total of 830 articles (cf. Table 2.1).[2]

Because enlargement mainly belongs to the domain of international politics, but also has a strong impact on national politics, national identity and the economy, the newspaper columns indicated in Table 2.2 were selected for further study.

In the distribution of the columns, the IP section is the most relevant, providing approximately 73% of the articles and a full 81% of the data. F/NP, in contrast, contributes to the corpus with approximately 17.5% of the articles and a mere 12.6% of the data. Concerning the different tendencies in portrayal within the respective columns (cf. Table 2.3), the corpus consists of 39.82% informative, neutral data, 32.49% negatively or skeptically connoted data and 27.69% positively connoted data.[3]

Table 2.1 Database structure

	Newspaper			
	Le Figaro (LF)	*Le Monde (LM)*	*Libération (Lib)*	*Total*
Articles	389 (46.86%)	253 (30.48%)	188 (22.65%)	830
Data	1,980 (48.60%)	1,019 (25.01%)	1,075 (26.39%)	4,074

Table 2.2 Selected newspaper columns

	Newspaper			
Articles	Le Figaro	Le Monde	Libération	Total
E	32 (4.20%)	37 (4.86%)	5 (0.66%)	74 (9.71%)
F/NP	64 (8.40%)	31 (4.07%)	38 (16.80%)	133 (17.45%)
IP	268 (35.17%)	159 (20.87%)	128 (16.80%)	555 (72.83%)
Total	364 (47.77%)	227 (29.79%)	171 (22.44%)	762 (100%)
Data				
E	87 (2.28%)	129 (3.38%)	19 (0.50%)	235 (6.16%)
F/NP	224 (5.87%)	85 (2.23%)	172 (4.51%)	481 (12.60%)
IP	1,574 (41.24%)	684 (17.92%)	843 (22.09%)	3,101 (81.24%)
Total	1,885 (49.38%)	898 (23.53%)	1,034 (27.09%)	3,817 (100%)

Note: E = Economics, F/NP = French national politics, IP = International politics

Table 2.3 Different tendencies in portrayal within respective columns

	Tone			
Section	Informative, neutral	Negative, skeptical	Positive	Total
E	87	82	66	235
F/NP	140	184	157	481
IP	1,293	974	834	3,101
Total	1,520 (39.82%)	1,240 (32.49%)	1,057 (27.69%)	3,817 (100%)

Note: E = Economics, F/NP = French national politics, IP = International politics

Given the fact that there is no equal distribution of data, neither with regard to the articles' derivation from various newspapers nor to their distribution in relation to thematic categories, we used a mean ratio calculation that levels the diverging figures for data and articles by focusing on their relation (cf. Table 2.4). This instrument, which can be understood as a specific value for public discourse in French newspaper coverage on EU enlargement, provides quantitative information on the way newspapers express their ideological position.

The newspapers' ratios for the subsets of informative, neutral portrayal (r_{inf}), negative, skeptical (r_{neg}) and positive portrayal (r_{pos}) deviate decisively from the ratio average ($r_{average} = 5.01$). In contrast to $r_{average}$, there is a remarkable difference between neutral texts ($r_{inf} = 4.04$) and rather biased texts ($r_{neg} = 5.41$; $r_{pos} = 6.73$): clearly, there more data are employed per article for a positive portrayal of EU enlargement. These

The Role of Metaphor in Shaping Cultural Stereotypes   19

Table 2.4 Mean ratio calculation for data and articles

Data/Article Ratio (r)	Newspaper			$r_{average}$
	Le Figaro	Le Monde	Libération	
r_{inf}	4.16	3.21	5.55	4.04
r_{neg}	5.93	4.39	5.51	5.41
r_{pos}	7.16	5.27	7.95	6.73
$r_{average}$	5.18	3.96	6.05	5.01

Note: r = ratio, r_{inf} = neutral, r_{neg} = negative, skeptical, r_{pos} = positive

numbers can be taken as an indication for a significant relationship of the tone of the articles and their editorial (and ideological) provenience.

As Figure 2.1 shows, there is a general tendency for texts with a positive tone to have a higher ratio than neutral, informative texts or even negative ones.[4] Second, the progressions of r_{inf} and r_{pos} are very similar, nearly parallel, differing by 1.46 points in April to 2.16 points in May. The only exception in which negative texts show a decisively higher ratio is in February (r_{neg_feb} = 6.57). Furthermore, r_{neg} does not show the same steady progression as r_{inf} or r_{pos}. After its peak in February, it reaches its nadir in March (r_{neg_march} = 3.62), then climbs to exceed $r_{average}$ in April (r_{neg_april} = 6.00), returning to a substandard ratio in May (r_{neg_may} = 4.65) and consolidating near $r_{average}$ in June (r_{neg_june} = 5.28).

The abundant use of linguistic means to conceptualize the EU in a positive portrayal appears to be symptomatic of the authors' intention to explain the benefits of the enlargement process. The overall occurrence of high ratios and their progression indicate that the apparent promotion

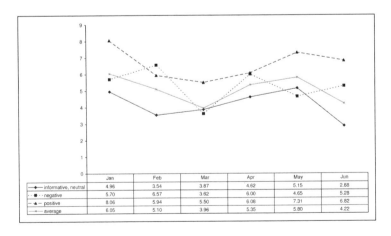

Figure 2.1 Mean ratio progression (January–June 2004)

of a positive image is more strategic than coincidental. The progression of the neutral, informative ratio (r_{inf}) must be seen as a backing of the positive portrayal. The use of a minor ratio ($r_{inf} < r_{average}$) corresponds with the ethics of an objective portrayal.

The progression of r_{neg} appears to be anticlimactic to r_{pos}. This especially applies to the months of January, February, March and, most considerably, May: the difference in ratio averages $r_{(pos-neg)\_jan} = 2.36$, $r_{(pos-neg)\_feb} = 0.63$, $r_{(pos-neg)\_march} = 1.88$ respectively, and increases up to $r_{(pos-neg)\_may} = 2.66$ in May as an explicit act of affirmative discourse at the very date of enlargement. Criticism conveyed via negative, skeptical texts seems to be uttered only with reference to specific incidents – for example, Cyprus' denial of the European Constitution. It could be argued that authors of negative, skeptical articles prefer to employ a rather 'covert' strategy in their effort not to clash with the predominant *doxa* of public opinion, which is generally pro-European.

Basic Conceptualizations

With his list of image schemas (e.g. CONTAINMENT, JOURNEY, PROXIMITY & DISTANCE and LINKAGE & SEPARATION), Lakoff (1987: 271ff.) provides the main frame for the classification of potential conceptual elements in discourse. When speaking about the structure of a state or a similar political entity, political rhetoric has manifested an astonishing stability since antiquity. According to Kurz (2004), this type of discourse is concentrated on a limited set of five base concepts: namely, ORGANISM, FAMILY, SHIP, MACHINE and ILLNESS. Depending on the particular thematic focus and perspective, not all of these are likely to be activated in any one political context. According to Musolff (2004: 173), the main scenarios for the linguistic representation of public discourse on Europe in Britain and Germany are FAMILY, JOURNEY, LIFE–HEALTH–BODY and ARCHITECTURE–HOUSE–BUILDING. In their study on political discourse in Germany and Poland concerning Poland's accession to the EU, Mikolajczyk and Zinken (2003) distinguish between four major metaphorical models: SOURCE–PATH–GOAL used for descriptions of the accession, LIFE–HEALTH–BODY in contexts referring to the enlargement as such, ARCHITECTURE–HOUSE–BUILDING and FAMILY representing the discourse on the design aspects connected therewith. Focusing on Switzerland as an EU-outsider and its relationship to Europe, Bärtsch (2004: 81ff.) finds the most relevant schemas to be INSIDE–OUTSIDE, DISTANCE and JOURNEY.

However, these observations are based on different cultural backgrounds and consequently convey different cultural as well as political attitudes toward Europe. As for the metaphors and other imaging devices in French press discourse, its focus on enlargement as a spatial frame leads to a heightened frequency of the CONSTRUCTION concept, the JOURNEY scenario and the INSIDE–OUTSIDE schema. Furthermore, French public discourse not only contains transnational and European conceptualizations, but also expresses certain specific French positions that have to be considered in context with their respective identification strategies concerning different member states.

The Construction of Cultural Identity: A Case Study

Means of construction and delimitation of group identities through imaging strategies are accompanied and supported by well-established devices of deictic mapping; for example, identification strategies that consist of attributing and appropriating facts or qualities to WE and THEY groups have been clearly defined through possessive pronouns or appositive phrases:

(1) our European project[5] (notre Projet européen, *Libération*, 9 April 2004)

(2) those that will function as a bridge between new Europe and Russia (ceux qui feront le pont entre la nouvelle Europe et la Russie, *Le Figaro*, 21 April 2004)

(3) The 'ten' that have just rejoined us (Les 'dix' qui viennent de nous rejoindre, *Le Figaro*, 25 May 2004)

(4) They have indeed received their European Union certificate of baptism this weekend. (Ils ont, certes, reçu ce week-end leur certificat de baptême de l'Union européenne. *Le Figaro*, 3 May 2004)

When based on the implicit or explicit juxtaposition of ideas and identities, the same device works as a contrasting strategy. In many cases, devices belonging to the centering WE concept occur in combination with positive imagery, whereas the othering THEY concept goes together with negative imaging strategies, suggesting a clear judgment to the readers:

(5) Instead of exporting stability, we will import uncertainty. (Au lieu d'exporter la stabilité, nous importerions l'incertitude. *Libération*, 9 April 2004)

(6) the impression that it is Brussels that obliges us to advance (l'impression que c'est Bruxelles qui nous oblige à avancer, *Le Figaro*, 26 April 2004)

This kind of strategy is often combined with a temporal (2, 3) or modal (7) inference of appeal, order, prognosis or expectation:

(7) The entry of the ten new member states, on 1 May, should reinforce its [US] influence. (L'entrée de dix nouveaux pays membres, le 1er mai, devrait renforcer leur [É-U] emprise. *Le Figaro*, 19 April 2004)

Table 2.5 WE concept vs. THEY concept

Tone, Type of text	We concept	They concept
Informative, neutral		
Essay	13	22
Interview	6	11
News	15	26
Negative, skeptical		
Essay	13	15
Interview	7	4
News	24	33
Positive		
Essay	46	13
Interview	17	3
News	20	13

Interestingly, these strategies can be aligned not only with the tone of the portrayal, but can even be traced back to the textual form of different text types. Most of our data has been derived mainly from three types of press texts: essay, interview and news. We found that the positively connoted WE concept is activated above all in essays (46), whereas in news (33) there is a tendency to focus negative identities through the THEY concept (cf. Table 2.5).

In-group identities: Concepts of France

References to France originate from a very rich conceptual inventory. In contrast to the portrayal of other countries, the concepts increase not only in number but also in detail. The concept of CONTAINMENT stands as a general prerequisite for other concepts – not only in the rather vague sense of ENTITY, but specifically in terms of PERSONIFICATION (8–9) as well as NATIONAL IDENTIFICATION (10–11).

> (8) Is France, too, sick of the European construction? (La France est-elle malade, aussi, de la construction européenne? *Le Figaro*, 14 February 2004)

> (9) France, Europe's former godmother (la France, jadis marraine de l'Europe, *Libération*, 30 June 2004)

> (10) This will be the end of France as a sovereign nation. (Ce sera la fin de la France en tant que nation souveraine. *Le Figaro*, 23 April 2004)

(11) This concerns France's future in Europe. (Il s'agit de l'avenir de la France en Europe. *Le Figaro*, 3 May 2004)

The relationship between France and Europe is either identified in terms of interpersonal linkage (9), or as a *pars-pro-toto* relation (12–14) that tends to become metonymical (15–16).

(12) Europe is France's future. (L'Europe est l'avenir de la France. *Le Monde*, 4 June 2004)

(13) France has no future outside of Europe. (La France n'a pas d'avenir en dehors de l'Europe. *Le Figaro*, 4 June 2004)

(14) In order to be big and strong, France needs Europe. (Pour être grande et forte, la France a besoin de l'Europe. *Le Figaro*, 4 June 2004)

(15) France full size (La France en grand, *Le Figaro*, 3 June 2004)

(16) Europe is ... : a French idea. (l'Europe est ... : une idée française. *Le Figaro*, 8 June 2004)

The interpretation of the EU as a Franco–German (European) Union[6] (17) is influenced by the concept of CENTRAL VS. PERIPHERAL STATES and intensified by the concepts of MASS or WEIGHT (18–20). In this context, France and Germany are conceptualized as Europe's (HARD) CORE (*noyau dur*) (21–23).

(17) a Franco-German Europe (une Europe franco-allemande, *Libération*, 10 June 2004)

(18) mighty Europe, indispensable counterbalance to American hegemony (Europe puissance, indispensable contrepoids à l'hégémonie américaine, *Libération*, 5 February 2004)

(19) Paris has been dreaming of a mighty Europe. (Paris rêvait d'Europe-puissance. *Libération*, 23 June 2004)

(20) France would have more weight than the 25-member Union? (en quoi la France pèserait-elle davantage que l'Union à vingt-cinq? *Libération*, 9 June 2004)

(21) The famous 'hard cores' that France and Germany wanted to relaunch (Les fameux 'noyaux durs' que la France et l'Allemagne voulaient relancer, *Le Figaro*, 25 March 2004)

(22) the emergence of a 'center of gravity' that consists of the most advanced states (l'émergence d'un 'centre de gravité' des Etats les plus allants, *Le Figaro*, 1 March 2004)

(23) Its core will be formed by the Franco-German coagulation. (Son noyau sera constitué par la coagulation franco-allemande. *Libération*, 25 June 2004)

The conceptual domain of SOCIAL & PERSONAL LINKAGE is frequently employed to demonstrate the closeness of France and Germany. The Franco-German union mentioned above goes beyond mere imagery of LINKAGE (24) and even shows signs of symbiosis (25). More than this, it is presented by means of a strong romantic relation, which is illustrated as a (strolling) couple (26–28) during their honeymoon (29).

(24)... around the Franco-German bond of friendship. (... autour du lien franco-allemand. *Le Figaro*, 14 February 2004)

(25) symbiosis between France and Germany (symbiose entre la France et l'Allemagne, *Le Figaro*, 27 April 2004)

(26) France and Germany are walking together on the European road holding hands. (La France et l'Allemagne marchent main dans la main sur la route européenne. *Le Monde*, 16 June 2004)

(27) the Franco-German couple (le couple franco-allemand *Libération*, 29 April 2004)

(28) Paris prefers to keep house together with Berlin. (Paris préfère se mettre en ménage avec Berlin. *Le Figaro*, 5 April 2004)

(29) the Franco-German relations in their honeymoon (les relations franco-allemandes en pleine lune de miel, *Le Figaro*, 10 February 2004)

From these two main conceptualizations, LINKAGE and CORE, derives the motivation for the political AXIS (30). This CORE–AXIS–LINKAGE is understood in terms of MOTION, which brings forth not only general procedural imagery (PATH, VELOCITY and JOURNEY) but also more specific concepts: for example, TANDEM (31–32), MOTOR & VEHICLE (33–35):

(30) Rather than a Franco-German axis (Plutôt qu'un axe franco-allemand, *Le Monde*, 11 May 2004)

(31) I will believe in the Franco-German tandem... (Je croirai au tandem franco-allemand... *Le Figaro*, 14 February 2004)

(32) the energy of the Franco-German tandem (la capacité d'entraînement du tandem franco-allemand, *Le Monde*, 29 April 2004)

(33) the European 'steam-roller' (le 'rouleau compresseur' européen, *Le Figaro*, 8 June 2004)

(34) not to adjust the velocity of the European convoy to its slowest part (ne pas aligner la vitesse du convoi européen sur celle de son élément le plus lent, *Le Figaro*, 1 March 2004)

(35) stimulated by an advancing, not a braking, Europe (stimulé par une Europe qui avance et non qui freine, *Le Monde*, 12 March 2004)

and PIONEERS & AVANT-GARDE (36–37), conceptually generalizing these aspects in the form of an elitist LEADERSHIP (38–40):

(36) the idea of 'pioneer groups' as motors of the enlargement (l'idée de 'groupes pionniers' comme moteurs de l'élargissement, *Le Monde*, 24 February 2004)

(37) to form an avant-garde (constituer une avant-garde, *Libération*, 30 June 2004)

(38) to resume leadership by prearranging affairs (reprendre le leadership, en se concertant, *Libération*, 2 March 2004)

(39) question of a directory of the big countries (question sur un directoire des Grands, *Libération*, 2 March 2004)

(40) the new triumvirate (le nouveau triumvirat, *Le Figaro*, 19 February 2004)

Apart from these ubiquitous conceptualizations, we find specific scenarios employed for biased portrayal. Negatively biased articles tend to focus on the political quarrels that are understood in terms of a structural DIVISION (41–42) leading to the DISINTEGRATION (43) of the European Union or, even worse, France (44–46):

(41) Europe, weakened by its division (L'Europe... affaiblie par sa division, *Le Figaro*, 13 April 2004)

(42) In its inner strife, Europe has been inaudible. (Déchirée, l'Europe a été inaudible. *Le Figaro*, 13 April 2004)

(43) the disintegration of the European community (la désintégration de l'Europe communautaire, *Le Monde*, 25 March 2004)

(44)...the progressive absorption, the dissolution of the French nation in the European magma. (...l'absorption progressive, la dissolution de la nation française dans le magma européen. *Le Figaro*, 30 April 2004)

(45) Europe is cooking France to rags. (L'Europe est en train de tuer la France à petit feu. *Le Figaro*, 23 April 2004)

(46) the European construction that leads 'to the destruction of France' (la construction européenne... que celle-ci conduisait 'à la déstruction de la France', *Le Monde*, 14 June 2004)

In articles with a positive tone, instead, the same aspects are treated with a shift in focus: The threat of DIVISION and DISINTEGRATION is negated (47–49), attenuated by modal auxiliaries (50) or neutralized by the attribution of a word with a contrary meaning (51):

> (47) no to the division of Europe into privileged and straggling countries (non à la division de l'Europe entre des pays privilégiés et des retardataires, *Le Figaro*, 25 February 2004)

> (48) We have no intention of cutting Europe into two pieces. (Nous n'avons aucune intention de couper l'Europe en deux. *Le Figaro*, 25 February 2004)

> (49) Europe doesn't replace our nations. It is a federation of nation states. (L'Europe ne se substitue pas à nos nations. C'est une fédération d'Etats nations. *Le Figaro*, 30 April 2004)

> (50) Europe could be perceived by many French citizens as a menace to French identity (L'Europe peut être perçue par de nombreux citoyens français comme une menace pour l'identité de la France, *Le Figaro*, 26 June 2004)

> (51) to overcome European division (surmonter les divisions européennes, *Le Figaro*, 17 March 2004)

Positive discourse especially invokes democratic values (52–53), RENEWAL (54), *history* (55) and FORTIFICATION (56), and turns the JOURNEY of European integration into an ADVENTURE (57):

> (52) A Europe of freedom and rights. (Une Europe de la liberté et du droit, *Le Figaro*, 30 April 2004)

> (53) peace, democracy, and stability, the French think that Europe can guarantee them best (paix, démocratie, stabilité, les Français pensent que l'Europe les garantit mieu, *Libération*, 26 May 2004)

> (54) Today, we enter a new age. (Aujourd'hui nous entrons dans un nouvel âge. *Le Figaro*, 28 January 2004)

> (55) the historical event (l'événement historique, *Le Figaro*, 30 April 2004)

> (56) The enlargement is a good thing: it strengthens Europe. (L'élargissement est une bonne chose: il renforce l'Europe. *Le Figaro*, 3 May 2004)

> (57) We have been mastering this adventure successfully for 50 years now. (Nous avons réussi cette aventure pendant 50 ans. *Le Figaro*, 28 January 2004)

Out-group identities: Concepts of Poland and Cyprus

The integration of Poland and Cyprus has been vividly and controversially discussed in the French press. As the biggest country of the ten new member states with regard to its territory as well as its population, Poland is described as a giant in terms of SIZE and at the same time as a dwarf with regard to its economy (58). As to the number of seats in the Council of the European Union, it is imagined as a (HEAVY)WEIGHT, although its influence is illustrated as not being as big as that of the old members – that is, France, Germany, the United Kingdom and Italy (59).

> (58) But, Poland, a giant within the new members' platoon, is an economic dwarf. (Mais la Pologne, géant au sein du peloton des nouveaux membres, est un nain économique. *Le Monde*, 29 April 2004)

> (59) Even Poland, a heavyweight among the 'newcomers', is very much mistaken. (Même la Pologne, poids lourd des 'nouveaux', est loin du compte. *Le Figaro*, 26 April 2004)

The debates about SIZE and WEIGHT do not solely result from inherently European issues, but also from the division the European Union suffered during the second Iraq war. Where European issues are concerned, the discussion about the pace of EU integration along with the CORE debate is relevant to understanding the rather negative portrayal that Poland receives in the French press. Its participation in the second Iraq war led to harsh criticism by French politicians and the media. This is the reason the established concept of SIZE in (60) is deconstructed and Poland is presented as a troublemaker (*trublion*). Press coverage of Poland is hence dominated by aspects of its supposed ethical and behavioral deficits: weakness (61), lack of eagerness (62), treason (63), mistrust (64), bad temper (65) and corruption (66):

> (60) Poland: Europe's new 'Great' or troublemaker? (La Pologne: nouveau 'grand' ou trublion de l'Europe? *Le Figaro*, 24 April 2004)

> (61) This country's problem is that it's too big to not be ambitious and at the same time still too weak to sit and vote among the big ones. (Le problème de ce pays est qu'il est trop grand pour ne pas avoir d'ambitions, mais encore trop faible pour siéger parmi les Grands. *Le Figaro*, 14 April 2004)

> (62) Poland's lack of eagerness to communicate the union's agreement (la Pologne pour son manque d'empressement à transporter l'acquis communautaire, *Le Figaro*, 29 March 2004)

> (63) the 'treason' by its Polish ally (la 'trahison' de son alliée polonaise, *Libération*, 27 March 2004)

(64) Poland has been backing America... By doing so, it only succeeded in deepening the lack of confidence within the union. (La Pologne misait sur l'Amérique... Elle n'a réussi qu'à creuser le déficit de confiance au sein de l'Union. *Le Figaro*, 14 April 2004)

(65) Poland continues to display its bad temper. (La Pologne continue de manifester sa mauvaise humeur. *Le Figaro*, 25 May 2004)

(66) Henceforth, the corruption in Poland will have an effect on the whole of Europe. (La corruption en Pologne aura désormais des effets dans toute l'Union. *Libération*, 27 April 2004)

This moral evaluation consequently leads to the EDUCATION scenario (67–69), in which Poland – like other new member states – is taken to be a pupil that still has to learn how to behave in the European Community:

(67) this country that the [European] Commission considers to be a bad student (ce pays [Poland] que la Commission désigne comme mauvais élève, *Le Figaro*, 24 April 2004)

(68) the apprenticeship of Europe's arcane secrets ([l']apprentissage des arcanes européennes, *Le Monde*, 29 April 2004)

(69) the 'almost grown-ups', those blocking Spaniards and Poles (les 'presque Grands', ces Espagnols et Polonais qui bloquent, *Libération*, 2 March 2004)

Poland is furthermore identified as the most Catholic of the new member state cultures. Polish Catholicism is hence stereotyped as a Polish collective symbol and serves as an explanation for Poland's and other countries' demand to include Europe's Christian roots in the constitution (70–72):

(70) the most Catholic of the new members (le plus catholique des nouveaux Etats membres, *Le Figaro*, 24 April 2004)

(71) Especially Poland insists on the future European constitution referring to Christian roots. (La Pologne notamment, qui insiste tant pour que la future Constitution européenne fasse référence aux racines chrétiennes. *Le Figaro*, 11 June 2004)

(72) They fight for the preamble of the constitution to refer to Europe's Christian heritage. (Ils se battent pour que le préambule de la Constitution fasse référence à l'héritage chrétien de l'Europe. *Le Monde*, 20 April 2004)

Given the fact that Cyprus is divided into a Turkish and Greek part, of which only the latter was to become an EU member, the pre-eminence of the concepts of UNION and DIVISION (73–74) concerning these new member states is not surprising:[7]

(73) to see their island rejoin Europe soon (voir bientôt leur île rejoindre l'Europe, *Le Figaro*, 2 April 2004)

(74) a line is cutting a member state in two (une ligne coupera en deux un Etat membre, *Le Figaro*, 27 April 2004)

Out of the repertoire of European history, the Berlin Wall is employed for comparison (75–78). This reference to a historical incidence helps create a positively connoted perspective on possibly overcoming the Cypriots' cultural division:

(75) final point in a process that started with the fall of the Berlin Wall (point final du processus né de la chute du mur de Berlin, *Le Figaro*, 3 May 2004)

(76) The island is divided by a demarcation line traversing the capital, Nicosia, like another Berlin Wall. (L'île est partagée par une ligne de démarcation qui traverse la capitale, Nicosie, comme un autre mur de Berlin. *Le Figaro*, 1 June 2004)

(77) 'the new Berlin Wall' that will determine the enlargement ('le nouveau mur de Berlin' que constituerait l'élargissement, *Le Figaro*, 22 April 2004)

(78) Five days after the enlargement, the European Union abuts on its first obstacle: the Cyprus Wall. (A cinq jours de l'élargissement, l'Union européenne bute sur son premier obstacle: le mur de Chypre. *Le Figaro*, 27 April 2004)

As an artifact of protection and shelter, the wall is also – not only practically but also conceptually – set to exclude those (Turkish Cypriots and Turks) who are not supposed to enter the EU and are thus excluded from its benefits (79–80). As in the case of Poland, we find characteristics of a moralizing discourse in the banning of the Turkish Cypriots (81):

(79) The Turkish Cypriots would be excluded from the benefits of the adhesion. (Les Chypriotes turcs seraient exclus des bienfaits de l'adhésion. *Le Figaro*, 23 March 2004)

(80) It would be paradoxical, even dangerous, if Turkey were part of the Union. (Il serait paradoxal, même dangereux, que la Turquie intégrât l'Union. *Le Figaro*, 23 March 2004)

(81) The Turkish Cypriots now find themselves banned by the EU. (Les Chypriotes turcs se retrouvent alors au ban de l'UE. *Le Figaro*, 24 January 2004)

Comparable to the portrayal of Poland, the French press takes Cyprus' denial of the constitution to doubt Cyprus' ethical and moral quality (82).

This evaluative attitude again yields SCHOOL metaphors (83–84) similar to those of the Polish context.

> (82) Cyprus. Disgrace for the European Union (Chypre. Embarras de l'Union européenne, *Le Figaro*, 26 April 2004)

> (83) Having become the bad students of the international class, they expose themselves to punishment. (Devenus les mauvais élèves de la classe internationale, ils s'exposent à des punitions. *Le Figaro*, 26 April 2004)

> (84) Good Student. He has to make an effort if he wants to succeed. (Bon élève. Doit poursuivre ses efforts s'il veut réussir. *Le Figaro*, 17 January 2004)

Conclusion

The effectiveness of metaphor as a typical device in persuasive argumentation is founded not only upon its intrinsic capacity to categorize, but also upon the cultural specificity of beliefs thereby transmitted. In the three newspapers considered in this study, French public discourse on European Union enlargement follows these premises via a limited and simple set of metaphorical clusters that convey a strong emotional impact.

As the strategies of identity-building show, France and (with some reservation) Germany are seen by the French press as legitimate, dominant and high-status group members. These insiders are identified as LEADERS and MOTORS. A subordinate status is assigned to the new, yet-to-be group members. Their change of status within the EU should coincide with a change of face in public perception. On the whole, the French press plays an active, albeit sometimes ambiguous, role in political legitimization discourse, thus conforming to the overall political goal of EU enlargement. French newspapers do not confine themselves to mere explanation by evoking the procedural aspects of this enterprise (i.e. the conceptual domain of ARCHITECTURE–HOUSE–BUILDING). By placing emphasis on emotional associations and moral qualities within the FAMILY concept, press discourse functions as a guideline for measuring the integrative capacity of future members and helps establish a framework for such a change in opinion.

Notes

1. For a detailed discussion of the incompatibility between France's traditional self-image as a nation, its vision of Europe on the one hand and its expected loss of influence within the new European paradigm on the Other, cf. Chopin (2005), Lieb (2008), Seidendorf (2008) and Vogel (2008). This loss of influence, in combination with overall fears concerning the respect for democratic values and concepts of security, explains the skeptical attitude of the French (among

both politicians and the general public), documented by *Eurobarometer 61* (spring 2004) just before the enlargement (37% in favor) and improving only slightly afterwards (*Eurobarometer 62*: fall 2004: 39% in favor), thus remaining rather low compared to the European average of 50% approval. This attitude again found its expression in the results of the European elections in June 2004, when French anti-European parties obtained a remarkable vote of 18% (cf. Höhne, 2005: 12).
2. At the level of data distribution, about 50% have been taken from conservative (*Le Figaro*) and leftist-liberal newspapers (*Le Monde, Libération*), respectively. This distribution provides an ideologically balanced basis for comparison, despite slight divergences in coverage by each of them.
3. The classification of press articles as informative (neutral) and evaluative (positive vs. negative, skeptical) is taken from Brinker (2000). By analyzing the textual and contextual indicators of a given text (cf. Brinker, 2000: 180), information about its communicative function is retrieved. In a second step, the author's thematic and evaluative attitudes (*thematische Einstellung* and *evaluative Einstellung*) are studied in order to identify the text's evaluative tone, which according to Brinker is the key category of textual analysis.
4. In one of the few studies on French press coverage of EU enlargement, Le (2002: 293), concentrating on *Le Monde's* editorial discourse, observed a similar development in tone: '... over a period of two years (January 2000–January 2002), *Le Monde* has evolved from a position of doubt about the appropriateness of enlargement to one of certainty.' However, she also stresses that 'this evolution and the strong position expressed in January 2002 must be seen in connection with the fact that France held the presidency of the EU from July to December 2000, and in this capacity prepared the Nice Summit that was supposed to provide the institutional reforms necessary for the enlargement.' The positive coverage in *Le Monde* is seen not only as part of the general legitimization discourse in accordance with the previous EU presidential function, but, furthermore, as a tribute to the political cohabitation of that time.
5. English translation for this and all other French quotations is provided by the authors.
6. Of the 286 entries that make statements about Germany, only in 56 cases is France not co-referenced simultaneously. This might already be taken as a strategy to portray the unity of France and Germany, thus strengthening their unquestionable public image. This accounts even more for the conceptual identification of Germany: We scarcely find image strategies that go beyond typical EU concepts.
7. The discussion of Cyprus' integration into the EU is portrayed mainly in the context of Turkey's possible future accession. In order to investigate the image of Cyprus in French press discourse, we consider only those articles that do not explicitly mention this debate.

References

Bärtsch, C. (2004) *Metaphernkonzepte in Pressetexten – Das Verhältnis der Schweiz zu Europa und zur Europäischen Union*. Doctoral dissertation, University of Zurich.

Brinker, K. (2000) Textfunktionale analyse. In K. Brinker, G. Antos, W. Heinemann, and S. Sager (eds) *Text- und Gesprächslinguistik. Ein internationales Handbuch zeitgenössischer Forschung* (pp. 175–186). Berlin, New York: Walter de Gruyter.

Chopin, T. (2005) *The European Social Model or the Creation of a European Social Identity* (= European Issues 6). Paris: Foundation Robert Schuman.

Eurobarometer (2004) = European Commission (2004) *Eurobarometer* 61/62. Public opinion in the European Union, national report, France – Online document: http://ec.europa.eu/public_opinion/standard_en.htm. Accessed 18 May 2006.

Höhne, R.A. (2005) Europawahlen in Frankreich 2004: Eine "europäische Ausnahme"? In DFI (Deutsch-Französisches Institut) (ed.) *Frankreich-Jahrbuch 2004: Reformpolitik in Frankreich* (pp. 201–218). Wiesbaden: Verlag für Sozialwissenschaften.

Kurz, G. (2004) Politische Metaphorik. In G. Kurz *Metapher, Allegorie, Symbol* (pp. 27–29) (5th edn). Göttingen: Vandenhoeck.

Lakoff, G. (1987) *Women, Fire, and Dangerous Things: What Categories Reveal about the Mind*. Chicago: University of Chicago Press.

Lakoff, G. and Johnson, M. (2003) *Metaphors We Live By* (2nd edn). Chicago: University of Chicago Press.

Le, E. (2002) The concept of Europe in *Le Monde*'s editorials. Tensions in the construction of a European identity. *Journal of Language and Politics* 1, 277–322.

Lieb, J. (2008) Die französische Kampagne zum Referendum über den Vertrag über eine Verfassung für Europa – Probleme mit der europäischen Wirklichkeit. In F. Baasner (ed.) *Von welchem Europa reden wir? Reichweiten nationaler Europadiskurse* (pp. 55–75). Baden-Baden: Nomos.

Mikolajczyk, B. and Zinken, J. (2003) Metaphern im politischen Diskurs. Die Rolle der Metapher in Vorstellungswelt und Argumentation (anhand von polnischen und deutschen Texten zum EU-Beitritt Polens). In L.N. Zybatow (ed.) *Europa der Sprachen. Sprachkompetenz – Mehrsprachigkeit – Translation. Vol. 1* (pp. 370–378). Frankfurt: Lang.

Musolff, A. (2004) *Metaphor and Political Discourse. Analogical Reasoning in Debates about Europe*. London: Palgrave-Macmillan.

O'Keeffe, A. (2006) *Investigating Media Discourse*. London, New York: Routledge.

Seidendorf, S. (2008) "Die Quadratur des Kreises" oder: Wie gehen Nation und Europa zusammen? In F. Baasner (ed.) *Von welchem Europa reden wir? Reichweiten nationaler Europadiskurse* (pp. 33–54). Baden-Baden: Nomos.

van Dijk, T. (2001) Discourse, ideology and context. *Folia Linguistica* 30 (1–2), 11–40.

Vogel, W. (2008) Narrative lost. Der Diskurs der EU-Kommission zur Zukunft Europas. In F. Baasner (ed.) *Von welchem Europa reden wir? Reichweiten nationaler Europadiskurse* (pp. 165–182). Baden-Baden: Nomos.

Chapter 3
Metaphors in German and Lithuanian Discourse Concerning the Expansion of the European Union

Sandra Petraškaitė-Pabst

Introduction

This chapter discusses the use of metaphors in discourse. Discourse is understood as a fabric of utterances that share a common theme and can be derived from texts (Busse & Teubert, 1994: 14). The key defining element of a discourse is the theme or, in the case of a comparative discourse, a common theme simultaneously discussed by two sides.

This chapter examines international discourse concerning the European Union's eastern enlargement. News articles from the most important German and Lithuanian print media comprise the corpus used in the comparative analysis. The selected media are significant in shaping public opinion in both countries and represent a broad spectrum of political opinion. The media play a decisive role in the propagation of politics, the dissemination of information, ideas and opinions, and thus also in the diffusion of metaphors. This discussion is taken up, presented and more or less critically reflected through and by metaphors (Schäffner, 1993: 13). Newspapers available online (and therefore convenient for computer analysis) were preferentially consulted. The German corpus consists of high-quality transregional daily newspapers (*Die Welt, Frankfurter Allgemeine Zeitung, Süddeutsche Zeitung* and *Frankfurter Rundschau*), as well as the weekly *Die Zeit*. The Lithuanian corpus also consists of high-quality transregional newspapers (*Lietuvos rytas, Lietuvos aidas* and *Kauno diena*) and weekly magazines (*Veidas, Atgimimas* and *Kulturos barai*). It is important to note that the mass media as determined by the Baltic survey (2001) by the Institute for Opinion Research is the institution most trusted by Lithuanian society and thus plays an important role in public-opinion formation. This survey has found that 75% of Lithuanians do indeed trust broadcasting, the press and television, whereas in Germany only 25% consider the mass media trustworthy. Metaphorical language use was analyzed for the period from 1995 to 2004. These years were marked by several important events for Lithuania, such as the negotiations on

EU membership from 1995 to 2004 and Lithuania's accession to the EU in 2004.

According to Lakoff and Johnson, 'metaphors play a central role in the construction of social and political reality' (1980: 159). In interpreting the typical metaphors used in German and Lithuanian discourse, focus is placed on those metaphors within the same text or even across different texts within a discourse that are picked up, further developed and combined with one another, and on those that advance to become catchwords or turn into the object of linguistic discussions. Such metaphors truly shape the content and concept of a text and, ultimately, a discourse.

This chapter has two main sections. Section one discusses several typical metaphorical expressions in German and Lithuanian used in the context of the European Union. Section two analyzes the role and self-perception of each country: Germany as an established EU member state versus Lithuania as a recent accession candidate and a new EU member state since 2004. In the case of Lithuania, it is particularly relevant to pose the question that has been formulated regarding all new members of the EU in the introduction of this book: Does the metaphorical inventory change with the changing images of insider–outsider relationships?

A comparison of typical metaphors used in German and Lithuanian discourse shows at a first glance that the majority of metaphorical themes such as HOUSE, JOURNEY, FAMILY or DISEASE are similar in both countries. They differ, however, with respect to the current political situation of the country in question. On the one hand, this is because Lithuanian discourse about EU eastern enlargement did not develop independently as something completely new, but naturally picked up and continued the language of pre-existing European political discourse. On the other hand, the Lithuanian discourse opens up entirely unexpected fields of metaphors that are not possible in German discourse; for example, negative sentiment against the European Union in Lithuania has led to comparison between the EU and the former Soviet system. Moreover, accession to the EU has been a major vehicle for Lithuania's internal reformers. However, quite often the accession debate turned into a dispute on keeping or loosing national identity. Increased prosperity in Europe will provide new challenges to national identity.

Numerous researchers have dedicated themselves to the studies of metaphors in international discourses about European politics in recent years: for example, Christina Schäffner (1993) and Andreas Musolff (2004) analyzed and compared the metaphors of European policies in the United Kingdom and Germany, and Beata Mikolajzcyk (2004) did the same for Polish and German.

In the case of geographically and historically distant discourse communities, such an investigation will be more of a typological enterprise, whereas for two political cultures as closely related to each other as the German and British one can assume that their range of conceptual metaphors is largely similar. But this does not mean that their metaphorical discourse has to be similar – even common conceptual source domains can be used for different argumentative and ideological purposes (Musolff, 2004: 5).

Metaphorical Expressions for the EU

The European Union is a highly complex structure that is essentially different in character from a state as defined by international law. The EU often appears to be detached from real life, something that is unfathomable in many ways. A multitude of metaphors have been employed to describe this 'something' in both German and Lithuanian discourse in an effort to make the European Union somewhat more tangible, that is, to bring it closer to peoples' everyday lives. It must be emphasized that the EU and its expansion are generally viewed positively as the project of the century, as a historic opportunity to which there exists no alternative. It stands for freedom, political security and economic benefit.

Metaphorization in German discourse

Nearly half of the metaphors relevant for the analyzed discourse about the enlargement illustrate the European Union as a *house* or *construction site*. Of the 198 metaphors documented in my doctoral dissertation (Petraškaitė-Pabst, 2006: 61) for the time between 1997 and 2002, 84 actually belong to the HOUSE and CONSTRUCTION metaphors. The analysis by Hülsse (2003: 78) also shows that construction metaphors are used for enlargement. Within Lithuanian discourse also, the European Union is seen as a *house*, but not with the same frequency and intensity as in German.

Within a study on the use of metaphors, Schumacher (1988: 61) was able to demonstrate that construction metaphors have been used ever since the beginning of European integration to characterize the process of unification. Musolff (2004: 122) notes that some metaphorical formulations have a history of their own and describes the development of the EUROPEAN HOUSE metaphor in British and German Euro debates between 1989 and 2001.

The most widely employed metaphor in German discourse is the *house* metaphor – the EU is described as a *house* and, to reflect current developments, is often called an *unfinished house* or *a chaotic building site*. Comments on the use of the *house* metaphor include explanations about the origin, frequency and popularity of this image of the *European house*. The political intention behind this strategy is to make the processes within the European Union seem simpler than they actually are, as illustrated by the following linguistic reflection:

> (1) The former President of the European Commission, Jacques Delors, once called Europe a UPO, or 'unidentified political object'. Most politicians do not like to admit this fact and prefer to talk about the *European house*, which, allegedly, is moving *'closer to citizens'*. As simple as this sounds, it does not make matters any less complicated. (Der frühere Präsident der Europäischen Kommission, Jacques Delors, hat Europa als 'Upo', also 'Unidentifizierbares Politikobjekt', bezeichnet. Die meisten Politiker geben das nicht so gern zu. Sie sprechen lieber vom *europäischen Haus*, das angeblich immer *bürgernäher* werde. Das klingt einfach, macht es aber nicht weniger kompliziert. *Frankfurter Allgemeine Zeitung*, 21 June 2002)

It is emphasized that the current phase within the EU eastward expansion process is a period marked by considerable tension that requires strong commitment from politicians, who need to submit a new *construction plan* for the enlarged house. The house of Europe we have lived in all these years has been turned into a gigantic *building site*. It is being *expanded*, *remodeled* and *reconstructed*. The cartoon by David Rooney, shown in Figure 3.1, which illustrates an article titled 'Plumbing for Europe' by Christian Wernicke in the weekly newspaper *Die Zeit*, is a visualization of this *construction* metaphor. The visualization of the European Union as a construction site not only contributes to a matter-of-fact understanding of the complexity of changes currently underway in the EU, but first and foremost poses the question whether it is actually possible to manage so many tasks at the same time. With the *construction* metaphor, enlargement is constructed as a fundamental change of the EU.

The EU member states now need to think about and decide how this enlarged union is to be organized to protect its existing structures from being damaged in the process and to preserve its ability to act. In German discourse, this challenge is illustrated by a combination of FAMILY, HOUSE and CONSTRUCTION metaphors:

> (2) The European Union is like a *scattered family* that tries to agree upon *refurbishing and expanding the house they have jointly* inherited in order to make room for *more family members*. (Der Europäischen Union geht es wie jener *weitverzweigten Familie*, die sich über *die Renovierung und den Ausbau des gemeinsam ererbten Hauses* verständigen wollte, in das weitere *Verwandte aufgenommen* werden sollen. Frankfurter Rundschau, 11 December 2000)

Metaphors that describe the EU as a *family* are used to postulate that old and new EU member states belong together by nature, and that this natural belonging is incontestable. By the same token, such metaphors imply

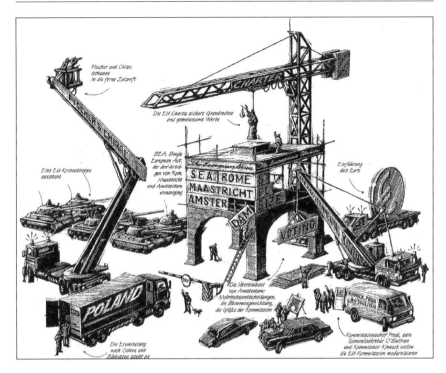

Figure 3.1 Visualization of the *construction* metaphor in the David Rooney cartoon

an innate trust and solidarity in the process of jointly shaping European politics. The European Union, sometimes portrayed in realistic family scenes, does not claim to be an ideal construction. Rather, it is presented as a process under development, a search for a better way of living together as Europeans.

It is argued that, in this process, future reforms are indispensable and are urgently recommended as the only possible cure for an expanded European Union – the EU *must undergo radical treatment*. There simply were no other alternatives. Should the reforms be delayed, the planned enlargement would have disastrous consequences for the already ailing European Union. The addition of new members might lead the EU to commit *suicide* or *choke itself*. The use of DISEASE metaphors indicating fatal conditions such as *cancer, heart attack, the plague* or *cholera* makes the need for reforms seem like a life-or-death decision.

The European Union is not a finished structure, but a continuously growing organism, and its final form remains uncertain. The principle that underlies the workings of the EU has been encapsulated in TRANSPORTATION metaphors. The *bicycle* metaphor, which refers to

European unification being a process, is surprisingly precise. On the one hand, it serves as a way to conceptualize characteristics of the EU such as movement, development and dynamism as its strengths, while drawing attention to the inherent danger of standing still.

> (3) The European Union is like a bicycle – 'It has to keep moving or it will fall over', said Verhofstadt to the Center for European Policy in Brussels. (Die Europäische Union sei wie ein Fahrrad: 'Sie muss sich vorwärts bewegen, sonst fällt sie um', sagte Verhofstadt vor dem Zentrum für Europäische Politik in Brüssel. *Süddeutsche Zeitung*, 23 September 2000)

Railway metaphors are used to stress that the expansion process is well-planned and headed toward a clear destination: for example, *a train at full speed*. The process of enlargement to the east is presented as the consequence, continuation and completion of the European integration process.

Metaphorization in Lithuanian discourse

In Lithuanian discourse, various metaphorical expressions are used to describe the EU in order to convey different intentions. For EU supporters, the EU is *a shared block of flats*, a *family, an express train* or *a rich groom*. For EU opponents, the EU is the embodiment of all things negative: *a people trap, a new Soviet Union*. Patterns of argumentation in the Lithuanian discourse differ from German ones. This is in line with the different motives and reasons for joining the EU. Some metaphorizations such as the EU as a *wealthy bridegroom* or as the *express train* to a better life do not appear in the German discourse.

> (4) Lithuania receives *a good dowry*. Lithuania is soon *to give its word of consent* – such were the witty expressions of the chief negotiator of the European negotiations, Petras Auštrevičius, after the negotiations between the EU and our country came to an end yesterday evening. *It seems that the bridegroom is going to bring along a significant dowry. Marriage means obligations, but it also promises an interesting and meaningful life.* (Lietuva gaus *gerą kraitį* Lietuva tuoj *duos pažadą ištekėti,* – vakar vakare pasibaigus galutinėms mūsų šalies deryboms su Europos Sąjunga juokavo vyriausiasis euroderybininkas Petras Auštrevičius. *Jaunikis, atrodo, atneša rimtą kraitį. Santuoka bus įpareigojanti, bet žadanti įdomų ir prasmingą gyvenimą. Lietuvos rytas*, 14 December 2002)

> (5) Therefore, the only real way to avoid lagging behind in the provincial backwater is *to board the express train of Europe and become a fully entitled passenger of this train* – with these words, in his yearly report President Valdas Adamkus admonishes striving after the all-but-easy goal of membership in the EU. (Todėl vienintelis realus būdas Lietuvai

išvengti provincijos atsilikimo – *įlipti į greitąjį Europos traukinį, tapti visateise šio traukinio keleive,* – šiais žodžiais negailėti jėgų siekiant labai nelengvo tikslo narystės ES metiniame pranešime ragino Prezidentas V. Adamkus. *Veidas*, 5 May 2000)

It is particularly striking in Lithuanian discourse how frequently the EU becomes metaphorized as a *strict teacher*. The dialogue between Lithuania and the EU, which has been emerging in yearly intervals from 1996 to 2002, and which shapes not only Lithuania's foreign but also its domestic politics is depicted in a way not unlike the relationship between a pupil and a teacher: The European Commission presented a report to the Lithuanian government every year since 1996, demonstrating and evaluating the country's progress. On the basis of these progress reports, it was determined whether the country had met the necessary criteria for starting accession negotiations with the EU, or whether the preparations had to be intensified further.

Following such a report in December 1999, Lithuania was invited to accession negotiations with the EU, and in December 2002 there was even an offer to become a member of the European Union. A good deal of patience was necessary on the part of the Lithuanian government until this invitation was finally extended. Prior to this, several times Lithuania had to cope with the disappointment of not being invited to accession negotiations.

The SCHOOL metaphor characterizes the phase of preparing for the EU by metaphorizing the aspiring country Lithuania as a *pupil*, the EU as a *teacher*, the preparations Lithuania has to make as *homework* and the EU's evaluation of these preparations as *grades*. Thus, a school scenario is generated by these metaphors for the negotiation process between Lithuania and the EU:

> (6) Negotiations with the EU are unpleasant because they do not take place between equal partners. The European Commission plays the role of *the teacher* and Lithuania the role of *the pupil. The teacher checks the pupil's homework and grades him.* His evaluation is decisive. An independent nation cannot be pleased by such a situation, but there is no other way. Lithuania needs the EU more than Brussels needs Lithuania. (Derybos su ES nėra itin malonios, nes jos nevyksta tarp lygiagrečių partnerių. EK perima *mokytojo,* Lietuva *mokinio* vaidmenį. *Mokytojas tikrina, ar mokinys gerai padarė pamokas, rašo jam pažymius.* Jo sprendimas lemiamas. Suvereniai valstybei ir Vyriausybei tai negali patikti, bet išeities nėra. Lietuvai labiau reikia ES negu Briuseliui Lietuvos. *Atgimimas*, 20 November 1998)

The school metaphor leads all the people of Lithuania into the school situation, including them in the learning process, and it reminds people that this situation, like every learning process in school, is only a limited phase, after which the pupil eventually benefits from what is learned. After completing all of the homework, prosperous life in the EU is waiting.

To make Lithuania's accession to the European Union more attractive to the Lithuanian people, the country's leading politicians, who set their foreign policy goal as leading Lithuania into the EU, first reached for metaphorical images that evoked positive associations.

Fast train and *EU express train* are metaphors that clearly point to the positive aspects of the EU. Some of the metaphors imply that accession to the European Union is the best way to achieve wealth for all citizens, and the EU is shown as a means to ensuring prosperity, security and a better life. This idea is expressed even more pointedly by FAMILY metaphors that describe the EU as a *rich groom* and Lithuania's accession to the EU as a *marriage of convenience*. Such metaphors reveal that the object of desire is not the groom himself, but his richness and the security of his wealth. These metaphors found in Lithuanian discourse tend to overemphasize and idealize the economic benefits of Lithuania's accession to the EU.

The following metaphorical description of the EU is a particularly creative and striking example. This description seeks to unite idealism and realism in one vision.

> (7) The way I look at Europe is the way I look at a woman one just has to love, not because of her richness but because of her charms – the charm that lies in the European way of life..... I know that this woman has flaws, too, that she is growing old as the years go by, but so am I. (Į Europą žiūriu kaip į *moterį*, kurią *reikia mylėti, mylėti* ne dėl jos *turto, bet dėl jos žavesio,* tas žavesys yra europietiškas gyvenimo būdas. Taigi, į tokią Europą aš einu ir vedu tuos, kurie su manimi eina. Žinau, kad ta *moteris turi daug trūkumų, kad ji po kelių metų pasens ir aš pasensiu*. Radio Free Europe, Vilnius, May 2001)

In addition, Lithuanian discourse is full of metaphors that reveal unrealistic beliefs, such as the false illusion that, with accession to the EU, life will miraculously improve overnight. Such disillusionment is prompted by fairytale metaphors – 'the EU is not an enchanted land' (*Lietuvos rytas*, 5 August 1997) – as well as metaphors linked to customs and tradition – 'the EU is not the Easter Bunny, who gives presents to all the good children' (*Kauno diena*, 14 April 2001).

Euro-skeptics employ historical metaphors, deliberately choosing terms that have acquired a negative connotation in history, such as *communism* or *union*. They use them as well-directed instruments to conjure up the memory of the Soviet Union, which is still alive in peoples' minds, and to frighten the Lithuanian people away from the EU.

> (8) I just don't understand how people can forget so fast about the aspirations that inspired us to fight for our country's independence.

And now, having barely left one union, we rush into the next one. The two of them may differ in style but not in purpose. (Nesuprantu, kodėl žmonės taip greit pamiršo, ko siekėme kovodami už savo valstybės nepriklausomybę. *Ir štai, vos ištrūkę iš vienos sąjungos glėbio, puolame į kitą.* Gal jos skiriasi savo manieromis, bet ne tikslais. *Kauno diena*, 7 March 2001)

Metaphorical Self-Descriptions

EU enlargement affects Germany and Lithuania in different ways: Germany is one of the most important member states of the EU and its positive attitude toward eastern enlargement has been of crucial importance. For Lithuania, membership in the European Union is a strategic test, not only for foreign policy but also for domestic policy, both of which necessitate fundamental changes in all areas of life. Seen from the outside, Lithuania seems exemplary – it was the first Baltic republic to liberate itself from the grip of the Soviet regime and one of the first post-Soviet countries to be accepted into the European Union. Moreover, today it is ranked as one of the economically more advanced countries in the region. Seen from the inside, however, many things turn out to be far more problematic.

Metaphors used in German

Two metaphors that appear frequently in connection with Germany's self-perceived role within the European Union and the union's planned eastward expansion are the concepts of ADVOCATE and ENGINE.

The *engine* metaphor is mainly used to stress France and Germany's equal partnership within the EU and to describe the current status of Franco-German relations in the context of EU eastward expansion: *the engine that starts* or *is picking up speed.* This *engine* metaphor is developed further in various other texts, often creatively adorned with typical engine characteristics. It is employed to point out that France and Germany share a joint responsibility for EU eastward expansion (*the engine that sets the pace*) or to criticize a lack of cooperation (*the engine that coughs and splutters, the engine idling, irregular engine operation*), and it is used to draw attention to the possible consequences for Europe as a whole should this engine fail, as in the following example:

> (9) One can question the efficiency of the *Franco-German engine* in the past, and why *breakdowns* have increased over the past few years. One thing, however, has to be acknowledged: *Whenever the engine failed, Europe stopped dead in its tracks.* (Man kann über *die Leistung des deutsch-französischen 'Motors'* in der Vergangenheit fragen, warum sich in den letzten Jahren *die Pannen* gehäuft haben. Eines muss man

jedoch feststellen: *Immer wenn der Motor aussetzte, trat Europa auf der Stelle. Die Welt,* 10 April 2000)

The second metaphor that appears consistently is that of the *advocate*; it emphasizes Germany's role in supporting the EU enlargement process on behalf of the countries of Central and Eastern Europe. The main argument in favor of rapid eastward expansion is the restitution of justice. The *advocate* metaphor fulfils an important function for Germany and the accession countries, and it guides their actions – Germany defines its responsibility to help new accession countries as an ethical and moral duty, and the countries of Central and Eastern Europe expect Germany to provide visible support in specific questions of EU expansion.

(10) In his speech, Fischer assessed Germany's role: In terms of enlargement, we are the *advocate of the Central and Eastern European countries in the EU*. (Fischer hat sich in der Rede über die Rolle Deutschlands geäußert: Wir sind *Anwalt der Mittel- und Osteuropäer in der EU*, was deren Erweiterung betrifft. *Süddeutsche Zeitung*, 1 December 1998)

When the theme turns to naming the position of the countries involved in the unification process or to depicting their tests or chances, the *train* metaphor is taken up and embellished. The *locomotive* metaphor describes Germany as having a leading role that entails responsibility for the development of the European Union; however, it is not used by German politicians, but by the politicians of other countries:

(11) An interview with Poland's prime minister: 'Germany was always a *locomotive* in the EU from the beginning, since Adenauer's time'. (Interview mit Polens Ministerpräsident: 'Deutschland war ja von Anfang an *die Lokomotive* in der EU, seit der Zeit Adenauers'. *Die Welt*, 26 April 2000)

Metaphors used in Lithuanian

The self-perception of the Lithuanian people in this transformation process seems double-sided. Culturally and geographically they feel like Europeans, whereas politically and economically they seem to be lagging behind most other European countries. The images of JOURNEY and HOUSE are the core metaphors found in discourse; they are employed to keep the Lithuanian foreign policy goal of EU accession fresh in the minds of the Lithuanian people and to mobilize Lithuanians to embrace and pursue this goal:

(12) *By taking the path towards Europe* we have *walked away* from former Soviet territory and have *entered* new ground. (*Eidami į Europą, mes išėjome iš* buvusios sovietinės erdvės ir *įžengėme į* visiškai kitą erdvę. Lietuvos rytas, 22 June 1995)

During the period of its candidacy, Lithuania presented itself as a self-confident and ambitious country in a variety of metaphors – as *standing at the door knocking*, or as *not allowing herself to be distracted from the right path to Europe* or as *a schoolgirl diligently doing her homework*, a country that does not shy away from difficulties, that will not give up its goal just because things are not going to be easy, but will pursue this goal all the more vigorously.

> (13) It really is a *tough school*.... True, we could steer clear of it... *True, we could refuse to learn what we were not allowed to learn for 50 years – but learn we must.* (*Griežta tai mokykla*.... Galime, žinoma, nuo jos ir atsiverti... *Galima, be abejo, ir nesimokyti, kaip mums ir neleido mokytis 50 metų. Bet mokytis reikia. Kultūros barai*, March 2000)

The stark contrast between the economic situation of Lithuania and that of the EU is a bitter reality. Lithuania often depicts itself as small and deficient: *a small schoolgirl, a primary school pupil, a forgotten disused train station* or a *flawed bride*. The dire political situation is met with fear of fate, fear of *being left sitting in the last carriage of the train*, or fear of *ending up an old maid* or a *deceived student*. As Lithuania received more praise and recognition for its achievements in the accession negotiations, its confidence seemed to grow, as indicated by the change in school metaphors. The major turning point was when Lithuania received its invitation to attend the Helsinki Summit in December 1999. This was the first time that Lithuania's progress was officially recognized:

> (14) The European Commission praised Lithuania for her diligence in doing her *homework*. (Europos Komisijos atstovai pagyrė lietuvius už *stropiai atliekamus 'namų darbus'*. *Lietuvos rytas*, 12 October 1999)

The teacher–pupil relationship still exists here, but it has taken on a new quality.

> (15) The figure of the *unhappy, insulted schoolgirl* has become a thing of the past. (Derybas šių metų pradžioje pradėjusiai Lietuvai pavyko atsikratyti *nepatenkintos, įsižeidžiančios mokinės komplekso*. *Lietuvos rytas*, 5 October 2000)

A huge transformation effort is required of Lithuania, a former Eastern Bloc country, to adapt to and join the European Union. The required reforms cover all areas of life and therefore involve all citizens of Lithuania in the transformation process. The first thing Lithuania needs to do in order to implement these reforms is to rid itself of the remnants of its planned socialist economy, to 'remove the metastases of communism and discharge the patient for full recovery on the free market' (*Lietuvos rytas*, 19 November 2000). Not everyone is convinced that the country really needs radical changes. Some accounts of the situation give the impression that these changes are merely accepted as an assignment given by a strict teacher whose orders are to be carried out obediently. In this context, it seems useful to emphasize those perceptions of the situation that help people understand that these reforms are inevitable and unavoidable for the best of their country:

> (16) We are doing our *homework* not *to receive a good grade* from Brussels, but because we want to reform our lives and live by European standards. (*Tuos namų darbus darome* juk ne todėl, kad Briuselis mums *parašytų gerą pažymį*, o todėl, kad norime reformuoti savo gyvenimą ir gyventi pagal europietiškus standartus. *Lietuvos aidas*, 12 November 1998)

As Vinogradnaite (2002: 189) puts it,

> At the same time, two conflicting identities are constructed – the identity of Lithuanians as Europeans and the identity of Lithuanians as non-Europeans. Such a contradiction appears because there are two different images of the community of Europeans. On the one hand, Europe is understood as a geographical and cultural space, which is a natural home of Lithuanians. On the other hand, Europe can be defined in terms of the principles of political organization. Such an understanding of Europe makes it a kind of 'enemy', defining the boundaries of national community, and precludes the articulation of European identity for Lithuanians.

In Lithuanian discourse, the particularly interesting metaphors are those referring to the cultural background knowledge of the Lithuanians. This most importantly applies to metaphors taken from Lithuanian folk tales: for example *Žilvinas ir Eglė* (Prince Žilvinas and Queen Eglė).

(17) is an allusion to the very popular Lithuanian fairy tale *Eglė žalčių karalienė* (Eglė, the Queen of the Grass Snakes). After 10 years of married life beneath the sea, Eglė, the wife of Žilvinas, makes plans to visit her parents on the land. Because her husband is strictly against it but does not want to overtly object, he assigns his wife three tasks. These tasks do not seem to be difficult at a first glance, but actually turn out be unsolvable. Eglė manages to fulfill them only with the help of a sorceress.

With reference to the level of difficulty of the tasks being a precondition for accession, former Lithuanian president Brazauskas describes the chance for Lithuania to enter the EU as an extremely delicate situation. On the one hand, the EU permits Lithuania's accession; on the other hand, it poses conditions that Lithuania can meet only with great difficulty:

> (17) The inquiries sent by the European Commission gave proof that there were more tasks to solve than had been assigned *by Žilvinas to*

(his wife) Eglė. (Europos Komisijos atsiųstas klausimynas liudijo, kad užduočių yra kur kas daugiau, *negu Žilvinas pateikė Eglei.* Brazauskas, 2000: 239)

Tradition and custom metaphors are used to ridicule and disarm the argument most frequently employed by Euro-skeptics against Lithuania's accession to the EU – the loss of its own identity and independence:

> (18) Maybe they themselves [the Euro-skeptics] are naively convinced of this and are now trying to convince others. We, however, will *erect fences around our courtyards, our sugar beets, and garden rue* [the national herb of Lithuania], *and cepelinai* [traditional Lithuanian potato dumplings] *will grow on every tree in our gardens.* (Galbūt ir patys naiviai tiki, o tuo patikėję ir kitus stengiasi įtikinti: *apsitversime savo kieme, auginsime cukrinius runkelius, rūtas ir ant kiekvieno medžio mūsų soduose augs cepelinai. Lietuvos rytas,* 21 April 2000)

Growing and fostering rue is an element the meaning of which can only be explained by referring to specific Lithuanian customs and traditions. Whereas such use of metaphor would remain incomprehensible to a German due to little familiarity with rue, it is immediately obvious to a Lithuanian: Rue is widely considered the national flower of the Lithuanians, traditionally grown right in front of the house, in front of the window, in the form of a rue garden. At weddings, it is still the custom for the bride to wear a small rue garland, which is burned after the wedding. Rue is regarded as a symbol of girls' purity and chastity.

> (19) It is said that the laws of the EU take precedence and only they matter. The Lithuanian, the saying goes, is not even allowed to *water his rue garden under the window,* with *tears* of course, what else. (Esą jos įstatymai ir viršesni, ir viską lemiantys. Lietuvis girdi, nebegalėsiąs net rūtų darželio palangėje palaistyti – ašaromis, žinoma, kuo gi daugiau. *Lietuvos aidas,* 9 July 1999)

Such metaphors create a surprise effect for the reader by juxtaposing two very different, distant areas – well-known Lithuanian folk tales, traditions and customs on the one hand, and the far less familiar political events of EU enlargement, often appearing alien to Lithuanian citizens, on the other hand. Moreover, they allow discourse about EU enlargement to be experienced as embedded in Lithuanian culture, so that personal concern with the problems of EU enlargement becomes perceptible. Zbierska-Sawala (2004: 416) also emphasizes the importance of such metaphors inspired by Polish culture in the context of European politics.

After Lithuanian accession to the EU, the crucial question is now which changes can be observed in the new situation. The moment of Lithuania's accession to the EU was first of all the crucial moment for the country in trying to define its new identity – an identity marked by optimism and pride, reflected by the old, well-known metaphorization of JOURNEY and FAMILY: 'We have come a *long way*. What seemed to be but a *dream* of a distant future has now become reality. We can be proud to have returned to *the family* of European democracies (From a speech by Lithuanian president Valdas Adamkus on the Day of Restitution of Independence, 11 March 2005).

The essence of this new Lithuanian self-image is expressed by the following declaration: 'Today we, the people of Lithuania, are fully-entitled members of the European Union and NATO' (29 March 2007, from a speech by Secretary of State Justinas Karosas). 'Undoubtedly, EU and NATO memberships signify a fundamental shift in the geopolitical status of the country. The symbolic comeback to Europe has occurred, but the actual one involves a day-to-day process of integration and transformation that has just begun' (Galbreath *et al.*, 2008: 76).

Meanwhile, another aspect of identity has been introduced into the country's self-image, an aspect that was hardly ever mentioned before its accession to the EU. This is seen in the following excerpt from a speech by a Lithuanian member of parliament during celebrations commemorating the 50th anniversary of the Treaty of Rome:

> (20) Europe is an opportunity for Lithuania and for other EU member states to not just think about getting something out of it, as we usually tend to do, but, more importantly, to contribute something of ourselves – our culture, our language, our past experience, and our vision for the creation of European values, European prosperity, and a European future. Thanks to us, Europe has now become a little more Lithuanian. (Gediminas Kirkilas, 29 March 2007)

Moreover, this change in Lithuania's self-perception finds expression in a different metaphor that is now employed in European political discourse – the image of a BUILDING SITE. In (21), it is even used as a prototypical description of the current state of Lithuanian domestic politics. What is striking here is the fact that a metaphor that was previously used only in connection with the European Union was assimilated by the new member state of Lithuania after the 2004 expansion. This indicates that the accession of the new member countries has turned the EU into an even larger building site:

> (21) The situation is best described by the metaphor of *building*. For the state, this situation opens a new angle on *building construction*. Lithuania now has this unique and historic opportunity to change radically within seven years.... Unfortunately, its citizens have so far only witnessed the beginnings of a less than convincing *building process* – nebulous projects, and lack of communication between *construction engineers and supervisors*. Voices are getting louder, the voices

of those that fear that Lithuania will turn into a *building site* controlled by *builders and construction workers* that are most concerned with pursuing their own selfish interests. Citizens that do not feel part of this *building project* of the Lithuanian state will become alienated and indifferent, they will have no qualms about turning their backs on their country to go somewhere else where they feel more needed. (Situacijai apibūdinti visiškai tinkama *statybos metafora*. Valstybei atsiveria *nauja statybos perspektyva*. Lietuva turi unikalią istorinę progą per septynerius metus neatpažįstamai pasikeisti.... Deja, kol kas jie regi tik *nelabai patrauklią statybos pradžią – miglotus projektus, tarpusavyje nelabai sutariančius vyriausiuosius inžinierius ir prižiūrėtojus*. Vis garsiau imama nuogastauti, ar valstybė netaps *statybos aikštele 'statybininkams'*, kuriems svarbiausia – iš jos kuo daugiau nugvelbti sau. *Valstybės statybos* nuošalėje atsidūrę piliečiai tampa jai svetimi, abejingi, nevengia traukti svetur, kur gali jaustis reikalingesni. *Veidas*, 9 March 2006)

Since the dual (EU and NATO) enlargement, there has been a marked change in Lithuanian foreign policy objectives. Lithuania's foreign policy objectives in the newly independent states are illustrated by three government documents following enlargement. First, the *Resolution on Directions in Foreign Policy* passed by the Lithuanian Parliament (*Seimas*) in May 2004 is a timely response redirecting Lithuanian foreign policy following the dual enlargement. This resolution declares that Lithuania seeks 'to continue expanding the zone of security and stability in Europe and its neighborhood'. Furthermore, the resolution aims to 'promote the policy of solidarity, confidence and transparency, to advance democratic values, to continue co-operation with the countries lying off the eastern border of the European Union, aiming at their rapprochement with the European Union, and to draw the three Trans-Caucasian republics – Armenia, Azerbaijan, and Georgia – into the European Union initiative of neighborliness'. Here we see the first explicit statement supporting future membership as leverage for reform in the region. Overall, the resolution is interesting because it illustrates the sudden change in direction of Lithuanian foreign policy objectives.

Second, the 'foreign policy section' of the *Program of the Government of the Republic of Lithuania for 2004–2008* offers some insight into the Lithuanian government's focus on the EU's eastern neighborhood. The program further aims 'to establish Lithuania as an expert of the European Neighborhood Policy'. No doubt Lithuania's role as an *expert* on this policy is an attempt to establish the Baltic state as a director of EU foreign policy toward the eastern neighborhood (Galbreath *et al.*, 2008: 122–123).

Six years of NATO and European Union membership have not brought Lithuania expected prosperity. Now a new idea is gaining increasing popularity: the idea of becoming a political and economic *bridge* between East and West. Galbreath and Lamoreaux identify three possible roles for the Baltic States vis-à-vis the EU and the eastern 'neighborhood': *bastion, beacon* and *bridge* (Galbreath & Lamoreaux, 2007: 115).

Conclusion

The discourse analyzed here with regard to the eastward expansion of the European Union is a continuation of the discourse about European unification that has existed in Europe for at least 50 years. By looking at the use of metaphors, one can observe how German discourse adjusted through the types of metaphors already employed early on, such as house, family and transportation. German discourse regarding eastward expansion linked up with the metaphors from the early stages of the European community and the arguments supporting it, urging that the half-finished European building site be finished. In this manner, the uninterrupted dynamic of the unification process is emphasized.

A comparison of typical metaphors used in German and Lithuanian discourse shows that the majority of metaphorical themes such as HOUSE, TRANSPORTATION, FAMILY and DISEASE are similar in both countries. This can be explained by the fact that Lithuanian discourse about the EU's eastward enlargement did not develop independently as something new, but naturally picked up and continued the language of pre-existing European political discourse. These metaphors are taken from the general European discussion and are simply placed into Lithuanian discourse as translations and quotations. In order to report and comment on the most meaningful political occurrences of the EU, Lithuanian journalists often use translations of articles from the best-known German, English or French newspapers. These previously used metaphors are repeatedly used in later publications, albeit adapted to and developed for Lithuania's political interests.

There are some differences in the use of metaphors that reflect the unique situation of each country. School metaphors, for instance, are specific to Lithuania. Even Lithuanian politicians acknowledge the fact that the people of Lithuania have a lot to learn and catch up with in many areas after 50 years of Soviet rule, and thus school metaphors sometimes oscillate between the literal and the metaphorical. Germany sees itself as a leader in the EU enlargement process, and consistently emphasizes its advocacy and responsibility for the success of this 'project of the century'. This leading role is asserted in the metaphors *locomotive, engine* and *advocate*. The German presidency of the EU in the first half of 2007 reinforced this discourse.

Lithuanian discourse abounds with metaphors relevant to EU eastward enlargement. Some of these metaphors only make sense in the particular context of the Lithuanian way of life. These are especially metaphors taken from Lithuanian fairy tales, traditions, customs and rites, as well as from the country's history. The use of such culture-specific metaphors enables Lithuanians to experience European political discourse as something that is embedded in their own culture. This makes them feel more directly involved in the processes of eastward expansion, which sometimes seems so distant and alien.

Lithuanian discourse shows that the Lithuanian self-image has undergone a process of change that began with the start of accession negotiations with the EU and was completed with the country's actual accession to the EU. One example is the change of metaphors in self-descriptions: School metaphors have now been replaced by building metaphors to reflect the current situation.

Both German and Lithuanian discourse reveal that the EU enlargement process is explained in political, pragmatic terms rather than idealistic, visionary language. Although originally the Eastern European countries' *return to Europe*, or the *building of the common European house* on the part of the Western European nations, was inspired by pure idealism, some idealism has been lost in the process now that the venture has almost become reality and political pragmatism has taken its place.

References

Brazauskas, A. (2000) *Penkeri Prezidento metai: ivykiai, prisiminimai, mintys*. Vilnius: Pradai.
Busse, D., and Teubert, W. (1994) Ist Diskurs ein sprachwissenschaftliches Objekt? Zur Methodenfrage der historischen Semantik. In D. Busse, F. Hermanns, and W. Teubert (eds) *Begriffsgeschichte und Diskursgeschichte* (pp. 10–28). Opladen: Westdeutscher Verlag.
Galbreath, D.J. and Lamoreaux, J.W. (2007) Bastion, beacon or bridge? Conceptualising the Baltic logic of the EU's neighbourhood. *Geopolitics* 12 (1), 109–133.
Galbreath, D.J., Lasas, A., and Lamoreaux, J.W. (2008) *Continuity and Change in the Baltic Sea Region. Comparing Foreign Policies*. Amsterdam: Rodopi.
Hülsse, R. (2003) *Metaphern der EU-Erweiterung als Konstruktionen europäischer Identität*. Baden-Baden: Nomos Verlagsgesellschaft.
Lakoff, G. and Johnson, M. (1980) *Metaphors We Live By*. Chicago and London: University of Chicago Press.
Mikolajczyk, B. (2004) *Sprachliche Mechanismen der Persuasion in der politischen Kommunikation. Dargestellt an polnischen und deutschen Texten zum EU-Beitritt Polens*. Munich: Peter Lang.
Musolff, A. (2004) *Metaphor and Political Discourse. Analogical Reasoning in Debates about Europe*. London: Palgrave-Macmillan.
Petraskaite-Pabst, S. (2006) *Metapherngebrauch im politischen Diskurs. Zur EU-Osterweiterung im Deutschen und Litauischen*. Tübingen: Stauffenburg.
Schäffner, Ch. (1993) Die europäische Architektur – Metaphern der Einigung Europas in der deutschen, britischen und amerikanischen Presse. In:

A. Grewenig (ed.) *Inszenierte Kommunikation* (pp. 13–30). Opladen: Westdeutscher Verlag.

Schumacher, N. (1988) Metaphern des europäischen Sprachgebrauchs. *Terminologie et traduction* 1, 55–79.

Vinogradnaitė, I. (2002) "The route to Europe": Construing European identity in Lithuanian public discourse in 1990–2000. In D. Staliunas (ed.) *Europos idėja Lietuvoje: istorija ir dabartis* (pp. 180–190). Vilnius: Lietuvos istorijos institutas.

Zbierska-Sawala, A. (2004) The conceptualisation of the European Union in Polish public discourse, 2002–2003. *Journal of Multilingual and Multicultural Development* 25 (5 & 6), 408–425.

Chapter 4
Domestic and Foreign Media Images of the Balkans

Ljiljana Šarić

Introduction

This chapter examines two corpora – one domestic (i.e. former Yugoslav) corpus and one foreign-media corpus – and discusses the identity-construction issues in them regarding the former Yugoslav countries. The first corpus comprises German media texts (i.e. written in German, whether from Germany, Austria or Switzerland), published from November 2007 to April 2008 that were gathered in a keyword search using Google™ News. The second corpus includes media texts from four prominent newspapers from the same period in Croatia (*Večernji list, Jutarnji list, Novi list* and *Slobodna Dalmacija*) and Serbia (*Politika, Danas, Dnevnik* and *Večernje novosti*). There is no search engine for former Yugoslav media for searching a large number of sources simultaneously, and so the relevant media can only be searched individually. These eight newspapers were selected based on their influence: They are papers that cover several regions, or that are widely read in other regions, even if they are considered regional.

The reason for focusing on this period was Slovenia's tenure in the rotating EU presidency for the first half of 2008. I expected this situation to give rise to new and strong discussions regarding the identity of the former Yugoslav countries. What is particularly interesting about the discourses related to Slovenia's presidency is that as of 2008 Slovenia is the only one of the former Yugoslav countries to have joined the EU. Moreover, one of the priorities for the Slovenian presidency was to strengthen the EU membership prospects for the western Balkan countries.[1] This chapter focuses on discourse representation strategies related to the terms *Balkan/the Balkans*. The rhetorical strategies linked to how these terms are used play an important role in constructing the identity of the South Slavs at home and abroad. Since Yugoslavia's disintegration, it has often been observed that these powerful terms can 'mold mentalities, channel political action, and script the fate of a region and its people' (Hyder Patterson, 2003: 110). These notions are frequently used in media discussions of the two topics that attracted the most media attention during this period: Serbia's early presidential election on 20 January and the subsequent run-off on 3 February 2008, and Kosovo's declaration of independence on 17 February 2008.

An additional issue considered is how the identity patterns ascribed to Slovenia relate to the terms *Balkan/the Balkans*, and how the identity patterns ascribed to Slovenia from abroad during its EU presidency differ from the identity patterns ascribed to other countries of the former Yugoslavia.

Discourse analysis needs more exhaustive research on both convergences and divergences regarding the discourse strategies of EU members versus the strategies of nonmembers, as well as whether and how the metaphorical models applied to and used by various EU members differ (e.g. old vs. recent members vs. nonmembers or potential members, see Petraškaitė-Pabst, this volume). So far, little research on the discourse representation of the EU integration process has focused on the Balkans. This analysis is a step in that direction.

Balkan: From Geographical Term to Cultural Concept

The effect of media texts stems from the interaction of various semiotic devices; in the case of newspapers, many of these devices are linguistic means. The intent of the semiotic devices employed is to influence the audience's opinion and behavior. Their effect is partly related to the intentions of those who create individual articles (e.g. journalists and editors) and their skill in convincingly mediating their intention. Lexical, graphic or pictorial devices create a specific image of a fragment of the world. To some extent, the directions for interpreting mediated images are predefined. Nonetheless, it is not entirely predictable how individual addressees will interpret a media text. Similarly, the effect of using the word *Balkan* in a particular media discourse cannot be predicted. The set of connotations related to this term varies among language users. In addition, how media texts apply this term and its role in the structure of media texts differ significantly from one text to another. I reflect on the general tendencies that can be traced in the corpus. Readers and discourse analysts interpret what a text (as a combination of semiotic devices) suggests. Of course, different interpretations of these representations highlight different aspects of media presentation.

The term *Balkan* is a semiotic, linguistic device that over time has evolved from a geographical term via a 'geographic metaphor' (Jansen, 2002) – that is, a metaphorical bundle of meanings – into a *cultural concept*. I avoid defining it as a metaphor because the idea of *Balkan* as metaphor (Bjelić & Savić, 2002) is vague and the metaphor's source and goal domains are fuzzy. As a cultural concept, *Balkan* involves knowledge and beliefs related to the Balkans that are activated in a concrete discourse situation.

The positive and negative connotation potential of seemingly merely 'geographic' names are examined below. Connotations evolve contextually: If there is a choice between multiple terms and one is consciously used in a particular context, this choice may have semantic implications. Choosing a name of an entity that has multiple names not only assigns names but also qualifies. In addition, the term acquires contextual meaning (i.e. meaning actualization). The choice of *the Balkans*,[2] or the actualization of its contextual meaning, involves connotations in the respective cultural model that are not always favorable. The power of this term, and also the potential dangers in its usage, lies in its vagueness – the rich but undefined spectrum of meanings it evokes.

Discourse representations of the Balkans, including media representations, are based on various knowledge frameworks. In turn, these rely on thorough study of the history and culture of the region, or on simplified images and/or disputed knowledge or fragments of knowledge. According to Đerić (2006), acknowledging differences between the Balkans and other parts of Europe is a legitimate action. Moreover, this process ascribes identity and should not be equated with how the difference is presented; that is, whether politically 'correct' or 'incorrect' language is used in the presentation. Media discourses contain opposing perspectives on representing the Balkans, ranging from representations based on certain facts and their interpretation to simplified images. Both representation types may use certain terms, including geographical ones, in an evaluative manner. The evaluative power of the terms linked to (*the*) *Balkan(s)* relates to the discourse practices of 'Balkanism'. Balkanism is the discourse practice of creating a southeast European 'Other' in literature, academia, journalism, diplomatic texts and so on, and has been widely observed in scholarship on the Balkans (e.g. Norris, 1999; Todorova, 1997). Todorova's study gave particular relevance to Edward Said's notion of Orientalism and applied it to the post-Yugoslav context (see also Bakić-Hayden, 1992; Bakić-Hayden & Hayden, 1995). Kiossev (2005: 180) argues that Western perceptions of the Balkans (a discourse known as 'Western Balkanism' – i.e. viewing the region from a 'macro-colonial perspective') are crucial in construing identities in the Balkans. Attempts by Balkan countries to "escape the image of the 'dark Balkans'" and their discourse attempts to differentiate themselves from other Balkan nations are a direct answer to 'Western Balkanist' discourses. The role of Balkanism in the region's own self-definition has also often been discussed in anthropology, the social sciences and linguistics (e.g. Jansen, 2002; Lindstrom, 2003; Lindstrom & Razsa, 2004; Mitani, 2006; Šarić, 2004).

Critical evaluations of Western 'Balkanist' discourses have sought to reveal these discourses' ideas and their politically incorrect language, and sometimes they themselves fall into the trap of perpetuating Balkanism. A passage from Luketić (2008) illustrates this:

(1) In Western collective representations, the Balkans are often considered to be the refuse, a menagerie of Europe, its dark and out-of-the-way part. They are the wild edge, Europe's appendix... Without this inverted, dark image of the Balkans, Europe, being itself also a phantasm notion, would lose the reference point that helps it construe itself.[3] (U zapadnim kolektivnim predodžbama Balkan se često smatra otpadom, zvjerinjakom Europe, njezinim mračnim i nepristupačnim predjelom. On je divlja margina, slijepo crijevo Europe... Bez te obrnute, mračne slike Balkana, Europa se – također pojam-fantazma – ne bi imala u odnosu na što konstruirati.)

The dark generalization of Western discourses above summarizes only part of them. According to Đerić (2006: 14), the main problem in deconstructing Balkanist discourses is that more attention is given to the manner of evaluation and presentation (i.e. construction) of the Balkans than to the fact that there are differences between the Balkans and other categories it is compared with. Simply put, it is implausible that the West invented *the Balkans* and their differences merely to enjoy its own positive image. Even in the 1990s, when Balkanist discourses were flourishing, it was possible to identify different discourse representations. However, these did not attract as much attention as Balkanist representations. Negative representations in various public discourse genres are much less frequent today, although Balkanist discourse practices can still be identified. Šarić (2007) examined negative representations of the Balkans in a single media source, the monthly online German journal *Eurasisches Magazin*. Here, *Balkan* is primarily a negative label (when it is not used as a plain connotation-free geographical term). Along with other rhetorical means of Other-presentation, it often appears in contexts with 'catastrophic' intercultural images (black holes, exploding bombs, etc.).

Balkan and Related Geographical Terms in German Media

Based on a corpus of German media texts (about 250 articles, mainly news and political commentaries) as a sample of Western media discourse, negative representations of the Balkans have been subsiding in comparison with media representations of the 1990s, along with the view of this region as an undifferentiated, dark whole, frequently conceptualized as a *Balkan vessel/pot*. The German term *Balkan* (referring to both *Balkan* and *the Balkans*) is often found when geographically characterizing Serbia – for example, *Balkan country* (Balkan-Land, Balkanstaat), *Balkan republic* (Balkanrepublik) – and significantly prevails over other geographical labels. *Balkan* is used mostly neutrally (even if some articles allow space for negative connotations) in articles discussing the Kosovo crisis: *Balkan war* (Balkan-Krieg, *Welt Online*, 18 January 2008) and *a Balkan crisis* (eine Balkankrise, *Tagesanzeiger*, 27 January 2008). The terms are often used neutrally when positioning and defining Kosovo, Macedonia and Bosnia: *a small Balkan province* (kleine Balkanprovinz) and *chain reaction in the Balkans* (Kettenreaktion auf dem Balkan, *Financial Times Deutschland*, 5 February 2008). The phrases *Balkanization of other areas* (Balkanisierung anderer Gebiete, *Süddeutsche Zeitung*, 22 January 2008) and *domino-effect in the Balkans* (Domino-Effekt auf dem Balkan, *Wiesbadener Kurier*, 29 January 2008) refer to strivings toward independence in Macedonia and Bosnia that could grow after Kosovo's independence declaration.

A rare example in which *Balkan* has explicit negative connotations is the headline 'Der Balkan strapaziert die Nerven' (Balkans Fray Nerves, *Welt Online*, 7 January 2008) of an article that discusses Kosovo as an EU protectorate. The negative connotation of the word is used in contexts that raise potential dangers and conflicts. Examples include headlines such as 'Explosiver Balkan' (Explosive Balkans, *Rheinische Post*, 22 February 2008), in an article analyzing the situation after Kosovo's independence declaration – in particular, tendencies toward a greater Albania in some parts of Macedonia and Montenegro with an Albanian majority.

The official EU term *the Western Balkans* (West Balkan/der westliche Balkan) is also used. In official EU terminology, this covers Croatia, Bosnia and Herzegovina, Macedonia, Serbia, Montenegro, Kosovo and Albania. It is noteworthy that the Western Balkans comprises all former Yugoslav republics except Slovenia. The term *southeast Europe* (Südosteuropa) occurs much less often than *the Balkans*. There are examples of the two terms appearing simultaneously in the same context – for example, *in the Balkans, in southeast Europe* (auf dem Balkan, in Südosteuropa, *Der Standard*, 5 February 2008) – suggesting that no negative charge is related to either of the two terms. Few contexts use or elaborate on the opposition *the Balkans* versus *Europe/the EU*.

The corpus does not precisely indicate which countries and regions are (or are not) included in *the Balkans*. In the media contexts examined, the region's scope explicitly includes Macedonia, Croatia, Albania, Serbia and Kosovo. After it declared independence, Kosovo is referred to as *the new country in the Balkans* (der neue Staat auf dem Balkan) and *the new Balkan country* (der neue Balkan-Staat)

Slovenia and the Balkans in German Media

Slovenia's presentation and its relation to the terms *Balkan/the Balkans* is of special interest because the Balkans have played an important role in constructing Slovenia's own identity. Before turning to how Slovenia appears in the German media, some comments on the role of the Balkans in constructing Slovenian identity outside and inside Slovenia are needed to illustrate how domestic and foreign discourses mutually influence this topic.

In Slovenian public discourse, *the Balkans* and its alternatives (or oppositions) *Central Europe* and *Europe* have played a significant role. Hyder Patterson (2003) argues that Slovenian discussions of politics and culture in Yugoslavia used these 'heavily freighted' concepts in order to construct a new sense of national identity in the late 1980s and early 1990s. The domestic discussion about the character of Slovenian society was ultimately aimed at foreign audiences, which proved crucial in securing Slovenian independence. Todorova (1997) excludes Slovenia from the Balkans, mainly because Slovenia does not share the Ottoman legacy with the Balkan peoples. Stokes (1997) acknowledges Slovenia's success in redefining itself as Central European rather than Balkan, which 'demonstrates the community-building power of the idea of Central Europe, but at the same time it validates Todorova's point that the idea has formed itself in part against a Balkan other'.

Implicitly, Slovenia's non-Balkanist discourse exemplifies the persuasive force of Balkanist discourse. During the final years of the Yugoslav federation, influential Slovenian articles on politics and culture were attracted to the new East European rhetoric of Central Europe and affirmed an identity based in traditions understood to be Western, not Balkan. Influential figures such as Taras Kermauner and Dimitrij Rupel joined together around the journal *Nova revija* as 'a platform for extraordinarily Balkanist readings of Yugoslav and Slovenian society' (Hyder Patterson, 2003: 118). Slovenia's links with Central Europe were related to political, social and intellectual factors common to the former Habsburg Empire. In contrast to the self-image of a democratic, ordered and stable society, Slovenian discourse portrayed *the Balkans* as a region characterized by authoritarianism, disorder, instability and violence. In 1989, Kermauner claimed that Slovenia was 'the Yugoslav Piedmont', and Rus (1995) understood Slovenia's mission to be the 'Europeanization' and 'enlightenment' of the Balkans (see Hyder Patterson, 2003, and sources cited therein). Vezovnik (this volume) states that discourse on Slovenian identity tends to differentiate it from the former Yugoslavia and communism; that is, the scenario in which the Balkans is cast in the role of the Slovenian Other. Šarić (2004) shows that Slovenian media discourse uses the concept of *the Balkans* to characterize other, southern former Yugoslavs, or in critical comments about problems in Slovenian society, in which the Balkans often serve as a contrast to Europe.

As Hyder Patterson (2003: 114–121) demonstrates, Slovenian discourse practices related to differentiation from the Balkans before and after Yugoslavia's break-up gained little attention in the immediate neighborhood (Austria and Italy), as though Slovenia's cultural belonging were less disputed for its neighbors than for Slovenians themselves.

How do foreign media present Slovenia today? Do foreign media discourses relate Slovenia to the Balkans and, if so, how? In other words, do Western discourse representations portray Slovenia as 'having departed' from the Balkans, and what kind of relation is assumed between Slovenia and the Balkans?

The symbolic geography of Slovenia that can be gathered from German media presentations is ambiguous. The most accurate geographic position implied in many texts, but not explicitly stated, is found in *Frankfurter Allgemeine Zeitung* (2 January 2008): *the country between the Alps and the Balkans* (das Land zwischen Alpen und Balkan). Generally, there is a clear demarcation between Slovenia and the Balkans, as in an article from *Frankfurter Rundschau* that explicitly defines Slovenia as *Central European* (mitteleuropäisch):

> (2) That space between Slovenia's southern border and Greece's northern border, which Foreign Minister Rupel characterized as 'undefined territory', represents the true challenge.... From its sorrowful historical experience, *Central European Slovenia* [can] contribute Balkan experiences. (Tatsächlich stellt jener Raum zwischen der Südgrenze Sloweniens und der Nordgrenze Griechenlands, den Außenminister Dimitrij Rupel als 'undefiniertes Territorium' bezeichnet, die eigentliche Herausforderung dar... *Das mitteleuropäische Slowenien* [kann] aus leidvoller historischer Erfahrung balkanische Erfahrungen beisteuern. *Frankfurter Rundschau Online*, 8 January 2008)

Which contexts use the term *Balkan* when discussing Slovenia? Individual media contexts show an awareness of Slovenia's tradition of constructing identity in discourse based on differentiating it from the Balkans:

> (3) He [Lenarčič] belongs to a generation that has consciously distanced itself from the Balkans and its conflicts. The two million Slovenians wish to be integrated into Europe and to leave behind them everything that lies further to the south. (Er [Lenarčič] gehört zu jener Generation, die sich bewusst vom Balkan und seinen Konflikten abgesetzt hat. Die zwei Millionen Slowenen wollten sich in Europa integrieren und alles, was weiter südlich lag, hinter sich lassen. *Aller-Zeitung*, 30 December 2007)

Slovenian discourse and the external view on Slovenia are best summarized in the article 'Der Musterschüler ist erwachsen geworden' (The Model Pupil Has Grown Up, *Welt Online*, 31 December 2007), which reflects on Slovenia's efforts to be an exemplary European country: Slovenia was the first 'new' EU member to adopt the euro, which is also interpreted as a symbolic act of a country desperately trying to break its connections with the Balkans. Discourses from the 1970s are recalled, in which foreign journalists reported that Slovenia was part of Central Europe and Belgrade was described as a 'semi-primitive south':

> (4) For a long time, it was the Balkans that Slovenia was running away from. Today it is Austria as a model of the future toward which this country is headed. Ironically, it is the Balkans that will be the focus of Slovenia's EU presidency. (Lange Zeit war es der Balkan, vor dem Slowenien weglief. Heute ist es das Zukunftsmodell Österreich, auf das das Land zusteuert. Ironischerweise wird ausgerechnet der Balkan die EU-Ratspräsidentschaft Sloweniens prägen. *Welt Online*, 31 December 2007)

Slovenia's current relation to the Balkans is historically contextualized – Slovenia's potential success in fulfilling one of the priorities of its EU presidency (i.e. strengthening the EU membership prospects of the western Balkan countries) is related to Slovenia's knowledge of the region based on shared history:

> (5) Slovenia counts on its relationships with and intimate knowledge of the region, its shared history, and its familiarity with the situation of the peoples of the Western Balkans. (Slowenien setzt auf seine Beziehungen und intimen Kenntnisse der Region, auf die gemeinsame Geschichte und die Vertrautheit mit den Befindlichkeiten der Völker im West-Balkan. *Welt Online*, 29 December 2007)

> (6) On the other hand Ljubljana, which itself broke away from Belgrade in 1991, sees the sparks of a new Balkan war more clearly than others. (Andererseits sieht Ljubljana, das sich selbst 1991 von Belgrad trennte, die Glutherde eines neuen Balkankrieges deutlicher als andere. *Frankfurter Rundschau-online*, 8 January 2008)

Most articles explicitly exclude Slovenia from the Balkans: the Balkan region begins at the Slovenian border, it neighbors Slovenia. For example, in a discussion about Croatia's proclamation of a protected fishing zone, *Slovenia...has the Balkans as its direct neighbor* (Slowenien...[hat] den Balkan als unmittelbaren Nachbar, *Märkische Allgemeine*, 8 January 2008).

When the terms *western Balkan countries* (Westbalkan-Staaten) and *Western Balkans* (Westbalkan) are used, they generally occur in contexts that explicitly discuss EU issues and, consequently, use EU terminology.

Based on the corpus analyzed, the past Slovenian discourse practices that aimed to create a demarcation between Slovenia and the Balkans have been successful. In the time frame analyzed, Slovenia is mostly characterized as a 'model pupil', with the Balkans and its burdens of armed conflicts as an immediate neighbor. The geographical and historical connection of Slovenia to the Balkans makes it an ideal mediator in Balkan countries' efforts to join the EU.

The Balkans in Croatian and Serbian Media

Accounting for the current discourse-based destiny of the terms *balkanski/Balkan* 'Balkan/the Balkans' in Croatian and Serbian media requires some reflection on the situation in the 1990s. From the beginning of the wars in the former Yugoslavia in the 1990s onwards, *Balkan/the Balkans* were the main terms used in discourses about identity. These terms were part of hate speech, although more subtle than the versions that Bugarski (1994) and Malabotta (2004) discuss – that is, they were negatively charged words and symbols. Occasionally burdened with various connotations, in many contexts they were also devoid of any concrete meaning. Used as metonyms, they replaced all other, more meaningful concepts. Many studies have been devoted to the 'Balkan-as-metaphor' complex, but few analyses concentrate on media images related to the symbolic potential of *the Balkans* as a term (one example is Močnik, 2005). Ambivalences in its media usage are discussed in Šarić (2004) based on media material from 1997 to 2003; here, I examine media presentations in 2007/2008 in a sample of Croatian and Serbian media.

Jansen (2002) and Lindstrom (2003), among others, argue that 'Balkanism' was at the center of nationalistic discourses on identity in Croatia in the 1990s. In Croatian discourses, *the Balkans* was the most frequent negative Other, usually representing Serbs. These discourses typically presented the former Yugoslavia as a *Balkan tyranny* related to the dark periods of communism. This image is diametrically opposed to that of a well-functioning multicultural and multiethnic community, applied to the same time period. This latter image of an open, culturally rich identity, filled with possibilities, a space between two opposing global blocs, still persists in the consciousness of the 'last Yugoslav generation' (Volcic, 2007). In the Croatian nationalistic discourse of the 1990s, however, the term *the Balkans* and its derivations symbolized a number of threats, which varied from context to context. Many Others existed (Serbs, Bosniaks or other Croatians – that is, political opponents), all of them under the metaphorical umbrella of *Balkan*.

Jansen (2002) identifies numerous post-Yugoslav discourse practices of the 1990s, in which the notion of *the Balkans* was part of the binary opposition *(the) Balkan(s)* versus *Europe*, employed in negative self-definition process. Both parts of this opposition were contested cultural constructs and, inevitably, parts of identity discourses. Attempts to construe the *Self* as different from the *Balkans* were interwoven with the feeling of being a part of the Balkan Other. The construct of *Europe* was equally ambivalent because it was situated both inside and outside the Self at the same time. The notions of Europe and the Balkans provided discourse material for subjects to relate their personal narratives to the larger stories of war and nationalism. In discourses during and immediately after the Yugoslav wars, *Balkan* was related to a collection of real and imagined social practices that generally implied primitivism, aggression and negatively connoted passion.

The semiotic potential and semiotic manipulation of *the Balkans* as used in Croatian media is directly related to Croatian official politics of the 1990s. *The Balkans* was a key term in Franjo Tuđman's discourse designed to create a Croatian identity. His opponents also used the term for their own purposes. Tuđman and his HDZ (*Hrvatska demokratska zajednica*, 'Croatian Democratic Union') claimed that Croatia was a part of the pro-Western world and Central Europe, and had little to do with the Balkans. This was reflected in various attempts to ban undesired phenomena, such as Serbian and 'Eastern' folk music. One significant move in the 'anti-Balkan' tendencies in 1990s Croatia included renaming the famous *Balkan* cinema (built in 1921) to *Europa*, an event that Jansen (2002) qualifies as 'ethnographically perfect'. The opponents and critics of the ruling party applied the terms *Balkan/balkanski* when they reflected on its '*Balkan* politics'. Antinationalist discourses therefore retained the discourse framework of Balkanism. The discourse-based antipode of *the Balkans* was *Europe*, whose features included Western, rational, modern, urban, developed and individualistic. *Europe* was a metaphor for a political/cultural ideal, often referring to the EU.

Less frequent positive evocations of the Balkans were explicitly subversive (e.g. in the journal *Arkzin*), with the function of destabilizing discourses that glorified Europe. *Balkan* had positive connotations mainly in the discourse of antinationalist dissidents.

Croatian media

In the Croatian media considered here (i.e. *Večernji list, Jutarnji list, Novi list* and *Slobodna Dalmacija*), the term *Western Balkans* (zapadni/Zapadni Balkan) and its derivations are much more frequent than *the Balkans* (Balkan). The term *zapadni Balkan* is used when *Balkan/the Balkans* are by and large avoided. In commentaries on EU issues, especially on foreign analyses and political events related to the region, the term *zapadni Balkan* is sometimes written capitalized, like a proper geographical name. The media seem to be aware of the catastrophic images that can be evoked by *Balkan* due to its discourse history since the 1990s. In comparison, *zapadni Balkan* has possible positive connotations because it comprises not only countries belonging to the former Yugoslavia, which itself tends to be associated with the cognitive framework of Yugoslavia's violent demise and wars after 1990. *Zapadni Balkan* appears to be a better choice, less dangerous and more neutral: It comprises Albania as a 'neutral' entity. As an administrative EU term for current EU non-members, it does not include Slovenia. Symbolically, its scope therefore corresponds to Slovenia's symbolic departure from the region, which was prepared in numerous discourse practices in the 1980s (Hyder Patterson, 2003).

According to Đerić (2006: 3), the use of the adjective *western* (zapadni) as a specifier of the Balkans is indicative of a destigmatization strategy that has developed during recent years. My media data suggest a similar interpretation. One reason may be the influence and awareness of foreign and domestic Balkanist discourses, and another is the fact that Romania and Bulgaria, as the 'eastern Balkans', are already in the European Union (which is metonymically often identified with *Europe*). The decisive difference lies in the qualifier *western*, which neutralizes the cultural model evoked by the negative connotations of *the Balkans*, relating to its symbolic opposite – that is, Western civilization. This symbolic power of the feature *western* relates to a widespread self-image of the Croats, Serbs and other Slavs: the idea that they were the most important bulwark of Europe protecting Western civilization from 'Eastern' barbarism for centuries (Hudabiunigg, this volume; Luketić, 2008; Žanić, 2007).

Let us take a look at the treatment of the terms *Balkan/the Balkans*. Only three Croatian newspapers are considered in greater detail because the fourth, *Jutarnji list*, does not offer any new tendencies related to the use of these geographical terms.

The Dalmatian daily *Slobodna Dalmacija* (*SD*) contains texts related to the former Yugoslav countries in the sections *World* (Svijet) and *News* (Novosti). The existence (or lack) of specific sections in newspapers is also meaningful. The absence of sections such as *Balkans* indicates the creation of a new identity, a wish to belong somewhere else and a desire to symbolically depart from the Balkans. This practice can be related to the discourse imperative of *leaving the Balkans* in 1990s Croatia. It is noteworthy that not only certain former Yugoslav countries insist on this symbolic departure: A similar phenomenon is also seen in Romania (e.g. Cioroianu, 2005).

The term *the Balkans* (Balkan) occurs in *SD* most frequently with neutral connotations, especially in articles discussing economics and culture. All of the Yugoslav successor countries may lie within the scope of *the Balkans*. The majority of texts in which I identified the term do not focus exclusively on Croatian issues, and so the position of Croatia remains ambivalent. Positive or neutral contexts are generally more inclusive regarding the scope of *the Balkans*. In these contexts, the *Balkan* umbrella may include Croatia as well as Slovenia. For example, the article 'Slovenski lider na hrvatskom tržištu' (Slovenian Leader on the Croatian Market, *SD*, 5 March 2008) with the subheadline 'Potencijal Balkana'

(Potential of the Balkans) explicitly defines the geographical scope of the Balkans:

> (7) The Balkan region – that is, Croatia, Slovenia, Bosnia and Herzegovina, Serbia, Montenegro, Macedonia, Romania, Bulgaria, Greece, and Turkey – has undergone remarkable development in recent years. (Područje Balkana, odnosno područje Hrvatske, Slovenije, Bosne i Hercegovine, Srbije, Crne Gore, Makedonije, Rumunjske, Bugarske, Grčke i Turske, bilježilo je posljednjih godina visoki rast.)

The feature that makes *the Balkans* a difficult concept in Self- and Other-representations of the Balkan region is the ambiguity in its geographical definitions – that is, its vaguely defined geographical scope (Cioroianu, 2005: 210–211). The cultural concept of *the Balkans* mixes knowledge of facts and related beliefs, as well as prejudices and misinterpretations. These all are possible components of individual metarepresentations. Every discourse activates different dimensions of this cultural model. The context activates it as a specific cultural model, but is rarely implied in its entirety. In the following passage, the model possesses an imagined center and periphery: the center relates to the Turks, Serbs and Yugoslavs. These last two categories are themselves fuzzy because it is not clear whether *Serbian occupation* and *Yugoslav occupation* are two different categories, or a single one. The media's awareness of possible implications when activating the Balkan cultural model is apparent in ironic comments on stereotypes and Balkanism discourses. The Bosnian/Croatian/Serbian idiom *pušiti kao Turčin* – literally, 'to smoke like a Turk' – relates to a South-Slavic image of the Turks:

> (8) The news of the day is that in Turkey itself one will not be allowed to '*smoke like a Turk*', given that Turkey is also starting to prohibit smoking in public places. Thus, smoking will not be 'in' any longer in the Balkans – which we blame for all our problems, including smoking habits. The so-called average Croatian believes that he does not belong to the Balkans: he was brought there in the course of Serbian and Yugoslav occupation; his behavior at all times has been European, characterized by respecting rules instead of looking for exceptions. (Vijest noći je da se više ni u Turskoj neće moći *pušiti kao Turčin* jer i ona uvodi zabranu pušenja na javnim mjestima. Pušenje tako više neće biti 'in' ni na Balkanu, koji okrivljujemo za sve svoje nedaće, pa i za slabost iliti snagu pušenja. Tzv. prosječni Hrvat vjeruje da ne pripada Balkanu, nego Europi jer je na Balkan doveden srbijanskom i jugoslavenskom okupacijom, da svojim ponašanjem oduvijek svjedoči europstvo, koje odlikuje poštovanje pravila, a ne traženje iznimaka. 'Pušačka vrdanja' 'Smokers' Stalling', *SD*, 21 January 2008)

It is not entirely clear if the remark about *the average Croatian* and his belief about where he belongs to is ironic, or simply a neutral comment.

The media are also aware of the power of *Balkan* as an attention-getter. The phrase *Balkan detonator* in the kicker[4] 'Balkanski detonator. Kosovo broji dane uoči proglašenja nezavisnosti' (A Balkan Detonator: Kosovo's Independence a Matter of Days), which introduces an article about the Kosovo prime minister's security guarantees to the Kosovo Serbs ('Thaçi: Srbi, ostajte ovdje', 'Thaçi: Serbs, Stay Here', *SD*, 7 February 2008), belongs to the group of catastrophic images discussed in Šarić (2004). This noun phrase shows a metaphorical view of Kosovo's approaching declaration of independence. The lexical choice activates a visual image, and the image further activates the cultural model (i.e. some of its components). The noun *detonator* may well carry the catastrophic meaning, rather than the adjective *balkanski* itself. Still, it is this very combination that produces the intended effect because other geographical terms sound odd in this combination: *southeastern European detonator* is not a likely lexical choice.

Another example of the term *Balkans* in contexts addressing difficulties and conflicts is the kicker of an article about local Serbs awaiting Kosovo's declaration of independence with barricades in Mitrovica in northern Kosovo: 'Recept iz hrvatske. Balkan na rubu novoga kruga krvavog nasilja' (A Recipe from Croatia. The Balkans on the Edge of a New Spiral of Violence), headline: 'Srbi i na Kosovu postavili balvane' (Serbs Put Up Barricades in Kosovo Too, *SD*, 14 February 2008). This is a historical analogy, a reference to the beginning of the war in Croatia. Later in the article, another noun phrase evoking the *Balkan* cultural model – *Balkan déjà vu* – is used: "Mnogi [se] plaše da će se dogoditi 'balkanski deja vu', jer ovako su počinjali i ratovi u Hrvatskoj i Bosni" (Many people fear a Balkan déjà vu because the wars in Croatia and Bosnia began the same way).

A similar example is the headline 'Balkanski horor-scenarij' (Balkan Horror Script, *SD*, 15 March 2008) of a comment on the Reuters' analysis of the situation in Kosovo, Serbia and Macedonia. Part of the kicker explicitly defines the scope of the Balkans: 'Crno im se piše. Reutersov urednik analizira aktualnu situaciju na Kosovu, u Srbiji i Makedoniji' (No Hope for Them. Reuters Editor Analyzes Current Situation in Kosovo, Serbia, and Macedonia).

The survival of the crucial dichotomy for identity construction in the 1990s – *Europe* versus *the Balkans*, which helped negotiate Croatia's identity – is attested in the commentary 'Duhovi prošlosti' (Ghosts of the Past):

> (9) Here, everything that is not Europe is usually *Balkan mud* and jealousy, manipulation and isolation.... If we cannot go further, to

Europe, we can go much deeper: into *the Balkan mud*, hatred, and new rivers of blood. This is why we need Europe much more than Europe needs us. (A sve ono što nije Europa, kod nas je obično *balkanski kal* i jal, manipulacija i izolacija.... Ako već ne možemo dalje, u Europu, možemo zato puno dublje: u *balkansko blato*, u mržnju i u nove potoke krvi. Tu leži odgovor na pitanje zašto mi puno više trebamo Europu nego ona nas. *SD*, 12 February 2008)

The dichotomy is strengthened by the catastrophic image *Balkan mud* (balkansko blato/kal). The semantic content of *balkansko blato* is defined through its metaphoric instances (*hatred, rivers of blood*), whereas the concept of Europe remains vague; the only certainty is that it comprises anything that is not *Balkan mud*.

The tendency of negative Other-representation (in this case, of neighboring Slovenia) by using lexical means that evoke the *Balkan* cultural model appears in the kicker 'Balkanska dežela. Po Financial Timesu, Ljubljana iskorištava EU' (Balkan Country: FT Says Ljubljana Exploits EU) of the article 'Slovenija izazvala negodovanje Unije' (Slovenia Provokes EU Disapproval, *SD*, 21 February 2008). This is a commentary on Slovenia's actions connected with the fishing zone unilaterally imposed by Croatia on 1 January 2008. It questions whether Slovenia is using its presidency to attain its own goals in its conflict with Croatia. The use of the Slovenian word *dežela* 'country' in the Croatian media is informal, ironic or derogatory.

Contexts discussing Slovenia's symbolic departure from the Balkans are also found in the Rijeka daily newspaper *Novi list* (*NL*). In the commentary 'Janša na Balkanu' (Janša in the Balkans, 24 November 2007), the discourse role of the adverb *balkanski* indicates Slovenia's symbolic reappearance on the Balkan scene after its (symbolic) running away from Yugoslavia and the Balkans:

> (10) Slovenia was the first to leave Yugoslavia and the Balkans, as soon as the chance arose. Recently, Slovenia has come back to those very Balkans.... The Slovenian prime minister has a problem understanding democracy. This means that also next year... Slovenia will continue to be a lively and overblown country with incidents, *full of Balkan political scandals*, and not boring and predictable, as it wishes to be. (Slovenija je prva zbrisala iz Jugoslavije i Balkana, čim joj se ukazala prilika, da bi se ovih dana – i to ne samo na simboličan način – na isti taj Balkan vratila.... Slovenski premijer ima problema sa shvaćanjem demokracije, što znači da će Slovenija i sljedeću godinu ostati živahna i ekscesna zemlja, *balkanski puna političkih skandala*, a ne dosadna i predvidljiva, kakvom bi toliko željela biti.)

Balkan characteristics as defined in the passage – *full of political scandals* (pun političkih skandala), *lively* (živahan) and *overblown* (ekscesan) – are contrasted with *boring* (dosadan) and *predictable* (predvidljiv), the latter relating to Slovenia's construction of its own identity seen through the eyes of its neighbor. Not all of the characteristics are unambiguously negative (e.g. *živahan*). Nonetheless, having problems with democracy is equated with *coming back to the Balkans*. Accordingly, the negative meaning of the Balkans is evoked.

Lexemes related to *balkan-* are not always free of negative connotations in *Novi list*; compare *political Balkanism* (politički balkanizam) in the article 'HDZ je opet prijetnja' (Croatian Democratic Union Again a Danger, 3 March 2008): 'It [the HDZ] is driven by its *political Balkanism*, and society is returning to a disaster of chaos, corruption, and political violence' (Ona pušta na volju svojemu *političkom balkanizmu*, pa zemlja tone natrag u kužnu jamu nereda, korupcije i političkoga nasilja). Polemical tones related to stereotyping and generalizing attitudes can be found in *Novi list*: This daily is most open to the critique of Balkanist discourse. One example is the commentary 'Bye-bye Balkan!' – an intertextual reflection on an article published in another Croatian newspaper, *Jutarnji list* on 5 March 2008: The article in *NL* problematizes the headline 'Šest uvjeta Hrvatskoj za odlazak s Balkana' (Six Conditions for Croatia to Leave the Balkans, 9 March 2008) of the article published in *Jutarnji list*:

> (11) [It] suggests that one day Croatia will move to a better, more secure location.... Our homeland, led by its confident navigators, will sail into a happy future. Nobody knows where it will land but, considering the far-reaching policy of our leaders, it will without doubt find an ideal destination. In any case, there will be no Serbs there, or anybody that has ever heard of Kosovo, let alone the left bank of the Dragonja and the curses of Slovenian Prime Minister Janez Janša. (... [to] sugerira da će se Hrvatska kad-tad preseliti s Balkana na neku bolju i izvjesniju lokaciju... Cijela naša domovina će... vođena rukom svojih sigurnih navigatora odjedriti u svijetlu budućnost. Teško je znati gdje će aterirati, ali s obzirom na dalekosežnu politiku lidera s Markova trga, nema sumnje da će se naći idealno odredište. U svakom slučaju takvo gdje nema Srbijanaca i gdje nitko nije čuo za Kosovo, a kamoli za lijevu obalu Dragonje i anateme slovenskog premijera Janeza Janše.)

The commentary reflects on undesirable social phenomena in Croatia, such as the lack of moral and political principles, and growing corruption. It ironically concludes that, despite all this, 'the Balkans is something we have never heard of'. At first glance, this passage seems like a critical account of Balkan-related stereotypes, but it is in fact an instance of Balkanist discourse itself because it criticizes the denial of acknowledging that negative social phenomena are in fact 'Balkan' phenomena.

Columns and commentaries often contain a self-assured treatment of Balkan stereotypes. In one commentary reflecting on the Schengen border (Slovenia joined the Schengen area in December 2007), the writer Slobodan Šnajder problematizes a tendency common to all former Yugoslavs to see themselves as better than their (eastern) neighbors. While 'We' (Croatians) are sad Others against whom Slovenians *put up barriers and locks*, our Others live to the east, and it is before them that we must *put up barriers and locks*, before they do it to their Others, the Turks. The author defines the aspiration patterns for the identity construction of all former Yugoslavs: What all Yugoslav 'Us' and 'Them' have in common is a wish to set up an imaginary or concrete border between themselves and their neighbors, trying to prove cultural supremacy at any cost, and, at the same time, attesting their self-derived immaturity:

> (12) Croatia has to discipline the Western Balkans; as a 'respectable regional force' it must lead it, civilize it, and, at the same time, it must leave the Balkans and enter the Schengen zone at least two months prior to Serbia and other competitors in Brussels' waiting room. If not, Croatian politicians will commit collective suicide ... All the Yugoslav successor states – including Slovenia, which 'ran away' – are immature. Some are doing better, some worse, but all of them have their tutors, as is normal for underage countries. (Hrvatska mora sada 'disciplinirati' Zapadni Balkan, mora ga kao 'respektabilna regionalna sila' predvoditi, civilizirati, uljuditi (uljudba!), a istodobno, mora se po svaku cijenu od njega 'odlijepiti', te ući u Schengenski prostor barem dva mjeseca prije Srbije i drugih suparnika u briselskoj čekaonici. Inače će hrvatska politička klasa počiniti kolektivno samoubojstvo ... Sve države proizašle iz rasapa Jugoslavije, inkluzive 'otperjalu' Sloveniju, nalaze se u stanju samoiskrivljene nezrelosti. Nekima ide bolje, nekima lošije, ali sve imaju svoje tutore, kako i priliči maloljetnim državama. 'Sve pod jednim ključem' 'Everything under One Key', *NL*, 5 January 2008)

To civilize (*uljuditi*) in (12) is a significant lexical choice relating to the construction of a distinct linguistic identity in Croatia in the 1990s; that is, a tendency to replace words of foreign origin that were commonly used up to that time (such as *civilizacija* and *civilizirati*) with words based on Slavic roots, which were considered 'better' Croatian words. The goal was to strengthen puristic tradition and create an opposition to Serbian linguistic tradition, which has not had a negative attitude toward loan words.

The general tendencies in *Novi list* and *Slobodna Dalmacija* can also be seen in the Zagreb daily *Večernji list* (*VL*). The attitudes to establishing metaphorical geography in the (non-)existence of newspaper sections are obvious. No news section relates to the very region that Croatia belongs to. For example, news about Serbia and Montenegro can be found in the section *Svijet* 'world', and no distinction is thus made between the importance of news from the 'near abroad' and distant places. The term *the Balkans* is infrequent. When it does occur, it usually refers to Croatia's eastern neighbors. It is more often used to paraphrase EU politicians' discourse than as the author's own term. *Western Balkans* (Zapadni Balkan) prevails over *the Balkans*. It is mostly used in quotations and references to European discussions, and is often marked as foreign usage with quotation marks. The same is true for the adjective *western Balkan* (zapadnobalkanski). The expressions *the region* (regija) and *countries from the region* (države iz regije) are also found as quotes or an author's own terms. Sometimes they can be interpreted as avoidance of more precise geographical terms.

Balkan occasionally carries negative connotations in articles where it is not part of EU discussions and EU-related issues. One example is the following context discussing Macedonia's NATO membership prospects and Greece's veto of Macedonia's application. The Greek decision to veto Macedonia's NATO membership is characterized as *Balkan small-mindedness* and a metaphorical *moving of the Balkans to NATO*:

> (13) Did *Balkan small-mindedness* really have to be stronger than the security and stabilization of a crisis region? It seems that after Greece's veto the Balkans have moved to NATO instead of NATO moving to the Balkans. (Zar je *balkanska sitničavost* zaista morala nadvladati nedvojbene izazove sigurnosti i stabilizacije jedne krizne regije? Čini se da se, nakon grčkog veta zbog imena, Balkan preselio u NATO umjesto da se NATO preseli na Balkan. 'Grčka voda na srpski mlin' 'Greek Grist for the Serbian Mill', *VL*, 4 April 2008)

Based on the corpus from the Croatian media, the tendency to use the term *Balkans* in contexts addressing difficulties and conflicts is generally subsiding. However, this decrease can be observed only if media texts from several years prior (Šarić, 2004) are compared to the 2008 media material examined here. The tendency of negative Other-representation using lexical means evoking the *Balkan* cultural model remains, but is generally weaker than in the late 1990s and the early part of the following decade. Direct reflections on Balkanist discourse are an interesting feature of some media contexts. However, some media texts simultaneously uncover and perpetuate this discourse.

Serbian media

Jansen (2002) argues that *Balkan* did not play a significant role in Serbian nationalist discourses of the 1990s: Serbia's geographical status as part of the Balkans was not questioned. However, the importance of this 'Balkan component' of Serbia's identity was ambiguous. It was linked to cultural pride related to resistance to foreign domination, for example, but was also related to negative social phenomena such as backwardness and ineffectiveness. This second notion prevailed in antinationalist Serbian discourses, carrying almost exclusively negative connotations (primitivism, laziness, rural culture and backwardness). It appeared in contexts in which 'European' values were seen as disappearing while the subjects of these discourses simultaneously presented themselves as loyal to these values. In general, *Balkan* was used ambivalently in self-definitions. Jansen notices an increase of rival, anti-Balkanist discourses in Belgrade during the NATO operation, which presented Serbs as victims defying every attempt at foreign domination – this being considered a *Balkan* characteristic. In everyday life, Jansen (2002) notices that many people oscillated between loving and hating the Balkans; that is, between the importance of what they considered good versus bad sides of the Balkans. Volčič (2005) addresses how the West has been written into the cultural practices of the post-Milošević era, considering poststructuralist arguments (e.g. Todorova, 1997) concerned with how the West (i.e. Western Europe) continually creates its identity in opposition to the Other of the Balkans. Volčič's analysis is based on interviews with young Serbian intellectuals and particularly focused on Serbian responses to Western discourses that portray the Balkans as primitive. It shows that the responses to Western stereotyping range from a simplistic Serbian Othering of the West to an internal Othering within Serbia, to the deployment of Western stereotypes about the Serbs in ways that cause them to be fully accepted.

In the mirror of uncertainties that reflect the notion of the Balkans, it is interesting to examine current tendencies of the relevance of *Balkan* terms in Self- and Other-identification processes in the Serbian media. In general, Serbian media (*Politika, Danas, Dnevnik* and *Večernje novosti*) only insignificantly contest the term *the Balkans*. It was not possible to identify many instances of Balkanist discourses – neither their critique nor further development – in the four newspapers analyzed.

Dnevnik uses the terms *Balkan/balkanski* in neutral contexts relating to geographical categories: for example, *Balkan countries* (balkanske zemlje) refers to Croatia and Serbia in the article 'Kako povući novac iz evropskih fondova' (How to Get Money from European Funds, 5 April 2008). In some contexts, the entire scenario depicted may evoke negative connotations, although the immediate contexts related to *the Balkans* do not: for example, *in the western Balkan ghetto* (u zapadnobalkanskom getu), in 'Srbija bez filtera' (Serbia Unfiltered, 5 April 2008), *Balkan narcotics sales corridor* (balkanski koridor trgovine narkoticima) and in 'Srbija i Kosovo na putu heroina' (Serbia and Kosovo on the Heroin Route, 5 March 2008). The same applies to neologisms, such as the phrase *a black Balkan saga* (crna balkanska saga), which carries negative connotations in an article commenting on an incident and a broken window at the Napredak Croatian Culture Association in Vojvodina:

(14) The village of Novi Slankamen the day before yesterday reminded us of *a black*, obviously unfinished *Balkan saga*, in which it is best to cause damage to a Croat because the Self is bothered by something. (Selo Novi Slankamen naksinoć nas je podsetilo na *crnu*, očigledno nezavršenu *balkansku sagu*, u kojoj je najpodesnije Hrvatu naneti štetu a konto nečega što tišti Onog Prvog. 'Mesto gde hrvatsko staklo najbrže puca' 'The Place Where Croatian Glass is Broken Most Often', 6 March 2008)

The negative potential of connotations is also related to variation on the theme *Balkan inn* addressed in Šarić (2004): *Unfortunately, on the Serbian political stage there are still people that would turn off the light in the Balkan inn* (Nažalost, na političkoj sceni Srbije još uvek ima onih koji bi da ugase svetlo u balkanskoj krčmi, in: 'Intervju: Armanijeva odela u balkanskoj krčmi' 'Interview: Armani Clothing in the Balkan Inn', 10 February 2008).

Danas, Politika and *Večernje novosti* use *the Balkans* and related lexemes neutrally in most cases. The phrase *western Balkans* (zapadni/Zapadni Balkan) is also often used. *The Balkans* is often explicitly used for Serbia's self-positioning, as in the following example from *Večernje novosti*:

(15) Why so much injustice toward us, *of all Balkan peoples*? Not one of our neighbors and former brothers has suffered as much as the Serbs in recent years. (Zbog čega toliko nepravde prema nama, *od svih naroda na Balkanu*? Niko od naših komšija i bivše braće se nije toliko napatio poslednjih godina kao Srbi. 'Kosovski nezaborav: Dirnuli i srce' 'Kosovo Unforgotten: The Heart Touched Too', 22 February 2008)

Slovenia is also explicitly within the scope of *the Balkans* in some contexts; compare an example from *Večernje novosti*: *Croatia is positioned more centrally than Slovenia in the Balkans* (Hrvatska je na Balkanu centralnije pozicionirana u odnosu na Sloveniju, in: 'Rusija kroji mapu' 'Russia Tailors the Map', 18 January 2008).

Đerić (2006) argues that constructivists' image-related approach to 'Balkan studies' failed to succeed as a genre in Serbian cultural and societal theory, while the dichotomy *(the) Balkan(s)* versus *Europe* has retained its strong symbolic force, relying on the political preferences of the discourse participants. In my media corpus, the concept of *Europe* is often used in identity-construction contexts with a positive symbolic force. Even so, it is rarely related to the concept of *the Balkans*.

In *Politika, Danas, Dnevnik* and *Večernje novosti*, the term *Balkan* and its derivations do not seem to play a significant role in either Self- or Other-presentation. In any case, the role these concepts play in identity-construction processes is much less significant than in the Croatian media.

Concluding Remarks

This chapter has examined how an originally geographical term can be used as an identity label. *The Balkans* is an indicative example, but there are certainly many more instances of metaphorical geography that deserve additional attention. The discourse presentation of Europe's integration process is a rich source of metaphors related to real and imagined geographies. My corpora (German, Croatian and Serbian media texts) are connected with the period when Slovenia held the EU presidency in 2008: I selected this period to examine how the identity patterns externally and internally ascribed to post-Yugoslav societies relate to metaphorical geography.

In most German media contexts, the equivalent of *(the) Balkan(s)* is used as a neutral geographical label. The geographic scope of the region referred to may not always be absolutely transparent, but the cultural model evoked is not intensively related to negative images. The situation in the Croatian and Serbian media differs. Although *the Balkans* and related terms are mainly used as geographic labels in neutral contexts, there are nonetheless many contexts dealing with Balkanist discourse practices, especially in the Croatian media. It is indicative that individual articles criticize these practices at a metalevel, but sometimes still fall into the trap of perpetuating Balkanism. Compared to the Croatian media, the Serbian media more often use *Balkan/the Balkans* in instant self-identifications. This is related to how the destiny of these terms has differed in the discourse of identity construction over the past two decades. The Croatian media are still struggling with Balkanism, and are criticizing the usage of *the Balkans* as a negative identity label and ascribing *Balkan* characteristics to unwanted internal and external societal phenomena. In contrast, the Serbian media contest *Balkan* and *the Balkans* much less. These findings indicate a need for additional research on identity labels that could bring together the perspectives of linguistics, anthropology, history and the social sciences.

Notes

1. http://www.eu2008.si/en/The_Council_Presidency/Priorities_Programmes/index.html. Accessed 20 July 2008.
2. The etymology of the word *Balkan* is debated. Folk etymologists tend to see in it an amalgam of two Turkish words, *bal* 'blood' and *kan* 'honey', a combination that seems convenient in evocations of typical stereotypes about the Balkans. Linguists generally point toward another stem, **balk* – 'wood', providing the etymology 'chain of wooded mountains' (Sekulić, 1999: 89).
3. All translations provided by the author.
4. I use the term *kicker* to refer to a headline typical for certain South Slavic newspapers. This headline is placed above the main headline. In *Jutarnji list*, kickers serve as article introductions.

References

Bakić-Hayden, M. and Hayden, R.M. (1992) Orientalist variations on the theme "Balkans": Symbolic geography in recent Yugoslav cultural politics. *Slavic Review* 51 (1), 1–15.

Bakić-Hayden, M. (1995) Nesting orientalism: The case of former Yugoslavia. *Slavic Review* 54 (4), 917–931.

Bjelić, D.I. and Savić, O. (eds) (2002) *Balkan as Metaphor: Between Globalization and Fragmentation* (pp. 165–190). Cambridge, MA: MIT Press.

Bugarski, R. (1994) *Jezik od mira do rata*. Belgrade: Beogradski krug.

Cioroianu, A. (2005) The impossible escape: Romania and the Balkans. In D.I. Bjelić and O. Savić (eds) *Balkan as Metaphor: Between Globalization and Fragmentation* (pp. 209–233). Cambridge, MA: MIT Press.

Đerić, G. (2006) Među javom i med snom. O balkanizmu i neuspehu konstruktivizma u Srbiji: pogled iz prošlosti. *Filozofija i društvo* 31, 195–219.

Hyder Patterson, P. (2003) On the edge of reason: The boundaries of Balkanism in Slovenian, Austrian, and Italian discourse. *Slavic Review* 62 (1), 110–141.

Jansen, S. (2002) Svakodnevni orijentalizam: Doživljaj "Balkana"/ "Evrope" u Beogradu i Zagrebu. *Filozofija i društvo* 18, 33–71. http://www.komunikacija.org.yu/komunikacija/casopisi/fid/XVIII/index_html?stdlang=dk. Accessed 20 May 2009.

Kiossev, A. (2005) The dark intimacy: Maps, identities, acts of identification. In D.I. Bjelić and O. Savić (eds) *Balkan as Metaphor: Between Globalization and Fragmentation* (pp. 165–190). Cambridge, MA: MIT Press.

Lindstrom, N. and Razsa, M. (2004) Balkan is beautiful: Balkanism in the political discourse of Tuđman's Croatia. *East European Politics and Societies* 18 (4), 628–650.

Lindstrom, N. (2003) Between Europe and the Balkans: Mapping Slovenia and Croatia's "return to Europe" in the 1990s. *Dialectical Anthropology* 27 (3–4), 313–329.

Luketić, K. (2008) Bijeg s Balkana. Zarez 224 – Online document: http://www.zarez.hr/224/z_temabroja.html. Accessed 20 May 2009.

Mitani, K. (2006) Balkan as a Sign: Usage of the Word Balkan in Language and Discourse of the ex-Yugoslav People. – Online document: src-h.slav.hokudai.ac.jp/coe21/publish/no15_ses/15_mitani.pdf. Accessed 20 May 2009.

Močnik, R. (2005) The Balkans as an element in ideological mechanisms. In D.I. Bjelić and O. Savić (eds) *Balkan as Metaphor: Between Globalization and Fragmentation* (pp. 79–115). Cambridge, MA: MIT Press.

Norris, D. (1999) *In the Wake of the Balkan Myth: Questions of Identity and Modernity*. Basingstoke: Macmillan.

Richter Malabotta, M. (2004) Semantics of war in former Yugoslavia. In B. Busch and H. Kelly-Holmes (eds) *Language, Discourse and Borders in the Yugoslav Successor States* (pp. 78–87). Clevedon: Multilingual Matters.

Rus, V. (1995) Uvod. In V. Rus (ed.) *Slovenia po letu 1995: Razmišljanja o prihodnosti*. Ljubljana: Fakulteta za družbene vede.

Šarić, Lj. (2004) Balkan identity: Changing self-images of the South Slavs. In S. Manz et al. (eds) *Discourses of Intercultural Identity in Britain, Germany and Eastern Europe*. Special Issue: *Journal of Multilingual* and *Multicultural Development* 25 (5 & 6), 389–408.

Šarić, Lj. (2007) Europe's black holes, economic ruins, lands back of beyond, and other objects of wonder. Workshop presentation. *Cultural*

Borders and (Re)formulations of Cultural Identities in Europe Oslo, 1–2 June 2007.

Sekulić, B. (1999) To remove the anathema of the Balkans. *Political Thought: Croatian Political Science Review (Politička misao)* 5, 78–92.

Stokes, G. (1997) Review of Maria Todorova, "Imagining the Balkans". HABSBURG, H-Net Reviews, September 1997 – Online document: http://www.h-net.org/reviews/showrev.cgi?path=1749878161715. Accessed 20 May 2009.

Todorova, M. (1997) *Imagining the Balkans.* Oxford: Oxford University Press.

Volčič, Z. (2005) The notion of the "West" in Serbian national imaginary. *European Journal of Cultural Studies* 8 (2), 155–175.

Volcic, Z. (2007) Scenes from the last Yugoslav generation: The long march from Yugo-utopia to nationalism. *Cultural Dynamics* 19 (1), 67–89.

Žanić, I. (2007) Nationale Symbole zwischen Mythos und Propaganda. In D. Melčić (ed.) *Der Jugoslawien-Krieg* (pp. 286–311). Wiesbaden: Der Verlag für Sozialwissenschaften.

Chapter 5
Naming Strategies and Neighboring Nations in the Croatian Media

Dubravka Kuna and Branko Kuna

Introduction

The main focus of this chapter is an analysis of various naming strategies for the neighboring South Slavic nations that lived together for 70 years in their common country of Yugoslavia. We analyze a conscious and deliberate name conversion, or a name modification of neighboring nations – Bosniaks, Serbs, Slovenians and Montenegrins – by different linguistic means. Up to 1991, these ethnic groups all lived in a common country (Yugoslavia) in which, according to the ideology of that time, they were named 'fraternal nations'. It must be pointed out here that among the speakers of their standard languages (with the exception of Slovenian, and to some extent Macedonian) 'a high level of understanding is possible'[1] because they share the same neoštokavian dialect basis.[2] Our interpretation is oriented toward structuring such naming, and the characteristics and features that have been ascribed to the other nations in the Croatian print media, as well as the ways of legitimizing the ethnic intolerance of individuals and groups toward others. The corpus consists of examples collected in 2007 from Croatian print media of various political affiliations: from the liberally oriented and most widely read daily newspaper *Jutarnji list*, the conservative regional daily newspaper *Glas Slavonije*, the moderately left-wing political news magazine *Nacional* and the right-wing political news magazine *Fokus*.[3] We examined around 400 issues of these newspapers: all issues of *Jutarnji list* from January to March 2007, all issues of *Fokus* and *Nacional* from July to December 2007 and selected issues of *Glas Slavonije* from March to July 2007. The search of *Glas Slavonije* was reduced because it provided only a few relevant examples.

Ethnic identity and language

In the transmission of a message it is never only the primary and neutral communication role of a language that is involved, but also the numerous symbolic functions of the language that manifest themselves at the same time. One of these is the identity function by which affiliation and loyalty to a certain social group are reflected and the relations among its members are strengthened. Language has a central function in the creation of ethnic identity and in reflecting its changes, whereas ethnic identity influences language choice and usage as well as language attitudes (Gudykunst & Schmidt, 1988: 11). Therefore, language and identity are reciprocally related. Individuals or whole groups are identified by names. Naming thus verifies the existence of ethnic varieties, but names can also be attributed or forced on recipients against their will (Valentine, 1998).

Attitudes about various nations are not universal or equally represented in different communities. When the proper name of a nation is exchanged for another name, or when a nation is named descriptively, inherited experience, value judgments and prejudices are also expressed. All the values and nuances that are not directly communicated, but are contained within an expression, are part of the implicit meaning that is one of the domains of pragmatics. If one agrees that 'a linguistic interaction is necessarily a social interaction' (Yule, 1996: 59), then the perception and naming of other nations is just one of the elements of social interactions. This analysis adopts a pragmatic point of view to analyze the linguistic means used in the Croatian print media for the names of neighboring nations and the countries they live in. We also examine the causes and effects of name modification and various renaming strategies. The major prerequisite for their understanding is context. Van Dijk (2003: 356) defines context as: 'the mentally represented structure of those properties of the social situation that are relevant for the production or comprehension of discourse', which includes various categories such as the overall definition of the situation, temporal and geographical settings, ongoing actions, participants and their knowledge, opinions, attitudes and ideologies. Contextual control includes the control over one of these categories, whereas control of the text or speech includes control of local details such as meaning, form and style.

Motivation of new names

The definition of the term *nation* poses a certain paradox: historians point out its objective modernity, nationalists emphasize its subjective antiquity and, in terms of anthropology, the nation is defined as an imagined political community, inherently limited and independent (Anderson, 1990). The creation of a sense of loyalty toward one's nation is also a result of the experience of other nations; it is deeply entrenched in the collective consciousness of a certain community and is often followed by value judgments, stereotypes and prejudices. No matter how relevant the objective facts for those convictions are, they are inherited by generations and they are the result of the need to organize the pertinent data – namely, social categorization. An attitude that functions as the overall evaluation of one social category, especially if it is negative, is called prejudice (Brown, 2001). The numerous prejudices and stereotypes about the relationship between language and race (black speech, white speech) have existed throughout history, even though there are no rational or psychological reasons for such attitudes. They are the result of 'learned' behavior and expectations (Trudgill, 2000). The constitution of an image about one nationality can originate from one's own nationality (an auto-stereotype) or the Other's nationality (a hetero-stereotype). In the constitution of modern identities and their stereotypes, Oraić-Tolić (2006: 31) points out the importance of the opposition Us/Our and Them/Their. Attitudes toward other nations are often reduced to the relationship between 'us' and 'them', which is a result of the viewpoint that 'our' manners of conduct, values and culture are the best, the only worthwhile ones and the standard of comparison by which others should behave or be judged. Stereotypes are usually regarded as negatively defined and are mostly associated with negative prejudices. However, stereotypes about Others – that is, the experience of somebody else's identity – are important for defining who we are and for constructing our own identity (Fehér, 2006). Although unverified, such historical experience of Others constitutes a certain type of earlier acquired knowledge necessary for communication. The individuals within a community, depending on age, education and other individual features, differ in respect to their exposure to these stereotypes. With regard to this, Foley (1997: 21) claims, 'If culture is the domain of cultural practices, those meaning-creating practices by which humans sustain viable trajectories of social structural coupling, it is obvious that culture should not be understood as a unified domain whose contents are shared by all.' Stereotypes are reserved for nationalities that are historically or communicationally closer to us, that we have or have had contact with. Images of distant and less familiar nationalities are often reduced to their mere biological markings, so the descriptions of a whole race are reduced to mostly offensive naming such as *yellow, slant-eyed* and so on (Anderson, 1990). It is assumed that the closer to us an ethnic group is, whether historically, geographically or in terms of language, the more numerous naming strategies for this community we will have.

Names as an Attitude about the Self and the Other

In this section, we discuss strategies and linguistic means that can be recognized in the naming of neighboring nationalities and countries based on corpus evidence. The term *strategy* implies 'a more or less accurate and more or less intentional deliberate plan of practices (including discursive practices) adopted to achieve a certain social, political, psychological, or linguistic aim' (Wodak & Reisigl, 2003: 386). Furthermore, the interpretation is oriented toward the linguistic organization and structure of such naming, the characteristics and attributes that have been ascribed to other nationalities in the Croatian print media and how individuals and groups, by using stylistic variations, legitimize the exclusion or discrimination of Others and justify their own attitudes. The referential strategy or naming strategy is the starting point in the discussion because it is used for the construction and presentation of social factors: nationalities, groups and their members.

Proper names

Names not only have the function of providing identification, but also are metaphorical, culturally marked, lexemes (Pintarić, 2002), the meaning of which is determined by the communicative situation and the characteristics of the communicators. In most cases, such names are emotionally charged. When ethnic groups are identified by name, a connotative charge can be achieved by different means. One of these is usage of various attributive and predicative expressions in order to define or (dis)qualify – that is, to sharpen or soften the attitude toward these groups, as in the following examples:

> (1) *Bosniaks/Muslims* take on an unitarianist position? Well, Alija Izetbegović himself declared at some time in the past that he was a 'Yugoslav.' (*Bošnjaci/Muslimani* nastupali su s unitarističkih pozicija? Pa i sam Alija Izetbegović se svojedobno deklarirao kao 'Jugoslaven.' *Fokus*, 12 October 2007)

> (2) We Croatians *have always been well-behaved and obedient boys*, whereas the Serbs *have always carried a chip on their shoulders* and needed to be calmed like naughty children and bribed, so that they would behave themselves and keep quiet. (Mi Hrvati *smo uvijek bili dobri i poslušni dečki*, a Srbi *su uvijek bili konfliktne bundžije*, koje je trebalo smirivati poput zločeste djece i nečim ih potkupljivati kako bi bili dobri i šutjeli. *Nacional*, 25 December 2007)

The author of the column from which the first example is taken does not accept the fact that the Bosnian Muslims chose the ethnonym *Bosniaks* (Bošnjaci) as the name of their nation some 20 years ago. This term is a historical expression for the citizens of Bosnia, regardless of their national and religious affiliation. By using the restrictive complement *Muslims*, the columnist narrows the group of *Bosniaks* whom he finds to be unitarianists, and excludes those that oppose such a political concept. Even though this is not said, it is still communicated. The effect of the relativization of the name *Bosniaks* is not merely a linguistic act, but it is at the same time evidence of the relativization of the group's identity. In (2), the author integrates himself into the positive self-presentation of his own nation by using stereotypical predications (Croatians are *well-behaved and obedient boys*), whereas the neighboring nation is excluded from such a perspective and is presented in a markedly negative fashion (Serbians *carry a chip on their shoulders*). The author uses arguments and justifies such an attitude toward Serbians that make profits for themselves (*and needed to be calmed like naughty children and bribed, so that they would behave themselves and keep quiet*), whereas Croatians allegedly gain nothing from the international community for their cooperation. Although the official proper names of the nations are mentioned, predications with them add to the already existing stereotypes. Referring to the facts and experience that are relevant to him, the author interprets the political reality.

Numerous variations of ethnonyms have been noted in Croatian lexicographic works. As a rule, these are suffixed derivations that convey positive or negative attitudes toward the members of a particular nation. The representation of the Serbian minority in some areas of Croatia, religious differences and numerous conflicts of political orientations and political groups over the last 150 years have left their mark in an increase in derivational variants of their name in Croatian. Such derivations are marked in terms of style and are derogatory. The following examples are all marked as derogatory in relation to the neutral name, *Srbin* 'Serb': *Srbadija* ('all Serbians', a collective noun), *srbenda* ('A Serbian that aggressively praises Serbia'), *Srpče* ('a child of a Serbian'; the suffix *-če* is characteristic of diminutives in Serbian, in contrast to Croatian *-čić*).

Due to historical and political relations with Bosnia-Herzegovina and the fact that Croatians are one of its constituent ethnic groups, various terms are used for the citizens of Bosnia: *Bosanac* (colloq.), *Bošnjanin*, *Bošnjak* and *Bosančero* (slang). For the ethnonym *Bosniak* (Bosnian Muslim), the expressions *muhamedanac* (hist.) and *balija* are also used. *Balija* is a Turkism that Muslim town classes originally used for Islamized Slavic cattle breeders. It was later adopted by Serbians and Croatians for extremely pejorative naming of all Bosniaks.

On the other hand, Slovenians and Croatians shared a common destiny in the Habsburg Empire for four centuries and then for 70 years in Yugoslavia without any conflict. Apart from the recent maritime border conflict, they have stable ethnic and political relations. According to Anić (2003), the only alternative name for a Slovenian is *Kranjac*, originally referring to an inhabitant of the Slovenian region of Carniola.

Various factors influence the number of such derivations: common history, religious differences and whether members of these nations live in Croatia. However, the fact is that due to the degree of media freedom and media standards achieved, as well as respect for social manners, explicitly pejorative expressions that would violate citizens' rights, or national and religious freedom, were not found in our corpus. We found only one piece of evidence with a humorous-ironic effect that was not noted in the dictionaries:

> (3) The Social Democratic Party has perhaps won even ten terms by its chauvinistic campaign towards Croatians (!) from Bosnia-Herzegovina. They have been continuously pushed into a nonexistent diaspora, which had been transformed into downy mildew a long time ago – this is sheer impudence, for the real downy mildew in its time depopulated the Adriatic coast and the islands – and recently following this SDP trend, there are some offensive talks about *'Bosancheros'* in the media (e.g. OTV). (SDP je proračunatom šovinističkom kampanjom prema Hrvatima (!) iz BiH osvojio možda i desetak mandata. Njih se uporno gura u nepostojeću dijasporu, odavno je preobražena u 'peronosporu' – što je čisti bezobrazluk jer prava je peronospora svojedobno raselila jadransku obalu i otoke – a u najnovije vrijeme na tom SDP-ovom valu javno se u medijima (OTV npr.) uvrjedljivo govori o *'Bosančerosima'*. *Fokus*, 30 November 2007)

The cited expression originates from a commercial television program and is not an exception to the stated rule. The neologism *Bosanchero* is a mocking expression referring to all citizens of Bosnia, but in this example it refers to the Croatians in Bosnia, whose participation in the Croatian elections causes divisions among the political parties. The markedness of this hybrid expression results from its derivational structure. It was coined with the Spanish plural form (*desperados, tupamaros*). In Croatian, it is used with a singular meaning (*Albanjeros* – 'Albanian', *komunjaros* – 'communist'), and the Croatian plural ending *-i* is added. The sound correspondence with certain Spanish words scornfully alludes to the citizens of Bosnia as outlaws, people who are in conflict with social values.

The use of a proper name is the most explicit way of referring to the Other. In Croatian, and in colloquial speech in particular, instead of the proper names of neighboring nations a whole set of stylistic variations and modifying expressions is used. Such practices can be found in media discourse as well:

> (4) Or [they think] that Slovenians will cross the Sutla River and annex Zaprešić, and that the greatest ship of the wartime navy, *Little Kekec*, under the command of a *Janez Ferhatović*, or whatever his surname is, will not only take the whole Bay of Piran, but also surround all of Istria. (Ili da će Slovenci forsirati Sutlu i anektirati Zaprešić, a da će najveći broj slovenske ratne mornarice *Mali Kekec* pod zapovjedništvom nekog *Janeza Ferhatovića* ili kako mu je već prezime, ne osvojiti Piranski zaljev, nego opkoliti cijelu Istru. *Nacional*, 9 October 2007)

> (5) *Janezi*, give us back our foreign currency deposits! (*Janezi*, vratite nam našu deviznu štednju! *Jutarnji list*, 8 March 2007)

After the collapse of Yugoslavia, Slovenia was the smallest newly formed country. Ever since, Croatia has had a slightly tense political relationship with it, due to the unresolved maritime border. Whenever a speaker wants to achieve a scornful effect, the 'largeness' of Slovenia is emphasized. Thus in example (4) the Slovenian ship is humorously named *Little Kekec* after a boy from a Slovenian children's novel, and its commander is given the common Slovenian first name *Janez*. However, a typical Bosniak family name, *Ferhatović*, is used. It suggests that there are so few 'genuine' Slovenians that naturalized Slovenians originating from Bosnia are needed to defend it. In mocking speech and street jargon, the name *Janez* is reclassified by metonymy and the meaning 'Slovenian' is assigned to it. According to Barcelona (2003), when a proper name replaces the entire class (i.e. when it is used as a paragon), it becomes countable and it can have a plural form, as in (5). Barcelona calls such a trope *pronomination*. In colloquial speech, common Serbian names (*Čedo, Jovo*) and Bosnian names (*Muhamed, Mujo, Alija*) can be used with mocking meaning for any Serbian or Bosnian (Pintarić, 2002: 186). In our corpus, evidence of such appelativization of proper names has not been noted.

Toponyms

Geographical names can also be metonymically used in various ways: for example, the names of capitals replacing the names of political organizations with executive power (government), institutions or events (Brdar, 2008). Metonymy has a primarily referential function because it is assumed that one entity is represented by another one and 'the grounding of metonymic concepts is in general more obvious than is the case with metaphoric concepts, since it usually involves direct physical or causal associations' (Lakoff & Johnson, 1980: 38). In the collected corpus there are cases of capitals metonymically denoting neighboring countries, nationalities and their representatives:

(6) Grandchildren export to *Vienna*, and grandfathers to *Belgrade*. (Unuci izvoze u *Beč*, a djedovi u *Beograd*. *Jutarnji list*, 23 January 2007)

(7) The decision of the international court in The Hague has provoked bitterness in *Sarajevo* and further, in contrast to the celebrations in *Belgrade* and *Banja Luku*, thereby deepened the gap among the ethnic groups in Bosnia-Herzegovina. However, the EU still naively believes that this decision should provide a basis for their reconciliation. (Iako je odluka ovog međunarodnog suda u Haagu izazvala ogorčenje u *Sarajevu*, pa i šire, a slavlje u *Beogradu* i *Banjoj Luci*, te time još više produbila jaz između etničkih skupina u BiH, EU naivno vjeruje da bi ova odluka trebala poslužiti kao osnova za pomirenje. *Jutarnji list*, 28 February 2007)

In (6), the names of the cities are a metonymic replacement for the countries Austria and Serbia, and the metaphorical terms *grandchildren* and *grandfathers* emphasize the viewpoints and experiential contrast between younger and older Croatian businessmen: the young are orientated toward Austria (i.e. the West) and the old to the linguistically familiar Serbia (i.e. the East). In (7), toponyms are denotations of nationalities and their national elites: *Sarajevo* for Bosniaks, and *Belgrade* and *Banja Luka* for Serbians in Serbia and Republika Srpska (one of the entities in Bosnia-Herzegovina). The evidence for that is the naming of the nation in the same sentence by a descriptive term: *ethnic groups*. The new political constellation and processes of integration and globalization result in new political wholes, so even their announcement or the mere possibility of establishing them imposes a need for the naming of new political alliances and groups. As an expression of opposition and disagreement, there are names that in terms of derivation appeal to some experiences from the past. Thus, the motives for the ad hoc creation of new toponyms are experiences from the former Yugoslavia, in which the Serbian political elite tried to maintain dominance in relation to the others:

> (8) As Kosovo and Albania incline towards a strategic partnership with the United States, the new version of the Balkans has been reduced to Croatia, Bosnia-Herzegovina, Serbia, Montenegro, and Macedonia, which might end up in a new *Serboslavia* that even the Yugocommunist machinery under the leadership of Slobodan Milošević did not manage to establish through war. (Kako Kosovo i Albanija sve više naginju strateškom partnerstvu sa Sjedinjenim državama, nova je inačica Balkana sad svedena na Hrvatsku, BiH, Srbiju, Crnu Goru i Makedoniju, što bi se u konačnici moglo pretvoriti u realizaciju nove *Srboslavije*, koju ni ratom nije mogao uspostaviti jugokomunistički aparat na čelu sa Slobodanom Miloševićem. *Fokus*, 6 July 2007)

Due to the twists and turns of national politics and numerous internal and foreign deterrents that have been slowing down Croatia's accession to the European Union, the author, by coining the neologism *Serboslavia*, expresses his fear for the coherence of his own identity and at the same time repulsion at the mere thought of integration into any new community with Serbia (the same is implied by *Balkanoslavia*). Through the second part of the compound *-slavia*, he reminds us that this would be a resumption of the former community of Yugo*slavia* and he alludes to the chaos in which communities carrying that name ended up (both the first and the second Yugoslavia broke apart in wars). In political discourse, the practices of such word formation are an effective substitute for presenting arguments, and they serve to create fear of the possible conspiracy of the imaginary 'international community', or they appeal to more authoritarian politics.

Ad hoc coined names that contain the toponym *the Balkans* and modifications of it at the word-formation level (*Balkanoslavia, Balkanistan*) or at the syntactic level (*the Balkan Union, the poor brothers from the Balkans*), and which indicate the possibility of forging new alliances, are also often used as a strategy that intensifies the illocutionary power of discrediting through naming. Even though Croatia is geographically situated in the Balkan Peninsula, the name *Balkan* is unwelcome and there is no institution or association that has this term in its name. From the 1990s onwards, Croatian politicians have been persistently making statements of belonging to Europe or Central Europe and not to the Balkans (Lindstrom, 2003), which is one of the key points in forming the national identity as well as the 'Croatian national trauma' (Luketić, 2008). This is not the case in the other South Slavic countries: Macedonia, Montenegro, Serbia and especially Bulgaria. Todorova (1997) argues that the Balkans also have some positive connotations: pride, love of freedom and independence. In the Croatian media, as a denotation of a geographical space, the expression *the Balkans* rarely includes Croatia. It is negatively marked even when it is a matter of ethnos because it implies the negation of neighboring borderlines, identities and names (e.g. the relationship between Greece and Macedonia), unresolved border conflicts or seizing another's territory (e.g. the Balkan wars or the Yugoslav break-up). When a proposal from certain political circles of the international community about a 'West Balkan' Customs Union, which would include all the countries of the former Yugoslavia except Slovenia, was submitted to the public, it was met with harsh criticism by both politicians and the public in Croatia. The stereotype about the Balkans 'as a region cursed with too much history per square mile, with an excess of historical memory, protracted hatreds, and a proliferation of obstinate and incompatible ethnic and religious identities', as Todorova (2005: 2) points out, is widespread. The adjective *Balkan* is mostly applied at the cultural level, in everyday and political life, and it denotes primitive behavior, conditioned by intuition and dishonorable deeds:[4]

> (9) We did not realize in the eighties that *balkanatry* in the middle of Zagreb was not and could not have been a manifestation of popular art or solidarity with the *poor 'brothers' from the Balkans*, but a plan to *balkanize* Croatians. (Nismo shvaćali onih osamdesetih godina da *balkanolatrija* usred Zagreba nije bila niti je mogla biti izraz popularne umjetnosti ili neke solidarnosti sa *siromašnom 'braćom' s Balkana*, nego plan *balkanizacije* Hrvata. *Fokus*, 28 September 2007)

The publication of the translation of the book *Language and Identity in the Balkans* by the American Slavic specialist Robert G. Greenberg

(2005) is another illustrative example. The reactions of Croatian linguists, published in a collection of articles (Peti-Stantić, 2008), were explicitly negative, partly because the author used a provocative and (for the English-speaking market) probably commercial title using the term *the Balkans*. He thereby equated the space and languages of the former Yugoslavia with the Balkans, not even mentioning Greek, Albanian, Romanian or Bulgarian, which are usually related to the Balkan Sprachbund.

Perspectivization

Discourse analysts use the term *perspectivization* to refer to a strategy by which speakers express their inclusion in discourse and the positioning of their viewpoints (Wodak & Reisigl, 2003). Applied to our corpus, it would refer to the observation (or perception) of geographical space from a particular perspective and its relation to nations and states. In terms of syntax, it is a case of the procedure by which geographical names and common nouns are modified and given additional meaning by using other expressions. Spatial relations are of special importance for everyday life. Therefore, there are numerous linguistic means and ways of denoting spatial categories. Spatial relations underlie numerous nonspatial meanings (cf. Langacker, 1987; Lyons, 1977) that can be well described in terms of spatial metaphors. In cognitive linguistics, metaphor is explained as being not only a linguistic structure, but as a universal cognitive pattern. Spatial metaphors, as the primary model of metaphorical thinking, 'are rooted in physical and cultural experience' (Lakoff & Johnson, 1980: 18). In addition, the advantage of metaphors based on the spatial model is that they represent a stable feature of discourse and a general means available to different participants in the discourse (Šarić, 2005). Space also has an important role in expressing attitudes toward ethnicities because the localization of the Others and their spatial definition is a path toward auto-localization; that is, the perception of the Self and of one's own ethnos in space. Regarding the aforementioned criterion, it is possible to apply four perspectives of space, which are related to *river, geographical orientation* (*east, west, north, south*), *mountain* and *distance* (Table 5.1). They serve as the starting point for a metaphorical and metonymical meaning transfer in the naming of neighboring peoples and their countries:

The perspective of space in relation to a *river* is expanded in many communities where the river is a natural borderline, and it implies the separating of one ethnicity from another or the beginning of something new (e.g. in the expression *to cross the Rubicon*). The river often metaphorically denotes the beginning and the end of an ethnic space, and the bridges over it symbolize the establishment of interethnic or international cooperation, whereas their destruction, either real or fictional, causes the interruption

Naming Strategies in the Croatian Media 83

Table 5.1 Spatial perspective in the function of naming nations and states

Concept	Croatian	English	Nations/states; meaning
River			
	obje strane *Drine*	both banks of the *Drina River*	Croatia and/or Bosnia and Serbia
	forsirati *Sutlu*	to cross the *Sutla River*	to attack Croatia
	rušenje mostova na *Sutli*	destroying bridges over the *Sutla River*	worsening the relationship between Croatia and Slovenia
Direction			
	istočni susjed/i	*eastern* neighbor(s)	Serbia/Serbians
	istočna braća	*eastern* brothers	"
	družina *s istoka*	the band from the *east*	"
	istočni uljez	*eastern* intruders	"
	južni susjedi	*southern* neighbor(s)	Montenegro/Montenegrins
	sjeverni susjed/i	*northern* neighbor(s)	Slovenia/Slovenians
	zapadni susjed/i	*western* neighbor(s)	"
Mountain			
	Alpski Slaveni	*Alpine* Slavs	Slovenians
	raja ispod *Trebevića*	the common herd below *Trebević*	citizens of Sarajevo/Bosnians
	narod podno *Lovćena*	the nation below *Lovćen*	Montenegrins
Distance			
	tamo *daleko*	there, *far away*	Serbians (Serbia)
	narodi *na ovim prostorima/na našim prostorima*	nations in *these spaces*/in *our spaces*	all (including Croatians) in ex-Yugoslavia
	narodi *na tim prostorima*	nations *in those lands*	all (excluding Croatians)

and suspension of relations. Although the Drina River is a border between Bosnia and Serbia today, due to historical reasons it is perceived as a border between Croatia and Serbia, between the East and the West;[5] in contexts such as (10) it is not a matter of territorial pretensions.

(10) Both banks of the *Drina* at Magelli's in Belgrade. (Obje strane *Drine* kod Magellija u Beogradu. *Jutarnji list*, 2 May 2007)

This is a newspaper headline about the Croatian stage director Paolo Magelli, who gathered Croatian and Serbian actors in a joint theater production after 15 years of noncollaboration. The metonymic connection of both banks of the Drina serves to metaphorically characterize the actors from the two countries. This is one of the rare examples in which national actors have been portrayed positively through the image of a river connecting the banks/nations.

The attribution of identity through reference to *geographical orientation* (*east, west, north, south*) is the most neutral and fastest way of localizing Others, so that in every community its members experientially and easily identify the neighboring nations or countries. With respect to geographical orientation, all but the Bosniaks are defined because Croatia borders Bosnia on three sides and such a renaming of the Bosniaks would be confusing for the citizens of Croatia from various regions because of their different spatial perspectives. In this kind of naming, a whole array of expressions has been applied to Serbians (the *eastern neighbors*): from *companionship* and *brothers* (an ironic reminder of an ideology in which the fraternal nations lived in a socialist 'idyll' that ended in the war) to *intruders*, as in the humorous example (11), which alludes to the invasion of Serbian words into the Croatian language, and also of Serbian soldiers in the war of 1991:

> (11)... they were pondering about introducing bills, all with a common goal: to place the Croatian linguistic soldier on the Croatian eastern border and never let the *eastern intruder* cross the Danube, the Una, or Triglav, either by boot or language. (... umovali su o zakonskim prijedlozima koji su svi imali isti cilj: smjestiti hrvatskog jezikoslovnog redova na hrvatsku istočnu granicu te ne dopustiti *istočnom uljezu* da ikad priječe Dunav, Unu i Triglav, bilo čizmom, bilo pravopisom. *Jutarnji list*, 24 February 2007)

The word *east*, used without any modification in Croatian media discourse, sometimes metonymically denotes Serbia (*totum pro parte*), and in most cases it refers to the cultural and political space:

> (12) Fifteen years ago Croatian ideology believed in rambling that 'we have always been in Europe' and the thought that the defense against the *east* is our lasting modus vivendi. (Prije 15 godina hrvatska je ideologija vjerovala u trabunjanje o 'mi smo uvijek bili Europa' i mislila da je obrana od *istoka* naš trajni modus vivendi. *Jutarnji list*, 24 February 2007)

Mountains as recognizable symbols of nations (if they have them) can be a perspectivization center in the localization of one's neighbors, and in such naming figurative speech becomes prominent (see Table 5.1). In the example *the nation beneath Lovćen*, Mount Lovćen is the mountain at the top of which is the mausoleum of the Montenegrin poet and ruler Petar II Petrović Njegoš. As a recognizable symbol, it is known beyond the borders of Montenegro. On the other hand, the expression *Alpine Slavs* can only refer to the Slovenians because Slovenia is the only Slavic country in the Alps.

The perspective of space with respect to *distance* (i.e. spatial deixis) can be included in the naming of countries of the former Yugoslavia. If the author and the addressees take part in the 'deictic center' (Yule, 1996) – that is, in the frameworks of the event for which particular expressions are used – then phrases of the type *in our/these spaces*, with a nuance of nostalgia for times past, can be used. When the author aims to exclude himself from events and places and expresses a certain degree of repulsion toward the area that is close to him or the nation that this region belongs to, expressions of the type *in those spaces* are used. The deictic expression *there, far away* refers to Serbia and Serbians because this is also the beginning of a well-known traditional Serbian song that was sung by Serbian soldiers far away from their country during World War I. Because Serbia is one of Croatia's neighbors, it also ironically alludes to the symbolic distance of the 'neighbors'. Such an effect is additionally emphasized by deviation from the orthographic norm because the adverbial expression *There, Far Away* (*Tamo Daleko*) is written in capitals as if it were the name of a country:

> (13) At this moment, if he hasn't fluttered away with his helicopter to *There, Far Away*, the famous Boba is sailing and swimming here with his even more famous wife Lepa Brena. (Trenutno, ako nije 'helihopterom' odlepršao *Tamo Daleko*, ovdje plovi i pliva poznati Boba i njegova još poznatija žena Lepa Brena. *Nacional*, 14 August 2007)

Culture-specific words

The experience of living in two Yugoslavias for 70 years has resulted in the fact that the speakers of the different standard languages have a specific stock of common words that, for various reasons, can metaphorically denote ethnic groups. Through their use, the obvious contrast of *Their/Our* words has been created, and by this simple concept the other nation is identified with certain vocabulary. The words in the examples cited below are mostly used in the deprecation or ironic naming of the nations. Although such examples are characteristic of spoken discourse, they also occur in less formal newspaper texts:

> (14) Our 'neighbors' have finally experienced a national catharsis, the repentance for the evil that their leaders did, by organizing the play in parliament called 'I'm a Chetnik and my name is Tomislav.' (Naši '*komšije*' konačno su doživjeli nacionalnu katarzu, pokajanje za zlo koje su njihovi voždovi učinili na ovim prostorima, organiziravši igrokaz u parlamentu pod naslovom 'Ja sam četnik, a zovem se Tomislav.' *Glas Slavonije*, 12 May 2007)

> (15) It is more lucrative for Moscow and Washington if *šajkača* [Serbian cap] and *keče* [Albanian cap] start a bloody feud for them. (Moskvi i

Washingtonu je unosnije ako se za njih zakrve *šajkača* i *keče*. *Jutarnji list*, 23 February 2007)

(16) All that, however, according to the author, puts *dežela* ['homeland' in Slovenian] into a delicate position when making important decisions about Kosovo. (Sve to pak, prema riječima autora, stavlja *deželu* u osjetljiv položaj pri donošenju važnih odluka o Kosovu. *Jutarnji list*, 8 December 2007)

The Turkism *komšija* 'neighbor' is a standard and neutral word in Serbian and Bosnian, but it is explicitly stylistically marked in Croatian. In this context, the word *komšije* is strikingly ambiguous; it is an affective expression alluding to the members of the neighboring Serbian nation and the not always good-neighborly relations between the two nations in certain periods of the twentieth century. In (15), the nouns *šajkača* and *keče* literally refer to soft head-coverings (caps), which are distinctive parts of Serbian and Albanian folk costumes. These are taken as the mark of the whole ethnic group. In rhetoric, such naming is defined as synecdoche, a subtype of metonymy. In Slovenian, *dežela* (example 16) means 'country, homeland'. Croatians, who are Slovenia's nearest Slavic neighbors and know its meaning, may use it in place of the name *Slovenia*. In this case, it does not have a negative meaning, but only suggests an additional stylistic effect.

Concluding Remarks

Media discourse as a part of public communication in modern society is a place where particular political and social ideas and ideologies meet. In the print media, the truth is never neutral because the sponsorship and the influence of specific political groups cannot be excluded, so that the work of media practitioners is a combination of an informative and persuading task at the same time (Christians *et al.*, 2001).

Discourse features of the Croatian media can be viewed as a reflection of the overall social structure. The analysis of naming strategies for neighboring ethnic groups in the Croatian media in this chapter included both the linguistic and conceptual structuring of these expressions and the analysis of the causes and contextual determination of their appearance. The origin of new names is often conditioned by prejudices and stereotypes about the Self and the Other, and their choice is defined not only by the genres of newspaper texts, but also by the personal convictions and political standpoints of the authors. By ascribing different names to the Other, various pragmatic effects are achieved, which reflect the authors' attitudes and moods. These attitudes and moods are not neutral, but have judgmental power in addition to their political and ideological impact.

In news items and extended reports, referential strategies with tropes that exclude valorization effects are manifested (*Belgrade* instead of

Serbia), and partly the strategy of perspectivization (*northern neighbors* instead of Slovenians). In less formal texts, such as columns and reports, strategies that aim at argumentation or strengthening of the illocutionary power of a statement are more common. In addition, discriminatory expressions from populist discourse toward neighboring nations, mostly with modifications and the metaphorical transfer of meaning, can be found (*eastern intruders, Bosanchero, eastern brothers, Janezi, Balkanistan*). The analysis of the newspaper corpus collected in 2007 shows that there are still reflexes and allusions to the four-year Croatian War of Independence, conflicts from the past and unresolved border disputes, even though the event reported and the communication situations themselves often do not have any direct connection with that period. The causes underlying the negative naming of some neighboring nations reach into the distant past. Media discourse shows that they remain in collective memory long after the disappearance of the objective reasons that generated them.

Notes

1. Cf. Croatian Academy of Science and Arts: http://www.hazu.hr/hrv-jez.html. Accessed 10 October 2007.
2. The štokavian dialect is named after the interrogative and relative pronoun *što* 'what'. The neoštokavian dialect is characterized by a special accentual system in relation to the more archaic old štokavian. Four standard languages in the successor states of former Yugoslavia are based on the neoštokavian dialect: Bosnian, Montenegrin, Serbian and Croatian. Greenberg (2005) reflects upon their formation. The formation of the Croatian standard language in lexical terms was influenced by the fact that two additional dialects are spoken in Croatia: kajkavian and čakavian (named after the pronouns *kaj* and *ča*, both 'what').
3. Both *Jutarnji list* and *Nacional* are sometimes judged to be tabloids; cf. Malovic and Vilovic (2003), Fisher (2005: 90).
4. An example of such an attitude is the expression *Balkan inn*, the leitmotif in numerous works by the prominent Croatian writer Miroslav Krleža. The meaning of this phrase is illustrated by the sentence: 'When the lights go out in the Balkan inn, then the knives flash.' (*Kad se u balkanskoj krčmi ugase svjetla, onda sijevaju noževi*), which is well-known in the countries of the former Yugoslavia. The expression *Balkan inn* is used in the Croatian media to refer to crises and social relations in the Balkans (cf. Mitani, 2008: 291; Šarić, 2004: 401).
5. The Drina River was first the borderline between the Western and Eastern Empire after 395 AD. After the church schism in 1054, it was the borderline between the Orthodox and Catholic churches.

References

Anderson, B. (1990) *Nacija: zamišljena zajednica; razmatranja o porijeklu i širenju nacionalizma*. Zagreb: Školska knjiga.

Anić, V. (2003) *Veliki rječnik hrvatskoga jezika*. CD-ROM. Zagreb: Novi Liber.

Barcelona, A. (2003) Names: A metonymic "return ticket" in five languages. *Jezikoslovlje* 4 (1), 11–41.
Brdar, M. (2008) *Metonymy in Grammar*. Osijek: Filozofski fakultet.
Brown, R. (2001) Međugrupni odnosi. In M. Hewstone and W. Stroebe (eds) *Socijalna psihologija* (pp. 427–455). Jastrebarsko: Naklada Slap.
Christians, C.G. et al. (2001) *Media Ethics: Cases and Moral Reasoning*. New York: Longman.
Fehér, I.M. (2006) Ni neutralnost ni poricanje sebe, nego otvorenost: Predrasude kao uvjet razumijevanja. In D. Oraić Tolić and E. Kulcsár Szabó (eds) *Kulturni stereotipi* (pp. 59–70). Zagreb: FF press.
Fisher, S. (2005) Croatia's rocky road toward the European Union. *Slovak Foreign Policy Affairs* 2, 81–94.
Foley, W. (1997) *Anthropological Linguistics*. Oxford: Blackwell.
Greenberg, R.G. (2005) *Jezik i identitet na Balkanu*. Zagreb: Srednja Europa.
Gudykunst, W.B. and Schmidt, K. (1988) *Language and Ethnic Identity*. Clevedon: Multilingual Matters.
HAZU (2007) *Hrvatski jezik* – Online document: http://www.hazu.hr/hrv-jez.html. Accessed 10 October 2007.
Lakoff, G. and Johnson, M. (1980) *Metaphors We Live By*. Chicago, London: University of Chicago Press.
Langacker, R. (1987) *Foundations of Cognitive Grammar*. Vol. I. *Theoretical Prerequisites*. Stanford, CA: Stanford University Press.
Lindstrom, N. (2003) Between Europe and the Balkans: Mapping Slovenia and Croatia's "return to Europe" in the 1990s. *Dialectical Anthropology* 27 (3–4), 313–329.
Luketić, K. (2008) Bijeg s Balkana. *Zarez* 224 – Online document: http://www.zarez.hr/224/z_temabroja.html. Accessed 20 May 2009.
Lyons, J. (1977) *Semantics*. Vol. II. Cambridge: Cambridge University Press.
Malovic, S. and Vilovic, G. (2003) Quality press in southeast Europe – Online document: http://soemz.euv-frankfurt-o.de/media-see/qpress/articles/sm_gv.html. Accessed 20 May 2009.
Mitani, K. (2008) Balkan as a sign: Usage of the word *Balkan* in language and discourse of the ex-Yugoslav people. *Acta Slavica Iaponica* 15, 289–313.
Oraić-Tolić, D. (2006) Hrvatski kulturni stereotipi. In D. Oraić Tolić and E. Kulcsár Szabó (eds) *Kulturni stereotipi* (pp. 29–45). Zagreb: FF press.
Peti-Stantić, A. (2008) *Identitet jezika jezikom izrečen*. Zagreb: Srednja Europa.
Pintarić, N. (2002) *Pragmemi u komunikaciji*. Zagreb: Zavod za lingvistiku Filozofskoga fakulteta.
Šarić, Lj. (2005) Metaphorical models in EU discourse in the Croatian media. *Jezikoslovlje* 6 (2), 145–170.
Šarić, Lj. (2004) Balkan identity: Changing self-images of the South Slavs. *Journal of Multilingual and Multicultural Development* 25 (5–6), 389–407.
Todorova, M. (1997) *Imaging the Balkans*. New York: Oxford University Press.
Todorova, M. (2005) *Balkan Identities: Nation and Memory*. London: Hurst & Company.
Trudgill, P. (2000) *Sociolinguistics: An Introduction to Language and Society*. London: Penguin Books.
Valentine, J. (1998) Naming the other: Power, politeness and the inflation of euphemisms – Online document: http://socresonline.org.uk/socresonline/3/4/7.html. Accessed 20 May 2009.

Van Dijk, T.A. (2003) Critical discourse analysis. In D. Schiffrin, D. Tannen and H. Hamilton (eds) *The Handbook of Discourse Analysis* (pp. 352–371). Oxford: Blackwell Publishing Ltd.

Wodak, R. and Reisigl, M. (2003) Discourse and racism. In D. Schiffrin, D. Tannen and H. Hamilton (eds) *The Handbook of Discourse Analysis* (pp. 352–371). Oxford: Blackwell Publishing Ltd.

Yule, G. (1996) *Pragmatics*. Oxford: Oxford University Press.

Chapter 6
Mujahiddin in Our Midst: Bosnian Croats after the Wars of Succession

Daphne Winland

Introduction

Globally, fears of terrorist acts perpetrated by 'Islamic fundamentalists' and 'Muslim extremists' have been seized upon by those with specific political and economic interests and agendas. Since the events of 11 September 2001, the image of Islam has become 'virtually naturalized in the discourse of Islamic terrorism' (Appadurai, 2006: 70). The conflation of the term *Islamic* with *terrorism* has become ubiquitous, laden with multiple misplaced assertions and misconceptions (Ali, 2003; Mamdani, 2002). The weight of these assumptions, coupled with the effects of 9/11, have proved challenging to those analyzing contexts with a history of Islamic traditions.

The history of Islam in Bosnia-Herzegovina (hereafter simply referred to as 'Bosnia') is a remarkably complex story of diverse national, religious and cultural influences and identities. The Yugoslav wars of succession in Bosnia in the early 1990s saw efforts to eradicate this history by force, and the flattening of this historical complexity by policy analysts and scholars of the region, as well as those broadly framed as the 'international community'. The result has been, at times, an overly simplistic rendering not only of Bosnian Muslims (hereafter referred to as 'Bosniaks') and their histories, but of the country and region more generally (cf. Huntington, 1996). Efforts to make sense of the rise of Islamic radicalism globally have spilled over into the Bosnian context, where hyperbolic claims about the nature and practices of Islam are circulated by those that stand to gain from all-too-common stereotypical assertions. Despite the paucity of evidence to support claims that anti-Western, fundamentalist Islamic groups and sentiments prevail in Bosnia, efforts to demonstrate their existence and the danger they pose persist. The abundance of balanced scholarship on the history of Bosnia is sometimes easily overlooked in favor of explanations that reinforce essentialist understandings of Islamic philosophies and beliefs, religious practices and historical and cultural variations.

The discourse of political Islam, characterized by most as that of extremism and militancy, holds little meaning for most Bosnians, regardless of ethnic and/or religious background (Qureshi & Sells, 2003). This, however, does not mean that there are not those that resort to inflammatory rhetoric about Islam in order to promote local, regional or national interests. This chapter asks how discourses that have emerged and/or have been popularized with the 'War on Terror' affect local populations in Bosnia. How do Bosnian Croats in particular, faced with slow postwar reconstruction and economic recovery, and changing political, economic and social institutions, see their future as a constituent nation/group in Bosnia? I investigate how anti-Muslim sentiments are strategically deployed by elites in the service of political, economic and other ambitions and how they are framed ideologically, culturally and historically to suit local contexts.

Although much of what has been reported in the media and other sources presents Croatian anti-Muslim sentiments as widespread across Bosnia, the analysis presented here calls attention to the need to think locally; that is, to consider those factors that, generated in localized contexts, contribute to the varied receptivity and relevance of these claims to Bosnian Croats. To examine politics in the Bosnian context is to recognize not only the centrality of history, however presented, but also the plurality reflected in but not limited to culture, religion, ethnicity, education and nationalism (cf. Lovrenović, 2001; Ramet, 1996). I consider the interrelationships between discursive (political) strategies and religion, culture, myth and legend in the configuration of local Croat responses.

Bosnia: A Brief History

As Roshwald (2001) states, 'Nowhere in Europe was the project of constructing national identity plagued by more ambiguity than among the South Slavs.' The history of Bosnia, like that of most other newly formed nations, is most often recollected as a series of pivotal chronological events, few of which have been immune from the narrativizing strategies of those that have a stake in promoting a particular version of the past and present. Throughout the history of this region, issues of territory and sovereignty have been at the center of disputes between numerous key players, few of whom were indigenous to the region. The region has had a long history of domination by foreign powers, beginning with the Hungarians and followed by the Ottoman and Habsburg empires. A review of the past three centuries thus reveals a profile of a region marked by a series of occupations, invasions and wars. The twentieth century, however, has been the most turbulent.

Although the literature on Yugoslavia's pre-1990 history provides the student of this region with a relatively rich and comprehensive picture of its past, nothing can compare with the explosion of literature since the break-up of the former Yugoslavia. Such titles as *Balkan Tragedy*

(Woodward, 1995), *Balkan Babel* (Ramet, 1996), *The Tragedy of Yugoslavia* (Seroka & Pavlović, 1992), *The Yugoslav Inferno* (Mojzes, 1994), *The Death of Yugoslavia* (Silber & Little, 1995) and *The Destruction of Yugoslavia* (Magaš, 1993) betray the tenor of shock and dismay. Scholarly perspectives on changes in the former Yugoslavia since 1989 ranged from geopolitical and policy-oriented analyses to personal accounts and reflective essays. Some became caught up in conflictive narratives of responsibility, sometimes characterized by accusations of guilt and culpability, as is evidenced in the arguments and critiques of Cushman (1997), Denich (1994), Meštrović (1996), Hayden (2005) and Magaš (1993). Ramet's analysis of the scholarly 'fault lines' still present in debates about the former Yugoslavia (2005) has also drawn criticism for being overly critical of Serbs. Thus, for some, like the Slovenian scholar Slavoj Žižek, it is pointless to even *try* to understand the Yugoslav conflict (2001).

Many have attempted to present a balanced analysis of the tragedy that befell Yugoslavia and, specifically, Bosnia, during a war that left over 4 million displaced and an estimated 200,000 dead, not to mention the resulting devastation to the country and its people. Although there is a great deal of scholarship chronicling the war, its causes and its effects (cf. Cigar, 1995; Malcolm, 1994; Sells, 1996; Silber & Little, 1995; Woodward, 1995), the greatest preoccupation of scholars and policymakers has been with how to mend Bosnia, from discussions of democratization or partition to the impact of external interventions in Bosnia and the perpetuation of conventional assumptions governing civil society, state-building and humanitarian initiatives.

Key to understanding those forces that have shaped the current political landscape has been the effects of the Dayton peace process. Since the Dayton Peace Accords were implemented in 1995, establishing a protectorate comprising two ethnically/nationally defined entities (the Republika Srpska and the Federation of Bosnia-Herzegovina), Bosnia became dependent on extensive international supervision and political engineering (Campbell, 1999; Chandler, 1999; Hayden, 2002). The decade since the Dayton Accords has thus seen innumerable international initiatives in Bosnia: humanitarian aid and refugee return, repatriation, governance and attempted reforms of local institutions such as policing. Significantly, though, the establishment of the two federal entities has meant the further entrenchment of ethnic/national divisions, and de facto partition among the three constituent groups – Serbs, Croats and Bosniaks – often serving to secure the power of ethnically based parties and local, cantonal and regional elites that have a stake in perpetuating the ethnic/nationalist and religious realignments of the war (cf. Bose, 2002; Oberschall, 2000; Søberg, 2006; Wooley, 2006). Ethnicity thus continues to be the major prism through which much of the analysis on the region has been filtered. The analysis of the war's effects through the recording of ethnically based statistics (evidenced in the oft-quoted 1991 Yugoslav census) demonstrates the reliance on ethnicity as the primary marker of difference in Bosnia (Jansen 2005). With some exceptions, specifically in anthropological literature (cf. Bougarel *et al.*, 2006; Bringa, 1995; Coles, 2007; Halpern & Kideckel, 2000; Žanić, 2007), this perspective has had the effect of detracting from a close examination of local power relations, economic and social pressures and realities as well as cultural influences and meaning systems that inform the ways in which people operate on a day-to-day basis.

Currently, Bosnians are coping with an international mandate largely unfulfilled, specifically reflected in stalled efforts to develop a new constitution and to institute significant reforms to local and national institutions. The future composition of Bosnia as an independent country thus remains uncertain. The effects of this uncertainty in Bosnia are experienced primarily by those who feel (or are made to feel) vulnerable, and most often it is those who have a stake in preserving or profiting from the status quo that attempt to manipulate uncertainty. This is true not only for Croats but also for Serbs and Bosniaks. For example, the leadership of the Republika Srpska (under the leadership of Serb nationalist Milorad Dodik) has consistently rejected the Dayton mission and agitated for the separation of Serb territory from Bosnia. The rationale used to bolster Serb political and territorial ambitions is built upon primordial claims of original status (Čolović, 2002; Judah, 1997), exemplified in Petar II Petrović-Njegoš' 19th-century composition *The Mountain Wreath* (1847), which was exploited by Bosnian Serb nationalists during the Yugoslav wars of succession (Cigar, 2003; Gordy, 1999; Jansen, 2003).

Nationalist Bosnian Croats, particularly political and religious elites, have consistently proclaimed the central historical role of Croats at the front lines in the war against Islamic terrorism in the Balkans. Portrayals of Bosniaks as *jihadist* and of the infiltration of radical *mujahiddin* into Bosnian politics are taken up by those political, church and community leaders eager to reinforce their economic and political bases. They do not have to look far for support in making these claims. Regardless of the limited degree to which such rhetoric holds sway with Bosnian citizens (cf. Bose, 2002; Bieber, 2003; Hoare, 2004; Loza, 2008), they are widely circulated and available in both local and international sources. There are numerous publications including newspaper commentaries and security reports that provide fodder for nationalists. Despite the exaggerated and often unfounded claims of al Qaeda infiltration and the presence of Islamic militants in Bosnia (Innes, 2005; Karajkov, 2006; Kohlmann, 2004; Schindler, 2007; Starr, 2004), Bosnian Islam has been characterized by some as extremist, fundamentalist and dangerous, bent on the destruction of nations in the Balkans (Cigar, 2003; Kuhner, 2005; MacDonald, 2002). Stories of Islamic radicals looking to create cells of 'white al Qaeda' (those that can presumably evade racial profiling used by police forces to locate potential terrorists) are available in the international press and reported locally ('Terrorist cells find foothold in Balkans' *Washington Post*, A16, 1 December 2005). Intelligence reports (some compiled jointly by American and Croatian military intelligence) of Islamic militants with ties to al Qaeda and other terrorist organizations crisscrossing the Balkans are reported internationally and contribute to concerns over the potential for regional destabilization. Recently, Richard Holbrooke, the chief architect of the Dayton Peace Accords, stated, 'We were concerned with the presence in Bosnia and Herzegovina of a little-known group of Islamist extremists who would later become infamous as al Qaeda. Without Dayton, al Qaeda would probably have planned the September 11 attacks from Bosnia and Herzegovina, not Afghanistan' (*Washington Post*, p. A21, 23, April 2008). Although Holbrooke is making reference to decade-old political concerns, the fact that Bosnia was considered a hotbed of Islamic extremism reveals the extent to which such fears were perpetrated by major international political players.

While in Bosnia in 2006 and 2007, I found headlines in several daily papers and weekly news magazines, some reproduced from international newspapers and local commentaries: 'An Islamist state in Europe?' recalling statements by Franjo Tuđman, the first president of Croatia and his defense minister, Gojko Šušak, in the early 1990s, and: 'Wahhabis are taking over Bosnia' in the liberal Sarajevo news magazine *Dani* (November 2006). Among the inventive terms used to describe potential developments in Bosnia are 'the coming Iraqoslavia' (Ivan Bačak, former Croat member of the Bosnian Defense and Security Board) and the 'Khomeinization' of Bosnia (in the Bosnian edition of the Croatian newspaper *Slobodna Dalmacija*).[1] The involvement of diaspora Croats also contributes to the heightened rhetoric of fear and intolerance. This is revealed in their lobbying and support for right-wing Bosnia-Herzegovina Croat parties and platforms evidenced in diaspora claims that Bosnia now serves as a 'base for al Qaeda operatives, where numerous terrorist cells are active and plotting attacks on targets throughout Europe' (Alliance of Croats of Bosnia and Herzegovina, 2006; Čuvalo, 2005). There is therefore no shortage of resources available for those wishing to capitalize on an international environment of fear generated through threats of impending terrorist attacks.

The way in which information of this kind percolates down to the local level is evidenced in the constantly shifting political landscape of Bosnia. Nationally, Bosnian Croats are represented by a range of parties spanning the political spectrum, including the right-of-centre HDZ BiH (*Hrvatska demokratska zajednica, Bosna i Hercegovina*) and the moderate and multiethnic SDP (*Socijaldemokratska partija*). Croat nationalists in particular have made numerous efforts to block internationally sponsored reforms and/or push for greater sovereignty in Bosnia. Thus, for example, there have been calls for the establishment of a third (Croatian) federal entity in the development of a new constitution. This is due to the fact that the Dayton constitution is seen by some Croats as primarily benefiting Bosniaks and one that effectively eliminates the provisions Croats have had protecting their rights, reflected in the following: 'Croats have been rendered subordinate to other nations in Bosnia-Herzegovina' (Dragan Čović, Leader of HDZ BiH, 4 September 2007, *Tanjug* News Service). However, although nationalist Croats are an important presence in Bosnian politics, so too are moderates. The current Croat president of the Federation of Bosnia-Herzegovina Željko Komšić is a moderate secular Croat from the multiethnic SDP party. When Željko Komšić was elected as the Croat member of the Bosnia-Herzegovina presidency, Croat nationalists were dismayed. Shortly after his election, the HDZ BiH (not HDZ 1990) wanted to nullify the results, accusing him of not being a real Croat (*pravi Hrvat*). Other Croat voices of moderation in Bosnia include Stjepan Kljuić, head of the multiethnic Republican Party of Bosnia-Herzegovina, who broke with Tuđman over his expansionist desires in Bosnia, and Komšić, who, like Kljuić, was a fierce opponent of Mate Boban, the founder of the short-lived Croatian Republic of Herceg-Bosna and a strong supporter of a united Bosnia. The outspoken writer and commentator Ivan Lovrenović has also long been a critic of Croatian ethnic nationalism. He has argued, for example, that the term *Bosnian Croat* is a recent construction dating from the nineteenth century. Furthermore, in his opinion 'Croatization' is a modern phenomenon, inseparable from nineteenth-century nationalist ideology originating with political events following Austria's annexation of Bosnia, pan-Croatism and the nationalist sentiments promoted by the church hierarchy. Clearly then, Croats are not politically united on the future of Bosnia and their place in it. Croats who live in villages and towns, far from the machinations of federal politicians and international agencies, have had to cope with the daily challenges and hardships of postwar Bosnia, revealed in perceptions and expectations that differ from the preoccupations of national leaders. Thus, national debates on the political future of Bosnia have limited appeal to Croats who are grappling with a different kind of politics at the local level. Control over local councils and the distribution of public services and resources essential to people's economic security are key to understanding the ways in which political alliances, voting strategies and opinions are forged at the local level, especially in a region that is economically and politically depressed. During and immediately after the war ended, in towns and villages with substantial Croat populations, Croatian political parties seized control of lucrative local assets with the result that control of local administration continues to mitigate against strengthening state institutions as well as systematizing local power dynamics and relationships. Political actors are often under the influence of elites at the national levels. This has been the case in the *Bosanska Posavina* region in northern Bosnia.

Bosanska Posavina

My preliminary research in the *Posavina* (Sava Valley) Canton supports the general assessment that Bosnian Croats feel increasingly marginalized in Bosnia's state-building process, producing (among other things) feelings of disaffection, apathy and/or resentment toward political actors involved in their fate (Grandits, 2006). Among the most common complaints are political and economic corruption and the slow process of refugee return. The resonance, if any, of anti-Muslim rhetoric for Bosnian Croats is seldom found in the language of the 'global terror threat' in Bosnia, but rather in local experiences, the aftermath of war and conflict, repatriation, difficult economic circumstances, local and regional histories and relationships among and between Bosnians. Of central importance, therefore, in understanding how and in what ways Croats in Bosnia respond to contemporary challenges is the complexity of local and regional histories. For example, Herzegovinian Croats in Western Bosnia are located close to Croatia and have a unique history in relation to the new Bosnian state. Emboldened by Croatian nationalists in the early 1990s, Herzegovinian Croats agitated for an independent state in Bosnia and for unification with Croatia,[2] whereas moderate Croats in Central Bosnia have typically been generally more supportive of a centralized Bosnia. My research in the towns of Orašje and Odžak (in *Posavina* Canton) focuses on how local residents conceptualize and narrate their pasts, cope with current uncertainties and see their future in the light of day-to-day postwar realities.

Despite a long history of imperial rule, wars, displacement and hardship, Croats in the *Posavina* region in northeast Bosnia respond variously to the efforts of local and national political, community and church leaders to mobilize their opinions concerning the future of *Posavina*. *Posavina* is a largely agricultural region located on a transit corridor that links central and southeastern Europe and (in part due to its geography) has a long history of sometimes brutal encounters with various imperial regimes in Bosnia. Historians have, for example, chronicled the flight of ethnic Croats from *Posavina* with the coming of the Ottomans. Some have even referred to this period as the 'ethnic cleansing of Croats from Bosnia' (Crkvenčić, 2004: 296). More recently, during the Yugoslav wars of succession, the *Posavina* region dominated key communication links between Bosnia and Croatia and also served as a strategic transit corridor for the transportation of weapons and ammunition by Serbs during their offensive in Bosnia. Before Serb forces launched their assault in Bosnia, Croats constituted the largest ethnic group in the *Posavina* region, with a population of 136,266. Five years after the Dayton Peace Accords gave the *Posavina* region to the Serb entity, only 10,881 Croats remained. The effects of the war and subsequent cantonal divisions resulting from the Dayton Peace Accords also represented significant shifts in the demographic distribution of Bosnians of all ethnic and religious backgrounds. This is clearly evident in the *Posavina* region, which was territorially divided after the war between Republika Srpska and the Federation of Bosnia-Herzegovina. *Posavina* Croats thus argue that they have been left out of the process of Bosnian reconstruction by both the international community and the Croatian state, which many felt was their natural ally. This sentiment was recently exacerbated by revelations of the central role of the Croatian government in precipitating the fall of *Posavina* during the war (Magaš, 2006). According to reports made public in the Croatian weekly news magazine *Nacional* (Šoštarić & Cvitić, 2007), *Posavina* was bartered with Serbian forces for western Herzegovina by Croatian defense minister Gojko Šušak (Šušak's birthplace is western Herzegovina).[3]

Posavina, like other areas of Bosnia with sizable concentrations of Croats, has not been immune to Croatian nationalist sentiments and initiatives. For example, shortly before Croats in Herzegovina declared their independence from Bosnia, eight communes in *Posavina* declared an autonomous (also short-lived) Bosnian Croat entity. In 2001, Croat separatists in Orašje (led by the HDZ and local Croatian veterans) also made an unsuccessful attempt to take control of the Federation barracks and weapons stores. However, despite *Posavina's* location a mere ten kilometers from the border with Croatia, their efforts to align themselves with Croatia have not been as aggressive as those of their compatriots in Herzegovina. Despite the history and experience of *Posavina* Croats, the responses of most of those whom I interviewed in Odžak (in the Federation) and Orašje (where part of the municipality lies in the Republika Srpska) are neither anti-Serb nor anti-Bosniak/Muslim. Croats are deeply attached to their regional identities, forged historically largely through hardship. Foremost in the minds of these Croats are not the grievances precipitated by the war or the prospect of a Muslim majoritarian state; rather, it is the dim prospect of reliable and sustainable financial and social security, the future of the younger generation (who are leaving the region for employment opportunities) and the return of those that fled during the war. How these are expressed and negotiated discursively necessitates an analysis of those factors that have historically provided frames of meaning for Croats.

For Croats faced with uncertain futures in Bosnia, the appeal of nationalist rhetoric, particularly making reference to the 'global terror threat', is mixed at best. In fact, mention of these discourses and questions about their relevance were frequently scoffed at by those I spoke to.

The lack of resonance of the language of fear popularized in the international press and by nationalist Croats lends itself to the investigation of those discourses that relate to the lived experiences. Local vernacular traditions and symbols reveal the interweaving of common histories and, more importantly, assumptions and expectations that are the product of ongoing negotiation among local inhabitants. By turning attention to the more common (and time-honored) referents familiar to Croats, it is possible to make greater sense of current realities. According to Ivan Lovrenović, ethnic nationalism, combined with and strengthened by its religious and confessional component, has been deeply implicated in all structures of social life although not in ways necessarily accessible or investigated by those that study Bosnian social and political life: the cultural sphere, the educational system, the media, official political discourse and the discourse of religious communities and their leaders (2008). It is therefore important to consider the roles of religion, history, symbols, myths and legends (and their politicization) in creating/reinforcing alignments and loyalties, and in establishing the foundations of support and coexistence.

The past as a social and political force has been theorized by a multitude of scholars including historians, philosophers and theologians (cf. Maier, 1988; Verdery, 1999). As Raymond Williams has argued, the past is 'an intentional selective version of a shaping past and a pre-shaped present' (1977: 115), wherein the passage of time smoothes out the wrinkles (Rushdie, 1991: 15). The discursive power of myths and legend has also long been understood as central to nation-building (Hobsbawm & Ranger, 1983). The reclaiming and celebration of old conquests and heroes has become commonplace all over the former Yugoslavia. These were catapulted to new heights and presented as authentic symbols of, for example, the Croatian national past, which Ramet (1996: 210) refers to as 'restored archaicisms'. The past, however configured, has always played an important role in informing local historical sensibilities and, as in the case of the former Yugoslavia, is often shaped into nationalist rhetoric of resistance, bravery, suffering and victimhood (MacDonald, 2002; Winland, 2007). The seminal work of the Croatian anthropologist Ivo Žanić (2005, 2007) is crucial to the analysis of contemporary politics in Bosnia if only to develop a richer and more contextually sensitive analysis of political and cultural communication there. Žanić's work focuses on the use of symbols, popular folklore and heroic epic traditions in mobilizing public sentiments in the former Yugoslavia:

> The heroic epic of the Serbs, the Montenegrins, the Croats, and the Bosniaks is the only example 'among all known literatures' where in the same language... and in the same form there are songs and poems about the same events and the same persons on both of the

belligerent sides – the other side being mainly the Muslim side of the former battlefield. (Žanić, 2007: 519)

Žanić demonstrates how nationalist politicians such as Franjo Tuđman, Slobodan Milošević and Alija Izetbegović (the first presidents of Croatia, the former Federal Republic of Yugoslavia and Bosnia, respectively) all identified in one form or another with epic, heroic traditions. The ubiquity of these narrative forms for the expression of local histories, grievances, alliances and experiences speaks to the centrality of shared symbols in making sense of current conditions and future prospects.

Hajduk i uskoci: Romantic Epic Tales

Traditions such as the *hajduk* and others have all been a source of fascination and veneration for centuries by Serbs, Bosniaks and Croats alike, especially since Ottoman rule. For Croats, the *hajduks* symbolized resistance to foreign rule, but the forms that they took differed widely between Croats in Bosnia and in Croatia. The folkloric/epic tradition of the Bosnian *hajduk* bandits (rebels) or *uskok* romantic figures that, according to Croatian legend, drove out Ottoman invaders has most recently been used to elevate the historical/civilizational status of Croats. These heroic figures are important not only for Croats, but have been resurrected by Serbs and Bosniaks in the assertion of contemporary identity claims. The symbolic power of the *hajduk* as a noble outlaw or brigand is entrenched in a variety of historical, cultural, regional and social contexts, infused with multiple and sometimes conflicting meanings in oral and literary traditions and local vernaculars. For example, the first president of Croatia Franjo Tuđman made frequent reference to the romantic notion of the *hajduk* as liberator, defender and freedom fighter, and also with reference to menacing characteristics of the enemy – Serb or Bosniak. Thus, these figures have had broad-based appeal albeit with distinctive regional and cultural variations (Lovrenović, 2001: 99). The Croatian media have also been complicit in the usage of epic metaphors and symbols, specifically the *hajduk*, particularly in the early years of the war. The Bosnian edition of the right-of-center newspaper *Slobodna Dalmacija* regularly featured articles and quotes on *hajduks* from political figures. HINA, Croatia's national news agency, *Večernji list* and *Vjesnik*, controlled by the ruling party HDZ (*Hrvatska demokratska zajednica*, Croatian Democratic Union) in the 1990s, also made use of traditional epic themes and narratives for political purposes. The use of heroic tales and epics thus became a potent and popular source of political mobilization during the Yugoslav wars of succession, inspiring nationalist ideologies and mobilizing popular sympathies. The reason for the frequent use of these and other folkloric symbols (including the musical instruments the *gusle* and *tamburica*) was that the language and significance of the *hajduk* is familiar, albeit in different guises to local inhabitants and their histories.

Antemurale christianitatis: Catholic Croat Heritage and Mission

Another potent symbol of resistance in Bosnia for Croats as well as for Serbs has been the motif of the *antemurale christianitatis* or 'bulwark of Christianity' against Ottoman/Islamic influence (Banac, 1996; Čuvalo, 1997; Žanić, 2005). For Croats, this builds on a historic Croatian claim (of providential destiny) that they are the guardians of western European traditions and provide an invaluable shield against the encroachment of eastern influences. This was and continues to be a central claim of the Catholic hierarchy in Bosnia (and Croatia); namely, that Catholicism provides a strategic barrier against Islamic expansionism in Bosnia, effectively positioning Croats as Catholic defenders of the faith and of the west. The potential for capitalizing on global concerns over Islamic extremism is evidenced in the fear-mongering displayed by such Bosnian Catholic leaders as the Catholic Archbishop of Bosnia Vinko Puljić, who has publicly acknowledged his worries concerning 'growing Muslim dominance in Bosnia which may wipe out or convert all Christians in the region' (*Catholic News Service*, 6 July 2006).

Rendering the Bosnian past in ways that reinforce the claims of nationalist Croats is reflected in discussions, or rather correctives, regarding the history of Croats in Bosnia. Hence the autochthonous claim that Bosniaks were originally Catholic Croats is vigorously defended. Statements that, for example, '50% of contemporary Bosnia has historically been part of the Croatian state in one form or another' (cf. Cvitković, 2006), are based on nationalist Croat claims beginning in the mid-nineteenth century (by nationalists including Ante Starčević and Eugen Kvaternik) that Bosnia is an 'old Croat land' (MacDonald, 2002) are also found in the work of the Bosnian-born Croatian Nobel laureate Ivo Andrić (1959), whose work belongs to both Serbian and Croatian literature. Croatian historiographers have long argued that the original inhabitants of Bosnia were Croats who were forcefully converted to Islam, a claim repeatedly disputed by noted scholars of Bosnian history (Cigar, 1995; Hadžiosmanović, 2006; Lovrenović, 2001; Malcolm, 1994).

Thus, headlines such as the following by Marcus Tanner of *The Independent:* 'Catholic Croats in Bosnia are feeling written out of the script' (2005) become public declarations of the continued historic plight of Bosnia's Croats. 'Ten years after the civil war, Catholics in Bosnia live amid violence, discrimination, and poverty. No one can dispute that the Catholic Church faces extinction in much of the country, outside a triangle of land in the barren hills of Herzegovina on the Croatian border, where

Bosnian Croats rule the roost' (ibid.). This plays into beliefs or fears that Bosniaks wish to establish supremacy over Catholic Croats and Orthodox Serbs.[4] The interpolation of nationalist discourses of Croatian victimhood with Christian tropes of suffering and redemption builds on the political importance of the idea of Croats as a long-suffering nation (Drakulić, 1993; Winland, 2007). Croatian trauma narratives and personal and collective memories work to mobilize for political and/or moral purposes (Baumann, 1995; Kolstø, 2005; Smith, 2003) and this is a political strategy familiar to Croatian politicians. The combination of lachrymosity (Dubnow, 1961; Winland, 1992), legends of heroism and histories of suffering become part of current religious and political elite efforts to cast Bosnian Croats as potential victims of a Muslim onslaught that easily tie into international concerns about Islamic fundamentalism. However, just as in the case of federal politics in Bosnia, so it is also with the Catholic Church hierarchy in Bosnia. Catholic clergy in Bosnia are not unified in making these assertions, as evidenced in the lack of support for this move by the Croatian National Council, led by the Franciscan father Luka Markešić and Marko Oršolić, who head the International Multi-Religious and Intercultural Center in Sarajevo. More often than not, grievances on the part of local religious leaders take the form of complaints (not necessarily substantiated) that Bosniaks have access to funding and permits to build mosques, whereas Catholics have none. Although these reflect the pragmatic concerns of local political and religious community leaders, they are undergirded by local processes of identity formation informed by symbolic referents, histories and relationships cultivated and/or damaged over the years of war, conquest and coexistence.

Conclusions

Perhaps the most significant lesson to be drawn through the analysis of political rhetoric in contemporary Bosnia is the continual contesting of the grounds of identity evidenced in the clash of competing narratives in the service of political aims. Bosnians of all backgrounds have faced radically different political and social agendas since the war ended. The problem of interethnic/religious relations in Bosnia began in pre-Ottoman times and has taken multiple forms over the centuries. At various times in history, Croats, Bosniaks and Serbs prevailed over the other, depending largely on the will of empires. The Catholic Croat hierarchy in Bosnia, for example, waxes nostalgic about the Austro-Hungarian occupation (1878–1918), when Catholics were favored politically over Orthodox Serbs and Bosniaks. Lovrenović has called this dynamic the 'domination-subjugation scheme' (2008) – one that has lasted to the present. More recent efforts to manage this pluralism have been given over to the international community, in the guise of the Dayton Peace Accords. As in the past, different and largely divided ethnic/confessional groups jockey for advantage (both nationally and regionally) in a system monitored and policed by the Dayton Accords. Bosnians from all backgrounds have been exposed to radically different and disjointed agendas for their country's future over the last 15 years. The mobilization of differences, while historically constant throughout Bosnian history (by both Bosnia's inhabitants and their occupiers) has proven most recently to have led to horrendously violent results (Bieber, 2003). To accept the enormous diversity of inter- and intraethnic/religious origins, histories and experiences in dealing with difference over the centuries (largely through the everyday experiences of conflict and coexistence) would signal a move forward in understanding moral and identity claims. Croat nationalists understand this and make appeals for support based on their intimate knowledge of these histories and symbolic referents. They have, with limited success, attempted to mobilize support against Bosniaks by accessing global discourses around terror by making links between the actions, past and present, of Bosnia's Muslims with Muslim extremists and terrorists. The resonance of these discursive strategies for local Croatian populations, while uneven at best, is as yet uncertain.

Notes

1. Erjavec and Volčič (2006) chronicle the prevalence of anti-Islamic rhetoric in Croatian and Serbian newspapers.
2. The Croatian Republic of Herceg-Bosna (Croatian: *Hrvatska Republika Herceg-Bosna*) was an unrecognized entity in present-day Bosnia existing between 1991 and 1994 as a result of secessionist politics during the Bosnian War. It was proclaimed a separate political, cultural, economic and territorial whole on the territory of Bosnia. Neither the Republic of Bosnia-Herzegovina nor the international community ever recognized Herceg-Bosna as a state. It was declared illegal by the Constitutional Court of Bosnia-Herzegovina in 1994 and it ceased to exist in 1994, when it became part of the Federation of Bosnia-Herzegovina. Following Herceg-Bosna's establishment in November 1991, and especially from May 1992 forward, the Herceg-Bosna leadership engaged in continuing and coordinated efforts to dominate and 'Croatize' the municipalities that they claimed were part of Herceg-Bosna, with increasing persecution and discrimination directed against Bosniaks. The HVO (Croatian Defense Council) took control of many municipal governments and services, removing or marginalizing local Bosnian leaders. Herceg-Bosna/HVO authorities and forces took control of the media. Croatian symbols and currency were introduced, and Croatian curricula and the 'Croatian language' were introduced in schools. Many Bosniaks and Serbs were removed from positions in government and private business; humanitarian aid was managed and distributed to the Bosniaks' and Serbs' disadvantage, and Bosniaks in general were increasingly harassed. One of the cantons of the Federation still uses the name Herceg-Bosna Canton to keep alive a memory of the former republic.
3. 'The circumstances under which the Bosnian *Posavina* area was lost marked the moment in which the leading role in Croatian policy making had been

entirely taken over by people from Herzegovina; that is, Defense Minister Gojko Šušak's people' (*Nacional* 2007). In Lovrenović's 2001 book *Bosnia: A Cultural History*, the author then stated, 'For reasons never yet explained the Croatian Army now withdrew from *Posavina*, allowing Serbs control of the corridor.... For equally unexplained reasons the HVO too withdrew' (198–199).
4. Alija Izebegović's Islamic Declaration (1972) became a benchmark moment for nationalist Croats of Bosniak plans for Islamic expansion in the region.

References

Ali, T. (2003) *The Clash of Fundamentalisms: Crusades, Jihads and Modernity*. London: Verso.

Alliance of Croats of Bosnia and Herzegovina (2006) Croats from Bosnia and Herzegovina in diaspora: Statement on the present and future of Bosnia and Herzegovina. 17 January 2006 – Online document: http://www.caausa.org. Accessed 15 May 2009.

Andrić, I. (1959) *The Bridge on the Drina*. London: George Allen Unwin Ltd.

Appadurai, A. (2006) *Fear of Small Numbers: An Essay on the Geography of Anger*. Durham, NC: Duke University Press.

Banac, I. (1996) Bosnian Muslims: From religious community to socialist nationhood to post-communist statehood. In M. Pinson (ed.) *The Muslims of Bosnia-Herzegovina: Their Historic Development from the Middle Ages to the Dissolution of Yugoslavia* (pp. 129–154). Cambridge, MA: Harvard University Press.

Baumann, Z. (1995) *Life in Fragments: Essays in Postmodern Morality*. Oxford: Basil Blackwell.

Bieber, F. (2003) Approaches to political violence and terrorism in former Yugoslavia. *Journal of Southern Europe and the Balkans* 5 (1), 39–51.

Bose, S. (2002) *Bosnia after Dayton: Nationalist Partition and International Intervention*. London: C. Hurst and Co.

Bougarel, X., Helms, E. and Duijzings, G. (eds) (2006) *The New Bosnian Mosaic: Identities, Memories and Moral Claims in a Post-War Society*. Burlington, VT: Ashgate Press.

Bringa, T. (1995) *Being Muslim the Bosnian Way: Identity and Community in a Central Bosnian Village*. Princeton: Princeton University Press.

Bosnia and Terrorism. *Večernji list*. 9 November 2005, 6.

Campbell, D. (1999) Apartheid cartography: The political anthropology and spatial effects of international diplomacy in Bosnia. *Political Geography* 18, 395–436.

Chandler, D. (1999) *Bosnia: Faking Democracy after Dayton*. London: Pluto Press.

Cigar, N. (1995) *Genocide in Bosnia: The Politics of "Ethnic Cleansing"*. College Station: Texas A&M University Press.

Cigar, N. (2003) The nationalist Serbian intellectuals and Islam: Defining and eliminating a Muslim community. In E. Qureshi and M. Sells (eds) *The New Crusades: Constructing the Muslim Enemy* (pp. 314–351). New York: Columbia University Press.

Coles, K. (2007) *Democratic Designs: International Intervention and Electoral Practices in Postwar Bosnia-Herzegovina*. Ann Arbor: University of Michigan Press.

Čolović, I. (2002) *The Politics of Symbol in Serbia: Essays on Political Anthropology*. London: Hurst.

Crkvenčić, I. (2004) The Posavina border region of Croatia and Bosnia and Herzegovina: Development up to 1918 (with special reference to change in ethnic composition). *Društvena istraživanja* 1–2, 293–314.

Cushman, T. (1997) *Critical Theory and the War in Croatia and Bosnia.* (= Donald W. Treadgold Papers in Russian, East European and Central Asian Studies 13). Seattle: Henry M. Jackson School of International Studies, University of Washington.

Čuvalo, A. (1997) *Historical Dictionary of Bosnia and Herzegovina.* Lanham, MD: Scarecrow Press.

Čuvalo, A. (2005) Tenth anniversary of Dayton. *Hrvatska Revija* 5 (45), 49–53.

Cvitković, I. (2006) *Hrvatski identitet u Bosni i Hercegovini: Hrvati između nacionalnog i građanskog.* Zagreb: Synopsis.

Denich, B. (1994) Dismembering Yugoslavia: Nationalist ideologies and the symbolic revival of genocide. *American Ethnologist* 21 (2), 367–390.

Drakulić, S. (1993) *Balkan Express.* M. Soljan, transl. New York: W.W. Norton and Co.

Dubnow, S. (1961) *Nationalism and History: Essays in Old and New Judaism.* K. Pinson (transl. and ed.) Cleveland: World Pub. Co.

Erjavec, K. and Volčič, Z. (2006) Mapping the notion of "terrorism" in Serbian and Croatian newspapers. *Journal of Communication Inquiry* 30 (4), 298–318.

Gordy, E. (1999) *The Culture of Power in Serbia: Nationalism and the Destruction of Alternatives.* University Park: Pennsylvania State University Press.

Grandits, H. (2006) The power of "armchair politicians": Ethnic loyalty and political factionalism among Hercegovinian Croats. In X. Bougarel, E. Helms and G. Duijzings (eds) *The New Bosnian Mosaic: Identities, Memories and Moral Claims in a Post-War Society* (pp. 101–122). Burlington, VT: Ashgate Press.

Hadžiosmanović, I. (2006) *Bošnjačko-hrvatski politički obračun.* CIP: Mostar.

Halpern, J.M. and Kideckel, D. (eds) (2000) *Neighbors at War: Anthropological Perspectives on Yugoslav Ethnicity, Culture and History.* University Park: Pennsylvania State University Press.

Hayden, R. (2002) *Bosnia Ten Years after "Independence": The Dictatorship of the Protectorate under Civicist Self-Management.* EES Special Report.

Hayden, R. (2005) Inaccurate data, spurious issues and editorial failure in Cushman's "anthropology and genocide in the Balkans". *Anthropological Theory* 5 (4), 545–554.

Hoare, M. (2004) Bin Laden in the Balkans? The Bosnian army and the *Mujahedin.* In M. Hoare *How Bosnia Armed* (pp. 131–135). London: Saqi Books.

Hobsbawm, E. and Ranger, T. (eds) (1983) *The Invention of Tradition.* Cambridge: Cambridge University Press.

Huntington, S. (1996) *The Clash of Civilizations and the Remaking of the World Order.* New York: Simon & Schuster.

Innes, M. (2005) Terrorist sanctuaries and Bosnia-Herzegovina: Challenging conventional assumptions. *Studies in Conflict and Terrorism* 28 (4), 295–305.

Jansen, S. (2003) "Why do they hate us?" Everyday Serbian nationalist knowledge of Muslim hatred. *Journal of Mediterranean Studies* 13 (2), 215–237.

Jansen, S. (2005) National numbers in context: Maps and stats in representations of the post-Yugoslav wars. *Identities: Global Studies in Culture and Power* 12 (1), 45–68.

Judah, T. (1997) *The Serbs: History, Myth and the Destruction of Yugoslavia.* New Haven, CT: Yale University Press.

Karajkov, R. (2006) The young and the old: Radical Islam takes root in the Balkans – Online document: http://www.worldpress.org. Accessed 15 May 2009.

Kohlmann, E. (2004) *Al-Qaida's Jihad in Europe: The Afghan-Bosnian Network.* Oxford: Berg Publishers.

Kolstø, P. (ed.) (2005) *Myths and Boundaries in South-Eastern Europe.* London: Hurst.

Kuhner, J. (2005) Islamist state in Europe? *Washington Times* – Online document: http://www.washingtontimes.com. Accessed 15 May 2009.

Lovrenović, I. (2001) *Bosnia: A Cultural History.* London: Saqi Books.

Lovrenović, I. (2008) Bosna i Hercegovina pred izazovom samostalnosti. *Duh Bosne/Spirit of Bosnia* 3 (1): 1–8.

Loza, T. (2008) Bosnia: A merry dance. *Transitions Online* – Online document: www.tol.cz. Accessed 20 April 2009.

MacDonald, D.B. (2002) *Balkan Holocausts: Serbian and Croatian Victim-Centred Propaganda.* Manchester: Manchester University Press.

Magaš, B. (1993) *The Destruction of Yugoslavia: Tracking the Break-Up 1980–92.* London: Verso.

Magaš, B. (2006) Gojko Šušak's gift to RS. *Feral Tribune* 16 April.

Maier, C. (1988) *The Unmasterable Past: History, Holocaust, and German National Identity.* Cambridge, MA: Harvard University Press.

Malcolm, N. (1994) *Bosnia: A Short History.* New York: New York University Press.

Mamdani, M. (2002) Good Muslim, bad Muslim: A political perspective on culture and terrorism. *American Anthropologist* 104 (3), 766–775.

Meštrović, S. (ed.) (1996) *Genocide after Emotion: The Postemotional Balkan War.* London: Routledge.

Mojzes, P. (1994) *The Yugoslav Inferno.* New York: Continuum Press.

Njegoš, P. II Petrović (1847) *The Mountain Wreath.* Vienna: Armenian Mechitarist monastery.

Oberschall, A. (2000) The manipulation of ethnicity: From ethnic cooperation to violence and war in Yugoslavia. *Ethnic and Racial Studies* 23 (6), 982–1001.

Qureshi, E. and Sells, M. (eds) (2003) *The New Crusades: Constructing the Muslim Enemy.* New York: Columbia University Press.

Ramet, S. (2005) *Thinking about Yugoslavia.* Cambridge: Cambridge University Press.

Ramet, S. (1996) *Balkan Babel: The Disintegration of Yugoslavia from the Death of Tito to the War for Kosovo* (2nd edn). Boulder, CO: Westview Press.

Roshwald, A. (2001) *Ethnic Nationalism and the Fall of Empires: Central Europe, Russia, and the Middle East, 1914–1923.* London: Routledge.

Rushdie, S. (1991) *Imaginary Homelands.* London: Granta.

Schindler, J. (2007) *Unholy Terror: Bosnia, Al Qa'ida, and the Rise of Global Jihad.* Osceola, WI: Zenith Press.

Sells, M. (1996) *The Bridge Betrayed: Religion and Genocide in Bosnia.* Berkeley: University of California Press.

Seroka, J. and Pavlović, V. (eds) (1992) *The Tragedy of Yugoslavia: The Failure of Democratic Transformation.* Armonk, NY: M.E. Sharpe.

Silber, L. and Little, A. (1995) *The Death of Yugoslavia.* London: Penguin.

Smith, A. (2003) *Chosen Peoples: Sacred Sources of National Identity.* Oxford: Oxford University Press.

Søberg, M. (2006) Empowering local elites in Bosnia and Herzegovina: The Dayton decade. *Problems of Post-Communism* 53 (3), 44–58.

Šoštarić, E. and Cvitić, P. (2007) Šušak je predao Posavinu. *Nacional* June (Issue 585) –Online document: http://89.201.163.71/articles/view/31061. Accessed 20 April 2009.

Starr, J. (2004) How to outflank al-Qaeda in the Balkans. *European Affairs* 5 (4) – Online document: http://www.ciaonet.org/olj/sites/ea.html. Accessed 20 April 2009.

Tanner, M. (2005) Losing their religion: Ten years after the civil war, Catholics in Bosnia live amid violence, discrimination and poverty. They say the west is ignoring their plight. *The Independent* – Online document: http://www.iwpr.net. Accessed 20 April 2009.

Tuđman, F. (1981) *Nationalism in Contemporary Europe*. Boulder, CO: East European Monographs.

Verdery, K. (1999) *The Political Lives of Dead Bodies: Reburial and Post-Socialist Change*. New York: Columbia University Press.

Williams, R. (1977) *Marxism and Literature*. Clarendon: Oxford University Press.

Winland, D. (1992) Native scholarship: The enigma of self-definition among Jewish and Mennonite scholars. *Journal of Historical Sociology* 5 (4), 413–461.

Winland, D. (2007) We are now a nation: Croats between "home" and "homeland". Toronto: University of Toronto Press.

Woodward, S.L. (1995) *Balkan Tragedy: Chaos and Dissolution after the Cold War*. Washington, DC: Brookings Institution.

Wooley, A. (2006) Bosnia: New survey shows country as divided as ever along ethnic lines – Online document: http://www.intermedia org. Accessed 20 April 2009.

Žanić, I. (2005) The symbolic identity of Croatia in the triangle crossroads-bulwark-bridge. In P. Kolstø (ed.) *Myths and Boundaries in South-Eastern Europe* (pp. 35–76). London: Hurst and Co.

Žanić, I. (2007) *Flag on the Mountain: A Political Anthropology of War in Croatia and Bosnia*. London: Saqi Books.

Žižek, S. (2001) *Did Someone Say Totalitarianism? Five Interventions of the (Mis)use of a Notion*. London: Verso.

Chapter 7
Construction of Serbian and Montenegrin Identities through Layout and Photographs of Leading Politicians in Official Newspapers

Tatjana Radanović Felberg

Introduction

The exact placement of the imaginary line of Europe's eastern rim has constantly been negotiated by various states, political parties, intellectuals and individuals (cf. all contributions to this volume). One such contested geopolitical area was the territory of the Federal Republic of Yugoslavia (FRY), which during its existence from 1992 to 2003 consisted of Serbia and Montenegro. In the public sphere of the FRY, several types of conflicting discourses served to help construct the relationship between the FRY and Europe. On the one side, there were discourses structured through the metaphor of a BATTLEGROUND on which European values – primarily democracy – were being fought for (Felberg, 2008). In this type of discourse, belonging to Europe was considered the equivalent of being civilized, democratic and forward-looking. In the background, there was also the strong component of potential financial and political support from the European Union. On the other side, the FRY was constructed as belonging to the east, having closer ties with Russia and China and thus not being a part of Europe (Felberg, 2009).

This chapter illuminates one example of a 'negotiation' concerning the placement of the eastern European rim:[1] The negotiation in question developed between the Serbian and Montenegrin governments, represented by the FRY's president Slobodan Milošević and Montenegro's president Milo Đukanović during the NATO bombing of the FRY (25 March–11 June 1999). This is analyzed by studying the front pages of two newspapers that supported the respective national governments: Serbian *Politika*[2] and Montenegrin *Pobjeda*.[3] The focus is thus on examining official voices. The corpus for this study consists of 79 front pages of both newspapers that came out during this period, with particular attention given to the photographs of Milošević, shown on 45 front pages of *Politika*, and Đukanović, shown on 39 front pages of *Pobjeda*. This chapter shows that the visual resources used on the front pages (i.e. layout and photographs) contribute to the construction of Montenegro as a 'democratic' state opposed to 'autocratic' Serbia, and of 'patriotic' Serbia as opposed to 'treacherous' Montenegro, depending on whose voice was heard. Such categorizations contributed to drawing the invisible line between Europe and non-Europe (i.e. including Montenegro while excluding Serbia from Europe). Because context is crucial for any type of interpretation, the first part of this analysis addresses some important political and media-related elements of context. Examples of the analysis are subsequently illustrated and connected with the ideological differences between Montenegro and Serbia.

Examining Some Elements of Political Context

The end of the Cold War influenced the political situation across the globe, and in particular in Eastern Europe. While some former communist countries of Eastern Europe entered what is referred to as a 'transitional period', the Socialist Federative Republic of Yugoslavia started to disintegrate into conflict (Mojzes, 1994). A combination of various internal and external factors contributed to the disintegration of the country.[4] The Serbs were allotted most of the blame and responsibility by the Western powers for the human suffering caused by these wars. This construction of Serb guilt established through cause-and-effect logic connects the global to the local political context of the NATO bombing, as explained from the official NATO point of view (Hemond & Herman, 2001). The Serbs' presumed atrocities in the past and expected atrocities in the future legitimized and justified the 'humanitarian bombing' in the given context. On the other hand, seen from the official Serbian point of view, the NATO bombing was understood as an act of aggression with the aim of conquering the nation as part of a more expansive plan to conquer the whole world (Ćurgus, 2003: 10; Nohrstedt et al., 2000: 390).

Serbia and Montenegro have a long shared history of periods of political integration and disintegration (Komatina, 1999; Petrović & Stanković, 2006). Politically speaking, Serbia and Montenegro were different states up to 1918. After that, they were united in a common state until 2006. In 2006, Montenegro became independent as a result of a peaceful referendum. Two predominant views on the relationship between Serbia and Montenegro have been in circulation: one that conceptualized Montenegrins as a part of the Serbian people and the other that conceptualized Montenegrins as a separate ethnic group/nation (Gallagher, 2003). The period of NATO bombing provided a snapshot in which these two leading views on the relationship between Serbia and Montenegro met in a crystallized form due to the war situation.

The political situation in the FRY prior to the NATO bombing involved a serious political rift between official Belgrade, represented by FRY president Slobodan Milošević, and official Podgorica, represented by Montenegrin president Milo Đukanović, after a period during which the two politicians had often been cooperating. The rift started to show during the Montenegrin elections in 1997, and became obvious during the NATO bombing.

The NATO bombing was referred to as military action, intervention, air-war, aggression or humanitarian intervention, depending on whose voice was heard. It entered military history under the code name 'Merciful Angel', considered by many to be an example of ironic nomenclature (Matić, 2005). The choice of name focuses on the 'humanitarian' nature of bombing through use of the adjective *merciful*, playing on a connection between NATO and religion through the religious term *angel*. Religion was thus used to endorse NATO's actions as good and accepted by a god because angels are seen to be messengers from God. Apart from resulting in human suffering and material destruction, 'Merciful Angel' generated different types of discourse about the legality and morality of the bombing and was also the triggering factor for more severe degrees of internal political struggle unfolding between the governments of Serbia and Montenegro and among different political parties in Serbia and Montenegro. It was also the time when the debates over Montenegrin identity (Roberts, 2007: 430) and over democracy as the demarcation line between Europe as positive and non-Europe as negative came to the foreground.

The relationship between Serbia and Montenegro was constructed both at an internal level and in relation to other powers that have been politically significant in the region at any given time: for example, Russia, Austria-Hungary, the Ottoman Empire, Germany, the European Union and NATO. Serbia and Montenegro thus present a microcosm of more global political relationships.

Examining Some Elements of Media Context

The importance of the media sources from which the average citizen of Serbia acquired information played a more important role in forming political views than any other sociological factor such as gender, education, age, income and so on (Branković, cited in Antonić, 2002: 443). The importance of media has also been shown through research on how media constructed different versions of reality during the NATO bombing (Gott, 1999; Hemond & Herman, 2001; Lakić, 2005; Nohrstedt *et al.*, 2000, 2002; Ottosen, 2002). The media landscape in the FRY was varied, consisting of both pro-government and opposition voices. The work of opposition media was severely restricted by the government. This situation became extremely difficult during the NATO bombing due to the physical threat posed by the NATO bombing itself and the restrictions imposed by both formal and informal FRY regulations (ANEM, 1999). The media were polarized into pro- and anti-Milošević factions in the FRY and pro- and anti-Đukanović factions in Montenegro. This analysis focuses on two broadsheet newspapers: *Politika*, which was pro-Milošević at the time, and *Pobjeda*, which was pro-Đukanović (for more on *Politika* and *Pobjeda*, see Felberg, 2008; Lakić, 2005; Marović, 1999, 2002; Nenadović, 2002).

It is significant to note that the topic of Montenegro was not brought up on the front pages of *Politika* at all. By backgrounding the country (i.e. discussing Montenegro in less prominent places), *Politika* played down the importance of Montenegro's different opinion. On the other hand, Milošević was backgrounded in *Pobjeda*, being shown on only three front pages.

Front-Page Layouts and Photographs as Meaning-Making Resources

The identities of Serbia and Montenegro as constructed and mediated in *Politika* and *Pobjeda* during the NATO bombing were constructed on the basis of historical, ideological, religious, political and legal differences/similarities between the two republics (Felberg, 2008). The following sections focus particularly on constructed ideological differences – or, in other words, the fact that Montenegro as a self-proclaimed democracy automatically belonged to Europe, and the proclamation of the other, Milošević/Serbia, as an autocratic regime consequently excluded it from Europe. These ideological differences are shown through analysis of selected semiotic resources such as layout and photographs found in *Politika* and *Pobjeda* during the NATO bombing.

Front-page layouts in *Politika* and *Pobjeda*

The esthetics of the various elements and the way they are placed on the page influence its interpretation. Pages are balanced through a complex combination of various features and their interaction. Such features may include proportionate size, scope of detail, tonal and color contrasts and so on (van Leeuwen, 2005: 198). Diverse factors are combined not only for esthetic reasons but also for pragmatic and ideological reasons (Macgilchrist, 2009). Newspaper size, traditional printing patterns, availability of photographs and so on play an important role in constructing front pages. However, irrespective of the reasons leading to the composition of front pages, the combination of various elements in the final product contribute to the construction of meaning. Here, I focus on three elements at the compositional level:

- *Information value*, or placement of various elements on the page
- *Salience*, or foregrounding of certain elements and

- *Framing*, or presence, absence and type of framing (Kress & van Leeuwen, 1996, 1998; van Leeuwen, 2005).

The recognizable, conventional global structures of the front pages of both *Politika* and *Pobjeda* were stable during the entire period of NATO bombing. Each newspaper followed its own patterns when combining verbal and visual resources (see Figure 7.1).

Politika front pages were dominated by texts with an average of fewer than two black-and-white photographs. Front-page photo coverage thus averaged approximately 8%. The front pages of *Pobjeda* were less dominated by text than those in *Politika*. On average *Pobjeda* printed three photographs per issue, covering on average 16.5% of the front pages. Black-and-white photographs were used in both newspapers, but only *Pobjeda* used cut-out photographs (on four occasions).[5] Headlines and photographs overlapped in some issues of *Pobjeda* (on 12 front pages), but not in *Politika*. Such differences highlight *Pobjeda's* tendency to integrate verbal and visual resources to a greater extent than *Politika*. The overall impression is that *Pobjeda* packaged information in 'strongly framed,

Figure 7.1 Representative examples of front pages of *Politika* (left) and *Pobjeda* (right), both from 11 June 1999, one day after the NATO bombing stopped

individualized bite-size morsels' (van Leeuwen, 2005: 219), thus presenting the information to the readers in moderated portions. Because the information is presented in different types of frames, it is presented in a hierarchy and thus some chunks of information are made to seem more important than others. This can also give the impression that a wider range of voices is represented on the front page. *Politika*, on the other hand, presents all the information pieces as belonging to the same order; in principle, each could be of equal importance as the others. The impression of having one uniform – and thus unified – voice on the front page could be conveyed by this type of layout.

When it comes to photographs, *Politika* gave more prominence (upper left corner) to the 45 front-page photographs in which Milošević was the main character due to the story's 'breaking news' character. He was clearly given preferential treatment whereas other Yugoslav government officials were rarely shown alone. For example, Milan Milutinović, the president of Serbia at the time, was shown on only four front pages, and Army General Dragoljub Ojdanić, the head of the Supreme Command HQ, was shown on two front pages.

Pobjeda, on the other hand, divided the front pages among three main Montenegrin politicians. Đukanović was present on 36 front-page photographs (46%), whereas Montenegro's prime minister, Filip Vujanović, appeared in 15 issues (19%) and the president of the Montenegrin Assembly Svetozar Marović in 11 issues (14%). At the same time, *Pobjeda* gave more salience to Đukanović by printing larger photographs of him, including cut-out photographs, and using marked boxes around photographs. This difference in spatial allocation and presence of the various politicians can be seen as the newspapers' construction of a 'strong man' versus a 'team-oriented' type of leader. The strong man Milošević did not allow any competition and made decisions alone, whereas Đukanović gave the impression of a leader who was working with others on an equal level.

The above differences may be understood as indicating *Politika*'s adherence to tradition and a way of positioning itself as stable element in a sea of postmodern instability, whereas *Pobjeda* showed more openness to change. Openness to change can be further connected to democracy, whereas reluctance to change may be more associated with the old regime.

Photographs in *Politika* and *Pobjeda*

Photographs in *Pobjeda* were more numerous and larger than in *Politika*, pointing at different newspaper styles: *Pobjeda* appeared more tabloid than *Politika*. Nevertheless, the photographs in both newspapers fulfilled several common functions. First, by way of repeating motifs, they entrenched and foregrounded certain political figures. Furthermore, they illustrated the actions of the political leaders, and by doing so they documented political events. By documenting and explaining political events in this way, both newspapers gave their readers clues as to how to understand the political situation.

The representation of the participants on these photographs, in this case Milošević and Đukanović, is achieved through:

- Narrative processes (participants are connected by vectors formed by, for instance, limbs, bodies, tools and gazes, which can represent action, events and change) and
- Symbolic conceptual processes (Milošević and Đukanović serve as symbols of the governments/nations they are leading).

In addition, participants' interpersonal relations – their imaginary relationship with other participants in the photographs – can be analyzed in terms of *contact* (gaze or absence of gaze at the viewer), *social distance* (close, medium or long camera shot), *attitude* (the camera's frontal, oblique, high or low angle) and *modality* (contextualization, texture, illumination, color, etc.) (Kress & van Leeuwen, 1996; van Leeuwen, 2005).

Depending on Milošević's and Đukanović's position in the photographs, it is possible to identify several different types of photographs: One group of photographs presents Milošević alone in *Politika*. Another group presents Milošević in the center of the photographs with other political figures. That central position is changed only in two photographs in which Milošević is given a position parallel to the representatives of the 'international community'. All the photographs are official photographs, apart from one, which could be characterized as semiofficial because it presents Milošević's family. Because these changes in the types of photographs are connected to certain political events, the following sections add more detailed comments about context.

The motifs in the photographs in *Pobjeda* followed a similar pattern to those in *Politika*. The main politician, Đukanović, is variously photographed alone, meeting other important political figures, or presiding over various meetings.

The main difference between the patterns found in *Pobjeda* and in *Politika* is that there are no semi-official photographs in *Pobjeda* and there are no photographs in *Politika* of Milošević meeting politicians abroad because he did not leave the country during the bombing.

Đukanović and Milošević portrayed alone

Figure 7.2 shows one example of 18 photographs in which Đukanović is portrayed alone, and one example of three photographs in which Milošević is portrayed alone.

Figure 7.2 Examples of Milošević, left (*Politika*, 25 March 1999) and Đukanović, right (*Pobjeda*, 28 April 1999)

Đukanović is shown with microphones in front of him (Figure 7.2, right), contextualizing elements that symbolize an official occasion, such as that of Đukanović giving a speech, an interview or a press conference. The microphones suggest the genre often used in the articles: the interview. Đukanović's gaze is directed outside the photograph, offering information and not demanding anything from the viewers. 'Screamer' headlines (in very large letters), which were regularly used in *Pobjeda*, overlap with the photograph, which itself is a cut-out. This overlapping connects the text with the photograph of the speaker; that is, it connects the visual with the verbal and foregrounds the verbal. Words overlap with the photograph, making the photograph a background or context for the words. This type of overlapping has almost a 'speech bubble' effect.

The use of the cut-out photographs is meant to make Đukanović more salient. This is done by removing Đukanović from the real background into a background that is simply gray. He is also lifted above the text. According to van Leeuwen (2005), this could indicate a shift in modality – from real to unreal – but in this case, the 'screamer' headlines, which are quotes by Đukanović, anchor Đukanović's photograph in the version of

Construction of Serbian and Montenegrin Identities 115

reality that the newspaper wants to convey. Modality is used to make Đukanović more salient rather than removing him from the real world.

Photographs of Milošević alone are meant to look 'official', as the example in Figure 7.2 (left) shows. Milošević is wearing a suit and tie and is positioned in front of the flags that symbolize the country. He is looking toward the horizon, in a visionary manner (cf. van Leeuwen, 2005). This is an offer of information; nothing is demanded from the viewers except passive observation.

Milošević and Đukanović with others

As a rule, Milošević is presented in a central position in most of the 33 photographs in which he is portrayed with other participants, as exemplified in Figure 7.3.

The central position signals the importance of the person positioned there. This importance is further emphasized by the vectors pointing at Milošević formed by other politicians' bodies, which are turned to Milošević, as well as their gazes, which are directed toward him. Their bodies are turned toward Milošević – away from the photographer and the viewers. The photograph is taken from a frontal angle – the photographer seems to be a participant in the meeting. The use of a long shot expresses social distance as impersonal. Because he is presented in the background, Milošević is removed from the viewer, possibly signaling reduced responsibility. However, Milošević's position changes, depending on the topic that *Politika* focuses on in a given day. For example, Milošević is foregrounded in the photographs that show the peace talks, signaling his increased responsibility (see Figure 7.9).

Going back to the example in Figure 7.3, where information is offered about this particular meeting, Milošević's gaze is not directed toward the

Figure 7.3 Example of a photograph with Milošević presiding over a meeting (*Politika*, 26 March 1999)

viewers, but somewhere between the two politicians on his left side. The objects in the photograph (e.g. the flowers and ashtrays on the table) are arranged symmetrically. The two rows of politicians are also symmetrical; their hands are folded on the table in front of them, signaling agreement of political views. In summary, Milošević is given the most prominent position by *Politika*. He is the one presiding over various meetings, receiving various guests and the only one constantly presented in all the photographs. The variables are the different guests that he is receiving. This is an important cultural point because the politician's power is signaled by the importance and number of other politicians that come to visit him. In this context, the similarity of Milošević's rule to a sultan-like leadership has been pointed out by Antonić (2002).

Đukanović is presented as though presiding over meetings on only two occasions, which is significantly less frequent than the 33 comparable photographs of Milošević. Examples of Đukanović leading meetings are shown in Figure 7.4.

The difference between these and similar photographs from *Politika* is that the attention of other participants is not aimed exclusively at Đukanović (Figure 7.4, left). Also, Đukanović is not exclusively positioned in the center. For example, he is positioned in the left corner of a photograph that shows him from one side (Figure 7.4, right). This could be interpreted as signaling a more liberal type of leadership than Milošević's.

As in *Politika*, the official nature of the meeting in *Pobjeda* is symbolized by Đukanović's official suit and tie, by the coat of arms visible in the center above Đukanović and by the flags in the background (Figure 7.4, left). The photograph is taken from a frontal angle, marking social distance. Đukanović is not in the center of the right-hand photograph in Figure 7.4 either, where he is chairing a meeting with religious leaders from Montenegro. The angle of the photograph is oblique and Đukanović is shown from the side, whereas more prominence is given to the religious

Figure 7.4 Đukanović leading meetings (*Pobjeda* left: 28 March 1999; right: 2 April 1999)

leaders whose faces we see from the front. All of the religious leaders are wearing clothes that symbolize the religion they represent. Thus, different religious leaders are united in the meeting and the unifier is Đukanović.

Figure 7.5 provides an example of a photograph in which Milošević is presented as talking to another important politician. The political background is as follows:

Figure 7.5 Milošević with an individual politician, here Rugova (*Politika*, 2 April 1999)

Milošević is presented in a relaxed position, his legs spread apart, his hands casually leaning on his thigh and the chair. The other politician Ibrahim Rugova, the leader of the Democratic League of Kosovo, representing Kosovo, has his hands in his lap; his fingers are intertwined, signaling a closed position. Approximately two-thirds of the photograph is occupied by Milošević, and the remaining third by Rugova. There is also a very small amount of space between Rugova and the right side of the photo – giving an impression of him being hemmed in and having less space to move. The background of this meeting is a luxurious room in *Beli dvor* (the White Palace).[6] The two politicians are looking at one other, smiling – thus expressing positive feelings toward each other and about the results of the meeting they have just had. To turn briefly to the political events that preceded the publication of this photograph, it should be noted that Rugova was the leader of the Kosovo Albanians, who led nonviolent resistance against Milošević's government. There were rumors that Rugova had been killed by the Yugoslav army or police in Kosovo. In order to dismiss these rumors, the photo was published on the front page of *Politika*, together with a statement signed by both Rugova and Milošević. The naturalistic coding gives the photograph a high degree of realistic modality. The photographs, signatures, date and joint statement were used to substantiate the reality of the meeting.

Đukanović is often portrayed in different positions from Milošević. Figure 7.6 is a further example of an oblique angle used by the photographer.

It shows the speaker from the side, more detached from the viewers, and the journalists at the press conference. Even though Đukanović is not in the center of the photo, he is salient because of his position as a speaker/sender of the message in contrast to the many journalists who are positioned as listeners. He is salient because he is closer to the viewer and his white jacket is in contrast to the darker background. Đukanović is portrayed as active because he is standing and talking, and the 'whole world' – represented by the journalists – is listening to him. 'Screamer' headlines overlap in this example as well. The overlapping gives an impression that the text is being spoken by the person in the photo. This photography is self-reflective, showing how the media work in a political context and at the same time positioning Đukanović as 'democratic'.

Figure 7.6 Example of a photograph of Đukanović taken from an oblique angle (*Pobjeda*, 17 April 1999)

Milošević in the personal sphere

The only semi-personal photograph of Milošević was published on 21 April 1999 in connection with a visit by Russian patriarch Aleksey (see Figure 7.7).

It shows Milošević, his wife Mira and their son Marko meeting with Patriarch Aleksey. The family is salient in this photo because the patriarch is portrayed from the back – only his head covering is visible. Milošević, his wife and his son are photographed from the side, the wife is shaking hands with the patriarch and the son is waiting for his turn. Marko, Milošević's son, is also dressed in a suit and his hair is cut short. For those aware of Marko's problematic behavior and his style of dress – as most readers that followed the daily press would have been – his presence in the photograph and his appropriate dress code is a powerful signal of obedience in times of trouble. The importance of this meeting is shown both by these photographs and by the text that appeared as an unusual genre: not 'news' as expected on that particular place on the front page, but a 'report' with elements of a personal story. The official sphere overlaps with the personal sphere. The reason for this was most probably the place and importance that religion was given in the political negotiations. Milošević was said to be one of those leaders who had used religion for his political aims (Veiga, 2004). Because the FRY was in a very difficult position, and Russia was seen as the most important ally of the FRY, Patriarch Aleksey, a religious leader, was a guest who potentially had substantial political influence. He was shown as a representative of the Russian people, carrying an appeal to the orthodox people in the FRY. All of the participants in the photograph look toward the patriarch, offering information to the

Figure 7.7 Example of a semi-personal photograph (*Politika*, 21 April 1999)

viewers; the camera angle is a medium shot, representing social distance (cf. van Leeuwen, 1996), but the motif of this photo has greater emotional potential than other photographs. Motifs of family and church symbolize the main pillars of society in times of crisis (Felberg, 2008).

Đukanović abroad and Milošević at home

Figure 7.8 shows three examples of photographs from Đukanović's series of visits to important foreign political leaders.

Figure 7.8 Đukanović meeting different political leaders (*Pobjeda*, left: 15 May 1999; center: 12 May 1999; right: 10 June 1999)

The common feature in these three photographs is the complementarity between Đukanović and the leaders he is photographed with. This complementarity is shown in Đukanović displaying the same body language as German Chancellor Schröder, in his shaking hands with French president Chirac and in walking down the stairs together with Secretary of State Albright. Complementarity suggests equality – if Đukanović is meeting these important political leaders, the very act of being photographed with them heightens his own importance. Đukanović is portrayed as active, shaking hands, signaling a promise or walking closely together with Albright, signaling agreement after a meeting. The headlines and captions contribute to the viewers' understanding by identifying the participants in the political action.

A change in the positioning of Milošević happened on 3 and 4 June 1999. The news articles published on those two days report on the peace plan that the negotiators Viktor Chernomyrdin and Marti Ahtisaari had brought to Belgrade. Milošević was no longer in the center of the photographs, but rather on one side of the negotiating table (see Figure 7.9).

The parallel position of the two sides indicates equality. There are two sides that are negotiating. On 3 June, Milošević is presented on the right side looking at Chernomyrdin and Ahtisaari and vice versa.

Figure 7.9 Example of a change in position – *Politika,* left: 3 June 1999; right: 4 June 1999

On 4 June, Milošević is photographed from a different angle, putting him in a central position again. This could mean the return to Milošević's more central position, reasserting his leadership role. This is a good example of how perspective can be used to foreground the same motifs differently. The gazes from Milošević and the people from his delegation form vectors that point at Chernomyrdin (see Figure 7.9, right). Even though he is photographed from behind, Chernomyrdin's important position is established by the vectors and the caption under the photograph. Chernomyrdin, being a Russian, is *a priori* accepted as a friend.

Esthetics in photographs in *Politika* and *Pobjeda*

In addition to human participants, there are a number of inanimate elements in the photographs that make up esthetic systems that are characteristic for *Politika* and for *Pobjeda*. Some of these elements have already been mentioned in the analysis: national symbols (flags), flowers, ashtrays, glasses, bottles and the luxurious interiors of *Beli dvor* in Belgrade with stylish tables, chairs, a fireplace and artwork. National symbols and luxury signal power. Most of the elements are presented as symmetrical (such as flowers, glasses and ashtrays on the table): Symmetry in this context signals order and discipline.

The system of esthetics in *Pobjeda* is low-key compared to that of *Politika*. The luxury of *Beli dvor* is replaced with the simplicity of meeting rooms in the Montenegrin parliament. Flowers are rarely shown, and papers and water glasses dominate. Microphones are another element more present in *Pobjeda* than in *Politika*, signaling connection with the audience. Concerning national symbols, the Montenegrin coat of arms is significant because it signals Montenegro's special status and hints at its possible future independence. Even though all of these elements that make up *Pobjeda's* and *Politika's* esthetics are perhaps not consciously noticed by the viewers, they in fact serve to contribute to the construction of political meaning.

Concluding Remarks: Democratic versus Autocratic Identities, Europe and Non-Europe

During the NATO bombing of the FRY, *Politika* was building and maintaining Milošević's identity as a strong leader and defender of the nation vis-à-vis major world powers such as the United States and NATO, whereas *Pobjeda* was building Đukanović's identity primarily in relation to Milošević and stressing the dichotomy of autocracy and democracy (Felberg, 2008). The examples presented in this analysis show connections between the visual representation of the political leaders and the newspapers' self-defined ideology. In *Pobjeda*, the Montenegrin government's ideology was presented as being emphatically democratic. If the term *democracy* is understood to refer to a society that gives space to different voices and opinions, then *Pobjeda's* presentation of Đukanović can be understood as supporting this view. Đukanović was not granted a monopoly on the front pages. Quite the contrary: Two other important politicians, Marojević and Vujanović, were allocated a significant presence. However, the majority of the photographs of Đukanović presented him alone, entrenching him as the default leader in Montenegro. In addition, the fact that Marojević and Vujanović shared Đukanović's political views and can be considered to be the same voice supports the notion that other voices were not given space after all.

In *Politika*, the main ideological focus was on the resistance toward the invasive new world order, which was to be achieved by the West, primarily the United States and its allies. Milošević was given an unquestionable monopoly on the front pages of *Politika*. His photographs were positioned in the most prominent place on the front page – the upper left corner – whereas the varying position of Đukanović's photographs suggested a sharing of important space with others. The strong leadership role of Milošević was illustrated by the type of photographs, the majority of which presented him leading meetings, and the centrality of his position in the photographs. Various domestic and foreign politicians were coming to see him, and not vice versa. In contrast to the presentation of Đukanović's fellow-politicians, none of the politicians who supported Milošević's political views were shown on the front pages in a significant manner.

The activities ascribed to Milošević through the photographs include his presiding over meetings, posing and mostly sitting – which, as a whole, implies a static or stable type of leadership. On the other hand, Đukanović is depicted giving interviews, press conferences, traveling abroad and often standing. This could be interpreted as the active type of leadership often connected with a Western style.

This wide range of semiotic features shows the variety of their functions in building political identities and relations. The various use of semiotic resources can, in this context, be connected to various ideological positions that these two newspapers held at that particular moment in time. *Politika* supported Milošević's government, which was considered by its critics to be an 'old communist regime', whereas *Pobjeda* was trying to build an image of Đukanović as a pro-Western leader. As such, Montenegro was aligned with Europe and the imaginary European rim was drawn between Montenegro and Serbia, primarily using democracy as the main component of a demarcation line.

Notes

1. This analysis is part of a larger research project (Felberg, 2008) which takes into account both linguistic (verbal) and semiotic (visual) resources, and argues that it is the combination and interaction of linguistic and semiotic resources that contribute to creating meaning (Baldry & Thibault, 2006; Kress & van Leeuwen, 1996; van Leeuwen, 2005).
2. *Politika*, the oldest newspaper in the Balkans, was the paper with the strongest influence on public opinion in communist Yugoslavia (Nenadović, 2002). It was under the influence of the ruling Communist Party until the multiparty system was reintroduced in 1990s. Then, *Politika* came under the direct control of Slobodan Milošević. *Politika* was sold in both Serbia and Montenegro. However, during the NATO bombing it was difficult to obtain in Montenegro due to logistic difficulties.
3. *Pobjeda*, the longest-running newspaper in Montenegro, had a strong influence on public opinion, albeit primarily in Montenegro. Like *Politika*, it was under the influence of the ruling Communist Party. After the reintroduction of the multiparty system, it came under the control of Milo Đukanović. *Pobjeda* was sold in Serbia, but at very few locations. It was almost impossible to obtain it in Serbia during the NATO bombing.
4. For a critical view of interpretations of the disintegration of Yugoslavia, see Jović (2001).
5. Cut-out photographs are photographs in which a person is removed from the original photograph and put into a single-color background.
6. *Beli dvor* is known to the readers as a power center. *Beli dvor*, which initially belonged to the Serbian royal family, was seized after World War II and used by Josip Broz Tito, and later by Milošević. All important national and international meetings were held there. *Beli dvor* belongs to the state, but was made available to the heirs of the royal family in 2001.

References

ANEM (1999) Serbia. In P. Goff (ed.) *The Kosovo News and Propaganda War* (pp. 304–344) Vienna: International Press Institute.
Antonić, S. (2002) *Zarobljena zemlja: Srbija za vlade Slobodana Miloševića*. Belgrade: Otkrovenje.
Baldry, A. and Thibault, P.J. (2006) *Multimodal Transcription and Text Analysis*. London, Oakville: Equinox.
Ćurgus, V.K. (ed.) (2003) *Brušenje pameti*. Belgrade: Medijska dokumentacija/Ebart konsalting.
Felberg, T.R. (2008) Brothers in arms? Discourse analysis of Serbian and Montenegrin identities and relations as constructed in *Politika* and *Pobjeda* front-page

articles during the NATO bombing of Yugoslavia in 1999. PhD dissertation, University of Oslo. http://www.duo.uio.no/sok/work.html?WORKID= 82491. Accessed 14 May 2009.

Felberg. T.R. (2009) Putovanje Srbije u Evropu na Đinđićevim metaforama. *Riječ*, Nova serija 1 (Nikšić), 43–60.

Gallagher, T. (2003) Identity in flux, destination unknown: Montenegro during and after the Yugoslav wars. *International Journal of Politics, Culture and Society* 17 (1), 53–71.

Goff, P. (ed.) (1999) *The Kosovo News and Propaganda War*. Vienna: The International Press Institute.

Hemond, F. and Herman, E. (2001) *Degradirana moć, mediji i kosovska kriza*. Belgrade: Plato.

Jović, D. (2001) Razlozi za raspad socijalističke Jugoslavije: kritika postojećih interpretacija. *Reč* 62 (8), 91–157.

Komatina, M. (1999) *Crna Gora i srpsko pitanje, Prilog izučavanju integrativnih i dezintegrativnih tokova*. Belgrade: Zavet.

Kress, G. and van Leeuwen, T. (1996) *Reading Images: The Grammar of Visual Design*. London: Routledge.

Kress, G. and van Leeuwen, T. (1998) Front pages: (The critical) analysis of newspaper layout. In A. Bell and P. Garrett (eds) *Approaches to Media Discourse* (pp. 186–219). Oxford: Blackwell.

Lakić, I. (2005) Diskurs, mediji, rat. PhD dissertation, University of Belgrade.

Matić, G. (2005) *U milosti anđela*. Belgrade: Mediagraf.

Macgilchrist, F. (2009) Imagining Russia: A cultural discourse analysis of news coverage in international media. PhD dissertation, European University Viadrina.

Marović, M. (1999) *Posrtanja "Stare dame": Crna Gora u Politikinom ogledalu mart 1997–januar 1998*. Podgorica: Kulturno-prosvjetna zajednica Podgorice.

Marović, M. (2002) *Politika i politika*. Belgrade: Helsinški odbor za ljudska prava u Srbiji.

Mojzes, P. (1994) *Yugoslavian Inferno*. New York: Continuum.

Nenadović, A. (2002) Politika u nacionalističkoj oluji. In N. Popov (ed.). *Srpska strana rata: Trauma i katarza u istorijskom pamćenju* (pp. 151–177). Belgrade: Samizdat FreeB92.

Nohrstedt, S.A., Höijer, B., and Ottosen, R. (2002) *Kosovokonflikten, medierna och medlidanhet*. Stockholm: Styrelsen för psykologisk försvar.

Nohrstedt, S.A., Kaitatzi-Whitlock, S., Ottosen, R., and Riegert, K. (2000) From the Persian Gulf to Kosovo – war journalism and propaganda, *European Journal of Communication* 15 (3), 383–404.

Ottosen, R. (2002) *Avisbildet av NATOs krigføring på Balkan; Norske avisers dekning av Kosovokrigen i 1999*. Oslo: Høgskolen i Oslo, Avdeling for journalistikk, bibliotek- og informasjonsfag.

Petrović, D. and Stanković, V. (2006) *Zajednička država Crna Gora*. Belgrade: Institut za političke studije.

Roberts, E. (2007) *Realm of the Black Mountain, A History of Montenegro*. London: Hurst & Company.

van Leeuwen, T. (2005) *Introducing Social Semiotics*. New York: Routledge.

Veiga, F. (2004) *Sloba – nedovršena biografija Slobodana Miloševića*. Belgrade: Naučna knjiga.

Chapter 8
Krekism and the Construction of Slovenian National Identity: Newspaper Commentaries on Slovenia's European Union Integration

Andreja Vezovnik

Introduction

This chapter explores the discursive construction of Slovenian national identity during Slovenia's EU integration process. It focuses on the period from January 2001 to December 2003, when public discussion on joining the European Union was at a peak. The texts analyzed here come from a more general body of texts (about 550) selected on the basis of three key words: *European Union*, *Europe* and *Slovenia*. These texts were initially selected for a quantitative analysis, but the results presented here are based on a qualitative analysis known as critical discourse analysis. For this analysis, the corpus was narrowed to the most relevant texts focusing on Slovenian national, cultural and political identities. Approximately 200 opinion articles, editorials, commentaries and columns from daily and weekly newspapers and political magazines were taken into consideration. The analysis includes all serious (i.e. not sensationalist or tabloid) Slovenian printed news[1] published in the specified period. This included both right- and left-wing oriented press. Generally, the press could be attributed to one or another political option; for instance, *Mag*, *Demokracija* and *Družina* could be categorized as right wing or more conservative, and *Mladina*, *Primorske novice*, *Dnevnik* and *Delo* as more left-wing press. However, there is a slight problem in categorizing the press under one or the other political option because often a generally left-leaning newspaper or magazine gives space to a right-leaning commentator and the other way around. Therefore, this chapter focuses instead on the production of meaning of discourses in general, rather than dealing with their belonging to one political option or another.

The majority of texts discussed the positioning of Slovenian identity toward Europe. With the dissolution of Yugoslavia's 'socialist utopia' in 1991, a conflict arose between Slovenian inclinations toward a parliamentary democratic system and the Serbian centralist and unitary model. This culminated in a brief military conflict between Slovenia and the Yugoslav People's Army, resulting in a Slovenian need for a new national identity different from its previous 'Balkan'[2] identity. Slovenia's secession from Yugoslavia and the breaking of ties with the 'Balkans' reflected Slovenia's reorientation toward a 'European' ethos. Laclau (1990: 50) states that in such periods, when a sociopolitical structure becomes dislocated, a contingent rearticulation of hegemonic positions may occur because the dislocated structure is an open structure in which the crisis can be resolved in the most varied of directions. However, even if an open structure does not theoretically bear in itself the conditions for possible future rearticulations, this analysis demonstrates that in the case of Slovenia, new articulations actually ushered in old discursive constructions on Slovenian national identity. Therefore, the construction of a 'new' Slovenian identity was a multilevel discursive process closely bound to Slovenia's relation to western Europe in its pre-communist period. Consequently, an intertextual perspective is introduced in order to demonstrate how discourses that construct contemporary identity are structured.

This chapter generally follows Fairclough's definition of intertextuality, which states that intertextuality is 'the property texts have of being full of snatches of other texts, which may be explicitly demarcated or merged in, and in which the text may assimilate, contradict, ironically echo, and so forth' (Fairclough, 1992: 84). It applies the notion of intertextuality, understanding it primarily in terms of Fairclough's interdiscursivity. This implies an interest not only in identifying linguistic properties of texts but also in ascribing them meaning that can be interpreted. In this sense, linguistic features are more likely to be understood at a more general level of discourse.

This analysis therefore explores the rearticulation of discourses on Slovenian national identity considering two different periods. It explores how the construction of Slovenian national identity starting in the nineteenth century – when the constitution of Slovenian identity was strongly connected with the establishment of modern European states and strongly bound to the Christian Socialist movement called Krekism (Sln. *krekovstvo*) – influenced the construction of national identity during the EU integration process, when Slovenia again related its identity to 'Europe'.

Historical Context

The most important period for the constitution of Slovenian national identity was the Slovenian national awakening, which occurred between 1848 and 1918. Although numerous Slovenian cultural, political and financial institutions were founded during this period, the formation of

Slovenian national identity was far from being autonomous. Instead, it occurred under the powerful influence of the Austro-Hungarian Empire, which at that time was Europe's strongest political, military, cultural and strategic center. As a consequence, Slovenia was seen as a rather marginal and unimportant part of the empire, mostly because of its small territory, economic dependence and predominantly rural population.

However, at the end of nineteenth century the Slovenian political scene also slowly began to coalesce. Although Slovenia was still part of the Austro-Hungarian Monarchy and subject to waxing German nationalism, the modifications to the Austro-Hungarian electoral system that developed after the end of Count Eduard Taaffe's government in 1893 worked in favor of two Slovenian political parties – one clerical and the other liberal. These parties consequently made their way into the political scene and began to shape the social and cultural character of Slovenia (Gestrin & Melik, 1979: 541–548, 560–561; Vodopivec, 2006: 111–115). Prior to World War I, Janez Evangelist Krek, the leader of the conservative Christian Socialist Party and the founder of the movement known as Krekism, was the leading politician among rural Slovenians (who represented about 70% of the entire Slovenian population between 1890 and 1910). The Christian Socialist Party focused on resolving the ongoing agrarian crisis by vigorously opposing the development of capitalism and liberalism. 'All devoted and reasonable Christians agree that individualistic and disunifying liberalism is to be blamed for social disorder. Fighting against this liberalism is our holy duty' (Krek, 1895: 168). Krek's sociopolitical program was strongly based on Catholic values and promoted the rural ethos (Gestrin & Melik, 1979: 561–568; Vodopivec, 2006: 115). At the same time, Krekism expressed devotion to the Austro-Hungarian Monarchy, convinced that the monarchy was the only regime that could protect the country from capitalism and preserve the agrarian Catholic population. '[It is] in the country's best interest to choose the monarchy, where only one hereditary sovereign is in charge that is supported by autonomous parishes, provinces, nations, and classes. The monarch can best guarantee peace and order in the country' (Krek, 1925: 193).

At a time when modern European states were being constructed – when the bourgeoisie should have been playing an active and crucial role, and when Slovenia should have been going through a modernization process – Slovenia's proto-bourgeois ethos remained strong and was promoted by Krekism as the leading movement. Žižek (1981–1982, 1984, 1987) therefore claims that Slovenia never completed the modernization process. The main problem was the underdevelopment of the Slovenian bourgeoisie, which was hampered by its lack of access to sources of capital. Consequently, Slovenia is frequently perceived as a nation of peasants that never really went through the process of modernization in a way that other European countries did – that is, through the constitution of the liberal bourgeois class. According to Žižek, a nation that is founded on a pre-modern ethos is only a 'half-nation' because it denies the basic principle of the nation – its foundation on the bourgeois demand for its own independent nationality. Because the liberal bourgeoisie lacked the strength to spearhead the establishment of Slovenia as a modern nation, there was a reaffirmation of pre-modern social relations. In contrast, Christian Socialism did not demand independent nationality, but instead emphasized submissive relations toward the Austro-Hungarian Empire. 'In the Habsburg kinship [*rodbina*] that leads Austria, we have a special protection of all the oppressed and the best preservation of justice. Therefore we emphasize that in our fight for social renovation we always wish to remain loyal Austrians and devoted subjects of the House of Habsburg' (Krek, 1895: 247). Consequently, the Slovenians were always perceived within a supranational totality (Žižek, 1984: 158).

After the collapse of the Austro-Hungarian Monarchy in 1918, the Slovenians initially joined the State of the Slovenes, Croats and Serbs, which during the following decades gave way to the Kingdom of the Serbs, Croats and Slovenes, then the Kingdom of Yugoslavia and then communist Yugoslavia after World War II. During the communist period, the state's pillars were the Communist Party, the army and the secret police (Pirjevec, 1995: 155), and obviously the Christian ethos was not in the party's interest.

Despite the communist repression of the Catholic ethos, the discourse of Krekism reemerged during the years when Slovenia prepared to join the European Union. The reinvention of Slovenian national identity consisted in differentiating Slovenia from the Balkans and in constructing its identity in relation to Europe. After the communist period, the rearticulated discourse of Krekism reemerged as the common denominator of the 'old/new' – but above all 'authentic' – Slovenian identity.

After a brief presentation of the construction of Slovenian identity in relation to 'Europe' and the 'Balkans', the chapter explains those elements of Krekist discourse that played an active role in the construction of Slovenian national identity during the European integration process.

Back to 'Europe'

Patterson (2003: 110, 114) states that since 1991, Slovenians have not regarded their country as Balkan, but may think of their land as belonging to 'Europe', and have affirmed an identity grounded in traditions understood to be 'Western', and not 'Balkan'. Similarly, Bakic-Hayden states that 'the implication is that the "real" identity of persons or groups is to be found in the pre-Yugoslav past.... What constitutes "real" identity in this context and is most often invoked ... are the religious/cultural "essences"' (Bakic-Hayden, 1995: 923). Taking into consideration examples from the

Slovenian press, the search for a 'European' identity might be exemplified in discursive and linguistic features concerning spatial (example 1), historical (examples 2 and 3), religious (examples 4 and 5) and cultural (example 6) dimensions:

> (1) First of all we should realize that we don't need to shove our way into Europe because we're already in it – and almost at its center, at that. (Najprej se je treba zavedati, da nam ni treba riniti v Evropo, ker v njej smo že, in to skoraj v njenem središču samem. *Primorske novice*, 7 February 2003)

Emphasizing Slovenia's geographical position legitimizes the Slovenian cultural and political aspiration in joining the European Union. The centrality of Slovenia's spatial position is metaphorically connected with its 'European' identity.

In addition to spatial metaphors, historical facts were found to be substantial for a reconstruction of Slovenian identity as a European one. In examples (2) and (3), the 'historical we' operates as a linguistic feature that refers to the collective history of the Slovenian nation:

> (2) ... we are forgetting that Slovenians lived in Europe long before. (... pozabljamo, da smo Slovenci že zdavnaj stanovali v Evropi. *Večer*, 24 October 2002)

> (3) From the days of Carantania, Trubar, the spring of nations in the mid-nineteenth century, the antifascist resistance in the mid-twentieth century, and the war of independence at the end of the twentieth century, it is clear that we are at home in the EU, although we never moved. (Od Karantanije, Trubarja, Pomladi narodov sredi devetnajstega, antifašističnega boja sredi dvajsetega in osvobodilne vojne koncem dvajsetega stoletja je jasno, da smo doma v EU, ne da bi se kaj prida selili. *Delavska enotnost*, 20 March 2003)

In these cases, 'we' includes the speaker, the addressee and other people who are not present. In order to construct an extended imagined 'we', the author refers to Slovenian people and combatants long dead, to whom the writer simply adds several people from the audience with Slovenian citizenship as well as other Slovenians who are absent and could be either alive or dead (Wodak *et al.*, 1999: 46).

In addition, religious arguments have been common, especially in the Catholic conservative press, which claims the importance of a shared religious identity in European unity:

> (4) Even today the European soul is united. In addition to its common origins, it also has the same Christian and human values. (Tudi v naših dneh ostaja evropska duša enotna. Poleg skupnega izvora ima tudi iste krščanske in človeške vrednote. *Družina*, 11 August 2002)

(5) ... but we have been in Europe for 1,200 years, ever since we have been Christians. (... saj smo v Evropi že 1200 let, odkar smo kristjani. *Družina*, 30 November 2003)

Example (4) uses religious rhetoric to connote Europe's spiritual unity, and the argument in (5) is a generalization that Christianity equals Europe, Slovenia equals Christianity and therefore Slovenia equals Europe.

Similarly, the argument for Slovenian integration into the EU and NATO is legitimized by presupposed facts about its historical and cultural essence:

(6) I think we are wasting far too much energy on debates over whether we should join the basic organizations of the Western world, to which we clearly belong historically and culturally. (Menim, da izgubljamo veliko preveč energije z razpravami o tem, ali naj se pridružimo osnovnim organizacijam zahodnega sveta, kamor zgodovinsko in kulturno nedvomno sodimo. *Delo*, 1 February 2002)

The construction of every collective identity (ultimately impossible) can be attempted only through a process of identification with socially available discursive constructions (Stavrakakis, 1999: 36). However, in addition to relating to similarities, identities are primarily constructed through differences – through relations to what one is not. Therefore, subjects can identify themselves as such because they can differentiate themselves from the 'others'. Slovenians perceive themselves as Slovenians only because they know they are not Italian or Austrian – but above all because they are not 'Balkan'. Derrida (2004: 130) claims that identity construction is always based on excluding something and establishing a violent hierarchy between the two resulting poles; Slovenian and Balkan discourses frequently result in negative stereotypes of the Other. Todorova (1997: 3) states that at the beginning of the 20th century, 'Europe' created its Other – the Balkans. Consequently, the Balkans were no longer seen only as a geographical region, but became a synonym for things tribal, backwards, primitive and barbarian. The Balkans became the 'other Europe'. As example (7) demonstrates, identifying Slovenia as European therefore also required opposing Slovenian identity toward Europe's Other – that is, the 'Balkans'.

(7) Just a few more days and everything will be over: successful referendums will push us Slovenians into another world, where we will breathe freely among other (equal) European nations and where our Balkan adventures will be just a recollection of memories (of extortions, wars, murders, assassinations, etc.). This will be an exceptional historic leap. (Še nekaj dni in vsega bo konec: uspešna referenduma bosta nas Slovence potisnila v drug svet, kjer bomo svobodno zadihali med [enakopravnimi] evropskimi narodi in kjer bo

ostal le še spomin na naše balkanske dogodivščine [na izsiljevanja, vojne, umore, atentate itd.]. To bo izjemen zgodovinski preskok. *Mag*, 19 March 2003)

After the dissolution of Yugoslavia, the concept of ideological uniformity on which communist Yugoslavia had been built could no longer be the common denominator. All that remained were the differences: cultural, linguistic, religious and economic. All the overlapping of territories, languages or customs were neglected or even denied. Slovenia began to differentiate itself from the rest of Yugoslavia by defining its national character as more European (i.e. more progressive, prosperous, hard-working, tolerant and democratic) than the ostensibly primitive, lazy and intolerant Balkans (Bakic-Hayden & Hayden, 1992: 8, 15). As Šarić (2004) determined, the Slovenian press avoids self-designations based on the word *Balkans*. This term has a negative connotation and is understood not only geographically but above all politically. The Balkans are brought into a relationship with crime and danger. 'Discussing the barbarity of the Balkans and the need for intervention helped create a sense of common identity and purpose in the European Union' (Šarić, 2004: 391).

However, further analysis shows that this impression of Slovenian identity is highly related to and marked by the ideological discourse of Krekism. In many ways, Krekism determined the relation of Slovenians to the universal symbolic field – that is, 'Western-Christian culture' (Žižek, 1987: 34–35) and 'Europe' in general. The next section explores how Krekist discourse was still present in commentaries on the EU integration process.

The Rearticulation of Krekist Discourse

Discourse of belonging

Having always been part of more powerful supranational structures (such as the Austro-Hungarian Empire and Yugoslavia), Slovenian national identity is commonly associated with smallness, marginality and provincialism. Musek (1994: 173–174) explains that Slovenians feel like children who are shaped by foreign influences. Therefore, the concept of the Other and alienation has a powerful presence in Slovenian cultural history and can frequently be found in Krekism. 'There is a stranger among us who is grazing and fattening, the Slovenian man has nothing – he leaves his country and moves all around the world to the detriment of his country and himself, in time and forever' (Krek, 1933: 33). Even Ivan Cankar, the most notable Slovenian writer from Krek's period and his political opponent, frequently addressed the dualism between the particularity of belonging (or ties to home) and the universality of alien erudition (e.g. Pirjevec, 1964; Žižek, 1987: 35). For Pirjevec, this duality poses difficulties for the identification of Slovenians with their nation because their identity is split between the two options. Cankar's characters are therefore frequently torn between the desire to visit and live in fascinating foreign lands, and by their guilt toward their homes, symbolized by the guilt they feel toward their abandoned mothers (Pirjevec, 1964). In Slovenian imagery, the symbol of the mother has a powerful presence. Musek (1994: 170–171) explains this symbolism through the absence of men in Slovenian families, especially in the nineteenth century. The main reasons for this male absence were military service, seasonal jobs and emigration, but a crucial role was played by the strong agrarian and rural ethos that delayed development of the bourgeoisie. Agrarian and rural cultures are typically more traditional and bound to feminine ideals.

However, the symbol of the mother in Cankar's novels can be interpreted at a more general level and seen as analogous to Slovenians' relation to their homeland. Cankar's complex of the mother is explained by Pirjevec (1964: 437) in psychoanalytic terms. He claims that one characteristic of Cankar is that his character's superego is not impersonated by the father, but instead by the mother. For Cankar, the mother is the supreme ethical principle and a symbol of liability and debt. However, if the basis of the superego is the mother instead of the father, this means that the father's superego, which is supposed to prevent incest between the child and its mother and open the particular toward the universal, actually fails. Consequently, the subject as such tends to close itself within the circle of home, but the superego acts as a traumatic break that forces the subject to distance itself from particularity (Žižek, 1982: 245–246). In other words, the Other appears as an external trauma to belonging, and therefore the crucial moment is when the subject identifies itself with what at first appeared as negativity. Once the subject has identified with the Other, he or she no longer experiences the Other as an external negative force, but the Other becomes the subject's position *par excellence*. Consequently, the identification with 'belonging' should no longer be possible. Therefore, Žižek (1982: 38) argues that Cankar's character of the mother is actually a symptom of suppressed resignation to the winning universality of law. The mother becomes embodied belonging, and as a consequence she becomes the bearer of God's name – that is, the bearer of the universal Law. 'The mother as the basis of the superego is . . . always a reaction formation to the fact that the Subject was unable to identify itself with the Other, so that he or she could carry out the transition to Universality' (Žižek, 1987: 247).

Following interpretations written by Žižek and Pirjevec, Cankar's descriptions of love for his mother symbolizes Slovenians' patriotic love for their original nation, manifested in the particularity and belonging that can be found in discourses of Krekism. However, this is not simply an arbitrary national problem; it is the problem of a small serf-like nation constantly threatened by other nations. Because of specific historical facts – for example, the economic and cultural weakness of Slovenians vis-à-vis the penetration of German capital – at the crucial moment of national identity formation, the prevailing ideological perspective perceived developing capitalism as a threat to the nation through the loss of rural rootedness. Therefore, the image of the diligent, hard-working and God-fearing peasant arose with the founding of the notion of Slovenian character (*slovenstvo*). The purest example of such an ethos is found in the discourse of Krekism (Žižek, 1982: 248–249), which was rearticulated in the period analyzed.

One of the most frequent linguistic features supporting the discourse of belonging versus the Other is the anthropomorphic metaphor (or personification) that constructs Europe as an entity representing a threat to the frailty of Slovenia. Anthropomorphic metaphors share the ability to give meaning to phenomena in a humanized form, and personifications possess high suggestive force. Regarding the mental construct of a nation, these metaphors also imply intranational uniformity and equality. Moreover, the vividness of such metaphors promotes identification of their addressees with that of the personified collective subjects (Wodak *et al.*, 1999: 44). They also enable speakers to dissolve individuals, and hence volition and responsibility, or to keep individuals in the semantic background. Abstract entities – for example, nations – are given a human form through personification (de Cillia *et al.*, 1999: 165), as demonstrated in (8):

> (8) I know and I understand that we are frightened of big partners that will overwhelm and 'consume' us. Will we be able to survive in the open world and preserve our Slovenian identity? (Vem in razumem, da nas je strah. Ali nas ne bodo veliki partnerji preplavili in 'pojedli'? Ali bomo sposobni preživeti v odprtem svetu in ohraniti svojo slovensko samobitnost? *Delo*, 1 February 2003)

The relation to Europe is bound to the Slovenian perception of Europe as alien and threatening. Europe is given a personified form, creating a heightened feeling of threat. As example (8) showed, Slovenia's main problem in relation to Europe seems to be the fear of losing sovereignty and national identity because of geographical smallness. Example (9) uses a marriage metaphor, which can also be related to an anthropomorphic view (cf. Musolff, 2004):

> (9) It is similar to envisioning sovereignty like a bride that is given away at the altar of the common European state. (Podobno je z merjenjem suverenosti in njenega oddajanja na oltar skupne evropske države. *Nedelo*, 6 May 2001)

Here, Slovenia is personified as a bride that is given away to the EU. Slovenia has a passive position, as though there is no possibility for initiative or action. The connotative meaning of marriage is obvious – the bride as a passive subject must be given away by her father in order to be validated by universal law, but at the same time she loses her independence and must henceforth serve her husband. Accepting universal law therefore implies relinquishing national sovereignty.

However, the distinction between Slovenia and 'Europe' is expressed not only through metaphors but also in most cases through the dichotomy between 'us' and 'them', which has a strong presence in newspaper commentaries, especially when they relate to national sovereignty versus European domination. *We* is used to indicate sameness and can be applied effectively in the service of 'linguistic imperialism' (Wodak *et al.*, 1999: 45). The author of a text can unite an audience 'into a single interest group by replacing differences in origin, confession, class and life-style with a simple "we"' (de Cillia *et al.*, 1999: 164). Slovenia's history of foreign dominance became topical during the EU integration process. Despite the pro-European element in Slovenia's position (just as during Krekism), there is also an accompanying fear of the foreign. Slovenia's relation to foreign countries today is therefore still presented as a threat to financial and economic sovereignty, as illustrated in (10):

> (10) We struggle against foreign capital like the devil struggles against lice. We would prefer to be the master of our own little field – the Slovenian way! – rather than offering our services to a soulless foreigner. (Tujega kapitala se otepamo kot hudič uši. Raje smo gospodarji na svoji njivici – Slovenska smer! – kot da bi se udinjali brezdušnemu tujcu. *Mladina*, 26 February 2001)

The pronoun *we* is used to create the idea of a large and cohesive community. The connotation of *little field* implies a small territory populated by peasants. The expression *the Slovenian way* shows the intention of presenting a common goal or modus operandi, or even acting by taking tradition into account.

Differentiating 'us' from 'them' can also be seen in the use of possessive pronouns such as *our* in (11) and (12):

> (11) You do not have to be a financial expert to see the fatal danger of selling off our banks... to foreign capital. (Ni treba biti ravno finančni strokovnjak, da bi dognali, da usodno nevarnost razprodaje naših bank... tujemu kapitalu. *Delo*, 1 December 2001)

> (12) In the proverbial servitude of our nation, my optimism is even less. Europe will not do Slovenia any favors on its own accord. We'll have to fight for our own rights... We'll even have to respect and protect our own language, and we'll have to know, promote, and be proud of our own culture. (Ob pregovornem hlapčevstvu slovenskega značaja se moj optimizem še zmanjša. Evropa sama od sebe Sloveniji

ne bo nič poklonila. Pravice si bomo morali sami izbojevati... Tudi svoj jezik bomo morali sami spoštovati in sami zaščititi, svojo kulturo pa sami poznati, promovirati in biti najprej sami nanjo ponosni. *Primorske novice*, 7 February 2003)

This example is full of possessive pronouns showing the exclusiveness of Slovenian culture and language – the two most important symbols of Slovenian national identity. Dolar (2003: 21) argues that Slovenian national identity is especially bound to Slovenian culture. During the last millennium, Slovenian identity has survived because of its relation to culture, and not because of its political, economic or military power. Culture was a substitute for more conventional sources of power that were more typical of 'large' European nations. Finally, the noun *protection* implicitly presupposes (cf. Fairclough, 1992) that Slovenia is threatened by something harmful or alien.

As the examples show, Slovenian identity is constructed in relation to Europe as the threatening Other. The fear of being dominated and losing sovereignty is substantiated by reference to historical facts before 1918 – although there were several periods of active, even military, resistance against occupying forces that were not made a subject of Slovenian identification because they were connected with communism. Fearing domination is therefore connected to the period of Krekism and the Austro-Hungarian Monarchy, and is rearticulated today as an essential part of Slovenian national identity.

Slovenians as hard-working, diligent and efficient

'The main values promoted in Krekist discourse are hard work, piety, modesty, frugality and efficiency. Krek (1895: 225) described the ideal farmer as follows: 'Ten years ago a very talented and diligent farmer in a certain Upper Carniolan valley... kept note of all his income and expenses... he mostly worked alone with the help of his wife. He did not waste anything, and only from time to time allowed himself a glass of wine' (Krek, 1895: 225). Whereas the Protestant bourgeois values of efficacy and economizing serve to accumulate capital, Krekism glorified the cult of the work as a ritual characteristic of a proto-bourgeoisie ethos (Žižek, 1981–1982). Labor is a man's obligation because only hard work can atone for man's sins: 'Work, pray, and live!' (Krek, 1993: 208). Commentaries frequently describe Slovenian identity as 'a God-fearing and obedient domain of "ora et labora"' (Bogaboječa in ubogljiva provinca 'ora et labora'. *Nedelo*, 6 May 2001).

Being a diligent and a hard worker therefore means being faithful to the sovereign and honoring God – similar to the relation between Slovenia and Europe. As example (13) shows, Europe frequently appeared in anthropomorphic metaphors of a pupil–teacher relationship used to symbolize the relation between Slovenia and the EU:

> (13) In recent years of preparation to enter the EU, Slovenia has demonstrated that it is the most diligent pupil in the class. (Slovenija se je v zadnjih letih v pripravah na sprejem v Evropsko skupnost izkazala kot 'najbolj pridna učenka v razredu'. *Večer*, 29 December 2001)

In such anthropomorphic metaphors, Slovenia always performs the role of a good student and the EU is represented as its teacher. Europe is constructed as an authority toward which Slovenia has a dual relationship. On the one hand, Europe is seen as a threat, but on the other hand, Europe is also constructed as an ideal to attain, as in example (14):

> (14) I believe that we have to...join all the organizations that want to accept us under equal conditions – from the European Union to NATO...if the rich and more powerful invite us to their table, we should thank them and sit down.... cooperating with the rich and more powerful, who also have more knowledge and experience, can help us. (Menim, da se moramo...pridružiti vsem organizacijam, kamor so nas pripravljeni pod enakimi pogoji sprejeti – od Evropske Unije preko NATA...če nas povabijo k svoji mizi bogati in močnejši, se zahvalimo in prisedemo.... sodelovanje z bogatimi in močnejšimi, ki imajo tudi več znanja in izkušenj, nam bo koristilo. *Delo*, 1 February 2003)

However, in order to attain the ideal of this well-developed Europe, Slovenia should work hard. Example (15) shows that Slovenians continue to view themselves as hard-working, obedient and efficient:

> (15) We hard-working Slovenians are the first and only ones among the candidate countries that have managed to establish a common agricultural policy system. (Mi pridni Slovenci pa smo prvi in verjetno še vedno edini med kandidatkami, ki smo vzpostavili sistem skupne kmetijske politike. *Finance*, 28 October 2003)

Slovenians as a nation of servants

However, the line between hard-working diligence and servility is very thin. Servility can be explained as a negative radicalization of a fundamentally positive characteristic. The claim that Slovenians are a nation of servants is derived from Cankar's critique of Krekism. Cankar viewed the Slovenians as incapable of free historical action and creating their own destiny. According to Cankar's plays and novels, the Slovenians missed this opportunity during the Counter-Reformation. As a consequence, Cankar referred to the Slovenians as servants. Because the Slovenians did not manage to take their own destiny into their hands, they never really became a nation and were relegated to serving an alien power (Pirjevec, 1968). In his play *Hlapci* (Servants), Cankar criticizes Catholicism, saying that during the Counter-Reformation the majority of honest people were killed or escaped from Slovenia. The ones that remained obviously sympathized with Catholicism, and Cankar referred to them as a 'stinking mob' (Cankar, 1994: 33). Further on in the play, he replaces the 'stinking mob' with 'servants': 'Servants! Born to be servants, raised to be servants, created for servility! The masters are changing, but the whip stays forever, because backs are bent, used to and in need of the whip' (Cankar, 1994: 56). When Cankar refers to changing masters, he means that the Slovenian nation was never independent, but always willing to be subjected to other supranational centers, as the following example shows:

> (16) Therefore: even if strangers start running things. That is still better than our political opponents gaining power over us. (Torej: tudi če tujci zagospodarijo pri nas. Še vedno je to bolje, kot da nam gospodarijo naši domači politični nasprotniki. *Delo*, 1 December 2001)

The connection between servility and sovereignty is also demonstrated in (17):

> (17) The Slovenians are a nation of servants. By gaining independence, we essentially rid ourselves of this stigma.... Moreover, they even planted the idea in our heads that the Slovenians were never able to stand up for themselves; that after the First World War we were liberated by the Serbs. (Slovenci narod hlapcev. Z osamosvojitvijo smo se te oznake bolj ali manj znebili.... Poleg tega so nam vcepljali v glavo, da se Slovenci nikoli nismo znali pošteno postaviti zase in da so nas po prvi svetovni vojni osvobodili praktično Srbi. *Demokracija*, 6 November 2003)

Cankar's reference to the Slovenians as a nation of servants remained an important signifier for constructing Slovenian identity and national self-identification. When commentators refer to the Slovenians as servants, they usually try to signify the Slovenians' subordinate position toward Europe or the Balkans, as in (17).

Other examples of constructing this Slovenian servant identity can be found in explicit cases of referring to the Slovenians as servants, as in example (18) – or as in (19), in which the naming is more implicit, merely listing several characteristics commonly connected with servility:

> (18) Servants on their way to Babylon. (Hlapci na poti v Babilon. *Primorske novice*, 29 March 2003)

(19) It will not be hard for Slovenians to become accustomed to new circumstances: once we had party commissars, now we have European commissioners. We are somehow used to dictatorships... but all those years we have showed that Slovenians manage very well under all circumstances. (Slovencem pa se na nove razmere niti ne bo tako težko privaditi: nekoč smo imeli partijske komisarje, sedaj imamo evropske komisarje. Nekako smo tudi navajeni na diktat... toda že nekajkrat smo pokazali, da se Slovenci v vseh razmerah dobro znajdemo. *Večer*, 1 October 2001)

In (19), the author presents all of Slovenian history and the EU as being under various dictatorships. The author therefore deterministically seeks to naturalize the servant position of the Slovenians, as if no other option had ever occurred (e.g. resistance to foreign powers during war) and, consequently, servility will remain the only option.

Masochistic internalization

It is also interesting to explore how the discursive construction of the Slovenians defined as a nation of servants was subsequently managed. Žižek (1987: 30) provides an interesting explanation. He says that the Christian Socialist conception of the Slovenian nation is actually the masochistic 'introjection' of the conflict between Slovenia and its dominator. Instead of extroverting the aggressive energy, it is introjected. Characteristic of Krekist discourse are lamentations about Slovenia's sad destiny, and complaints about the Slovenians being suppressed by foreign capital that exploits Slovenian workers and takes land away from the Slovenian peasants, who are always portrayed as suffering victims (see Krek, 1895). However, this victimization discourse is not transformed into increased national consciousness or aggression toward the oppressors, but into a masochistic internalization of the problem, as the following example shows:

(20) The European public has placed us at the tail end of all the candidates for entering the EU, among the most unpopular. As a matter of fact, we should not be surprised that Europe does not care for us. (Evropska javnost nas je spet uvrstila na začelje med vsemi kandidatkami za vstop v Evropsko unijo, med najmanj priljubljene države. Pravzaprav se ne bi smeli čuditi, da nas Evropa ne mara. *Tednik Ptuj*, 10 May 2001)

Žižek (1984: 159) argues that the Christian Socialist conception of Slovenians never calls for an aggressive reaction or active resistance toward the enemy. However, the source of the problem becomes internalized because the Slovenians and their weaknesses were the reason that the enemy was able to enter the system. Therefore, the solution lies mainly in hard work, parsimony and Christian patience. The solution is not in resisting the Other, but in an inner change in the subject. Finally, example (21) illustrates this masochistic internalization:

> (21) Slovenia...will just have to beautify and improve herself. (Slovenija...le polepšat in izboljšat se mora. *Slovenska panorama*, 23 July 2003)

This means that the subject must be and remain docile, hard-working, obedient and submissive toward the master that holds the authority.

Conclusion

Slovenia has experienced significant historical changes in the past 100 years – from being part of the Austro-Hungarian Empire, then Yugoslavia, to an independent state in 1991 and finally an EU member state in 2004. During the post-Yugoslav period, Slovenian national identity could no longer be associated with its communist Yugoslav past, so a 'new' process of identification based on the rearticulation of the pre-communist discourses occurred. An interdiscursive perspective was adopted in this analysis to demonstrate the analogy between the discourse of Krekism and its rearticulation during Slovenian integration into the EU. The main characteristics of the 'original' Krekist discourse promoting belonging, submissiveness and servility toward 'Europe' were summarized, and it was shown how influential the ideological notions of Krekist discourse were in the identification process while Slovenia prepared to enter the EU.

However, in addition to the Krekist discourse, another discourse was present, closely connected with the first one. This is based on the constructions of differences between Slovenia and its Others – the 'Balkans' and communism. Therefore, Slovenian national identity found itself trapped between submission to a threatening 'Europe' and the process of othering the 'Balkans'. It somehow found itself in the symbolic transition exemplified in one of the headlines: *Identity from the Balkans to Europe* (Identiteta od Balkana do Evrope. *Mag* 26 March 2003), or expanded in the following example:

> (22) Slovenia has a great historic opportunity on 1 May 2004 to finally renounce its communist roots, which extend deeply into times before 1991.... Joining the Union represents a unique opportunity to break with the ruined Yugoslav mentality forever.... Starting on 1 May 2004, when it joins the EU, Slovenia will have the opportunity to unconditionally reject the pernicious Balkan habit of inflation and to accept the basic economic rules of the Western world.... At the same time, this day will be a great defeat for all Yugo-nostalgics that

cannot or do not want to cut their Balkan umbilical cord connecting them to the communist heritage of the ruined Yugoslavia. (Slovenija ima veliko zgodovinsko priložnost, da se 1. maja 2004 dokončno odreče svojim komunističnim koreninam, ki sežejo globoko v čas pred letom 1991... Priključitev Uniji pomeni enkratno priložnost, da za večno prekinemo s propadlo jugoslovansko miselnostjo... Slovenija bo s prvim majem 2004 in pridružitvijo EU dobila tudi priložnost, da se nepreklicno odreče pogubni balkanski inflacijski navadi in sprejme temeljno ekonomsko pravilo zahodnega sveta... Hkrati bo ta dan velik poraz za vse jugonostalgike, ki ne morejo in nočejo pretrgati svoje balkanske popkovine s komunistično dediščino propadle Jugoslavije. *Mag*, 27 November 2002)

Clearly, the universality of 'Europe' stands opposed to communism and the 'Balkans', stylized as a system of values in which communism is not included. The myth of Europe is a bright narrative of values such as freedom, democracy, welfare, solidarity, modernization and, above all, high culture (Puntscher Riekmann, 1997: 64). However, in order to make a claim for the European character of Slovenian identity, the roots for its reconstruction had to be found in Slovenia's relation to Europe before the communist era:

(23) Havel said that Communism was a period of lies in which identity could not be established. (Havel je čas komunizma označil kot čas laži, v katerem se identiteta ni mogla vzpostavljati. *Mag*, 26 March 2003).

Although, on the one hand, Slovenia certainly identified itself with Europe to the point that it also adopted the construction of the 'Balkans' as 'Europe's other', on the other hand, discourses on Slovenian belonging, servility and diligence toward Europe showed that Europe was also constructed as an authority to be followed, with all of its constructed characteristics listed above. Therefore, as Salecl (1994: 226) points out, 'A return to Christian values, the family, the "right to life" and so forth, is presented as a rebellion against immoral real socialist authority which, in the name of the concept of communism, permits all sorts of state invention into the privacy of the citizen.' The idea of preserving privacy could probably explain the contradicting nature of discourses relating to the relationship between Slovenia and 'Europe'. There is a strong identification with supposed European values that help distance Slovenia from the 'Balkans'. However, at the same time, the fear of alien erudition that could threaten national sovereignty and ruin the uniqueness of Slovenian national character appears as a reemerging national complex of being unimportant, small, servile and 'without our own identity'.

Notes

1. Although it is sometimes difficult to distinguish between serious news and tabloid news, one could generalize and say that *Mag, Mladina, Nedelo* and *Demokracija* sometimes tend to introduce certain tabloid features.
2. This chapter distinguishes between the Balkans, Europe and the west as geographical regions versus the notions of the 'Balkans', 'Europe' (denoting the EU until 2004) and the 'West' with all the ideological imagery that these concepts designate today. The terms *Europe* and the *EU* are used interchangeably both in this text as well as in the sources.

References

Bakic-Hayden, M. (1995) Nesting orientalism: The case of former Yugoslavia. *Slavic Review* 54 (4), 917–931.

Bakic-Hayden, M. and Hayden, M.R. (1992) Orientalist variations on the theme "Balkans": Symbolic geography in recent Yugoslav cultural politics. *Slavic Review* 51 (1), 1–15.

Cankar, I. (1994) *Hlapci*. Ljubljana: Mihelač.

de Cillia, R., Reisigl, M., and Wodak, R. (1999) The discursive construction of national identities. *Discourse and Society* 10 (2), 149–173.

Derrida, J. (2004) *On Deconstruction. Theory and Criticism after Structuralism*. London: Routledge.

Dolar, M. (2003) Slovenska nacionalna identiteta in kultura – navodila za uporabo. In N. Pagon (ed.) *Nacionalna identiteta in kultura* (pp. 21–36). Ljubljana: Inštitut za civilizacijo in kulturo.

Fairclough, N. (1992) *Discourse and Social Change*. Cambridge: Polity Press, Oxford: Blackwell Publishers.

Gestrin, F. and Melik, V. (1979) Demokratična in socialna prebuja na Slovenskem. In Z. Čepič and D. Nećak (eds) *Zgodovina slovencev* (pp. 527–597). Ljubljana: Cankarjeva Založba.

Krek, J.E. (1895) *Črne bukve kmečkega stanu: Jedro kmečkega vprašanja*. Ljubljana: Tisek Katoliške Tiskarne.

Krek, J.E. (1925) *Izbrani spisi: Socializem. (III. zvezek iz l. 1901)*. Ljubljana: Jugoslovanska tiskarna.

Krek, J.E. (1933) *Izbrani spisi: Prvikrat v državnem zboru (IV. Zvezek, 1987–1900)*. Celje: Družba Sv. Mohorja.

Krek, J.E. (1993) *Izbrani spisi: Življenje in delo v letih od 1900 do 1907 (V. Zvezek)*. Celje: Mohorjeva družba.

Laclau, E. (1990) *New Reflections on the Revolution of Our Time*. London and New York: Verso.

Musek, J. (1994) *Psihološki portret Slovencev*. Ljubljana: Znanstveno in publicistično središče.

Musolff, A. (2004) The heart of the European body politic. British and German perspectives on Europe's central organ. *Journal of Multilingual and Multicultural Development* 25 (5 & 6), 437–452.

Patterson, P.H. (2003) On the edge of reason: The boundaries of Balkanism in Slovenian, Austrian, and Italian discourse. *Slavic Review* 62 (1), 110–141.

Pirjevec, D. (1964) *Ivan Cankar in evropska literatura*. Ljubljana: Cankarjeva založba.

Pirjevec, D. (1968) *Hlapci, heroji, ljudje*. Ljubljana: Cankarjeva založba.

Pirjevec, J. (1995) *Jugoslavija (1918–1992): nastanek, razvoj ter razpad Karadjordjevićeve in Titove Jugoslavije*. Koper: Lipa.

Puntscher Riekmann, S. (1997) The myth of European unity. In G. Hosking and G. Schopfin (eds) *Myth and Nationhood* (pp. 60–71). London: Hurst & Company.

Salecl, R. (1994) The crisis of identity and the struggle for new hegemony in the former Yugoslavia. In E. Laclau (ed.) *The Making of Political Identities* (pp. 205–232). London: Verso.

Šarić, Lj. (2004) Balkan identity: Changing self-images of the South-Slavs. *Journal of Multilingual and Multicultural Development* 25 (5 & 6), 389–407.

Stavrakakis, Y. (1999) *Lacan and the Political*. London: Routledge.

Todorova, M. (1997) *Imagining the Balkans*. Oxford: Oxford University Press.

Vodopivec, P. (2006) *Od Pohlinove slovnice do samostojne države: Slovenska zgodovina od konca 18. stoletja do konca 20. stoletja*. Ljubljana: Modrijan.

Wodak, R., de Cillia, R., Reisigl, M. and Liebhart, K. (1999) *The Discoursive Construction of National Identity*. Edinburgh: Edinburgh University Press.

Žižek, S. (1981–1982) Kako so slovenci postali pridni in kako bodo to, če bodo pridni, tudi ostali. *Problemi razprave* 81–82 (11–1), 85–97.

Žižek, S. (1982) *Zgodovina in nezavedno*. Ljubljana: Cankarjeva založba.

Žižek, S. (1984) Krekovstvo. *Družboslovne razprave* 1, 147–164.

Žižek, S. (1987) *Jezik, ideologija, Slovenci*. Ljubljana: Delavska enotnost.

Chapter 9

The Linguistic Image of the Balkans in the Polish Press in Discourse on European Union Expansion

Paweł Bąk

Introduction

This analysis reflects on the linguistic presentation of southeast Europe in the most prominent Polish newspapers. The considerations below are based on an analysis of 40 news articles published during the past decade and will contribute to research on insiders and outsiders' images of southeastern European societies. This analysis uses a descriptive approach to examine a corpus excerpted from the following weekly publications: the Polish edition of *Newsweek*, *Polityka*, *Wprost* and *Gość Niedzielny*. The articles examined come from 'quality' publications published between 2003 and 2007. Particular emphasis is placed on articles published after Poland's accession to the European Union. This context clearly has an impact on the way other countries aspiring to EU membership are perceived. This discussion focuses on Croatia, Montenegro and Serbia, as well as Bulgaria and Romania, the two most recent countries to join the EU.

Metaphorical Models in Polish Discourse before 2004

Some of the Balkan countries are referred to as EU candidates today. This chapter examines the metaphorical models present in the description of the Balkan countries. It confirms the existence of the metaphorical models presented by Mikołajczyk and Zinken (2003) and Mikołajczyk (2004) in the context of European integration. The models are as follows:

– Joining the EU (the *Beitrittsmodell*),
– EU expansion (the *Erweiterungsmodell*),
– EU integration (the *Gestaltungsmodell*; cf. Mikołajczyk & Zinken, 2003: 369–378).

The first strategy (*joining the EU*) played a significant role mainly in German press discourse; the remaining two also appeared in Poland. According to Mikołajczyk (2004), Polish press discourse described

Poland's accession to the EU as a building, using either the *integration model* or the *expansion model* (cf. Mikołajczyk, 2004: 151). The expansion model could even be placed within the anti-integration context found in the Euro-skeptic press (e.g. *Nasz Dziennik*).

This study seeks to determine whether:

- the contemporary Polish press made use of metaphorical models in discourse before the 2004 EU expansion;
- the discourse used in Poland confirms changes in the perception of other countries seeking to join the EU; and
- descriptive methods as well as unique stylistic means are used.

In particular, stylistic means are represented along with other language characteristics that imply an emotional attitude to the issues concerning the Balkans. This makes it possible to determine whether the language used by the Polish press demonstrates solidarity or distance in the approach to the Balkans since Poland joined the EU.

This chapter also investigates whether the language of the press presents the societies of the Balkans as active or passive, as deserving EU membership in the future with all their cultural heritage, or as societies that are simply allowed to join the EU within the model of *joining the EU* as described in German discourse before 2004.

The Balkan region has not been called a 'Balkan pot' (cf. Šarić, 2004: 389–407) without reason because it constitutes a mosaic of numerous cultures. I therefore take a closer look at the texts that deal with individual countries' situations.

My premises presuppose that conceptual metaphors are common to different languages. Here, I refer to the theory by Lakoff and Johnson (1980), and their depiction of orientational and ontological metaphors in particular. The very concept of the EU's *expansion* makes it possible to think of the European Union in terms of the *container* metaphor.

General Tendencies in Creating the Image of the Balkans in Polish Discourse during the Past 10 Years

Before embarking on an analysis of the related texts, I briefly discuss the presence of the Balkans in the daily *Rzeczpospolita*. A search for collocations of the adjective *bałkański* 'Balkan' on Polish website archives of this newspaper yields many hits. These include phrases such as *Balkan problem* (problem bałkański), *ghouls of the Balkans* (upiory Bałkanów) and *demons of the Balkans* (demony Bałkanów).

Of course, search engines provide neutral geographical names as far as the connotation is concerned, but at the same time, they also give numerous word connections with adjectives that are related to the Balkan wars and carry negative connotations. These connotations are consistent with

Polish films of the 1990s, which contain extreme brutality and vulgar language: for example, the films by Władysław Pasikowski *Psy 2* and *Demony wojny wg Goi* (Demons of War after Goya). Films of this sort, apart from their descriptions of the former Yugoslavia, may be responsible for creating and sustaining stereotypes concerning the Balkans, just like the picture of the *Balkan pot* (kocioł bałkański) – created in the movies, introduced then and still present in the language of Polish society. Interest in these countries was also motivated by the Balkan war that broke out at that time. Although the term *Balkans* covers all of the southeastern European countries, in Poland it often functions as a name for the former Yugoslavia (cf. Olejnik, 2004: 125–130). The topic of the Balkans is eagerly dealt with in the press. The journalists at *Rzeczpospolita* know the specific nature of the region very well. They have also authored some books about this region (cf. Ryszard Bilski, *Kocioł bałkański* [Balkan Pot], 2000). The following reflections not only cite individual *Rzeczpospolita* lexemes,[1] but further develop the content of certain texts. Since 2000, a certain change has taken place regarding the image of the Balkans. This evolution has shifted the image to other thematic areas (e.g. economics, tourism, cuisine or science), which is undoubtedly linked to the time that has elapsed since the Balkan wars. The region is also discussed in other newspaper sections besides political ones. The image of the Balkans in the Polish press is far from stable: It did not stop during the war, as it is believed about the Western press (cf. Todorova, 2008: 394–396), but continues to evolve. Pejorative terms concerning the Balkans are relatively rare in the press nowadays. More on this topic can be found elsewhere (cf. Bąk, in press). To examine this change in journalistic perception, I include an analysis of what I feel are journalistic texts representative for all of Poland.

Metaphorical Models in Polish Discourse on the EU after 2004

This section takes a closer look at the attitude toward non-EU members presented in *Gość Niedzielny*, a weekly Catholic paper. Unlike the Euro-skeptic *Nasz Dziennik*, *Gość Niedzielny* rarely voices controversial opinions about politics and international relations. It is a widely read paper and perceived as being neutral, and does not make prominent use of stereotypes. Unlike numerous other papers (not only tabloids), it does not contain provocative headlines or photos.

Gość Niedzielny published the article 'Dokańczanie Europy' (Completing Europe) by Jacek Dziedzina, which discussed European Union expansion during the accession of Bulgaria and Romania. What attracts attention is its conceptual metaphoricism. Terms such as *history, structures, process of integration* and *reforms* are presented by means of metaphorical imaging. The way history and the passage of time are presented can be reduced to the concept of a *road*:

> (1) There will not be any further EU expansion without deciding the direction of integration.[2] (Nie będzie kolejnego rozszerzenia UE bez określenia, w jakim kierunku ma iść integracja. *Gość Niedzielny*, 7 January 2007)

Descriptions concerning the entire process often include the concept of *expansion*:

> (2) During the process of EU expansion, the EU has to answer some important questions. (Unia Europejska przy okazji tego rozszerzenia musi odpowiedzieć sobie na najważniejsze pytania. Ibid.)

> (3) During backstage discussions, it is frequently said that at this stage of EU expansion new candidates have to meet less demanding requirements. (W kuluarach unijnych instytucji często mówi się, że ten etap rozszerzenia Wspólnoty będzie niedobrym obniżeniem poprzeczki wymagań dla kolejnych kandydatów. Ibid.)

> (4) The awareness of western Europeans has increased considerably. (Świadomość mieszkańców zachodniej Europy znacznie się poszerzyła. Ibid.)

Here the 'awareness of western Europeans', depicted as the contents of metaphorical container, is said to benefit from the process of expansion. Now and again, a conceptual metaphor is accompanied by concepts from discourse on 20th-century history:

> (5) Expansion is yet another stage in raising the iron curtain. (Rozszerzenie jest kolejnym etapem zwijania żelaznej kurtyny. Ibid.)

The *container* metaphor prevailed in Polish media discourse on integration before 2004 and was visible in both the *EU expansion* model and the *EU integration* model (cf. Mikołajczyk & Zinken, 2003: 369–378). In the article 'Dokańczanie Europy' (Completing Europe), the strategy of *EU integration* stood in first place. This emphasizes the position of the intellectual contribution made by the new members in creating a common European home, which takes place within the model of European *integration*:

> (6) Despite all the damage done to the countries [Bulgaria and Romania] by communism, they have an incredible intellectual and spiritual potential. (Mimo wyniszczenia krajów [Bułgarii i Rumunii] przez komunizm mają niesamowity potencjał intelektualny i duchowy. Ibid.)

The example indicates that eastern Europeans have something special to offer to the rest of the EU. The title of the article 'Dokańczanie Europy'

(Completing Europe) has a justified function – presenting the following stages of European integration as an obvious consequence of the breakthrough as well as a matter of historical justice:

> (7) Bulgaria and Romania's presence in the structures of the integrating continent is a complement to the greatest expansion in the history of European integration, which took place in 2004. (Obecność Bułgarii i Rumunii w strukturach jednoczącego się kontynentu jest dopełnieniem największego rozszerzenia w historii integracji europejskiej, jakie miało miejsce w 2004 roku. Ibid.)

Croatia and other Balkan countries are further described in the following terms:

> (8) Their membership in EU structures may be treated as the raison d'état of all Europe. The integration of this war-ravaged region into a now peaceful part of the continent could be the first attempt to quench a burning flame in a number of years. (Ich przynależność do Unii można uznać za rację stanu całej Europy. Integracja tego poranionego przez wojnę regionu z żyjącą w pokoju częścią kontynentu może być pierwszą od dawna szansą na wygaszenie wrzącego kotła. Ibid.)

Since 2004, Poland has been a participant in the events taking place in Europe. The persuasive function, which literature has attributed to the model of *EU integration* (Mikołajczyk, 2004: 152), has been a voice in favor of allowing other countries (except Bulgaria and Romania) to become EU members. The article was published in January 2007, soon after these two countries became EU members.

Bearing in mind the source's worldview (as a Catholic weekly), we can expect argumentation in favor of a mission in secularized Europe. However, the text does not address the issues encountered in more conservative newspapers. The Polish Euro-skeptic press often talks of the dangers that the EU entails (cf. Mikołajczyk, 2004: 151). *Gość Niedzielny* articulates the advantages of EU membership expressed from the position of a new member state – advantages that can also be derived from old inhabitants of the EU. Regarding the linguistic aspect, the idea of *integration* along with the metaphorical model of *expansion* can be observed.[3] Now and again, there are characteristics typical of the model *of joining the EU*. Nonetheless, the author barely ever uses expressions that would contrast with the model of the *integrated* Europe and would give a description of passively *joining* the EU, which were typical for German discourse before the new countries joined the EU in 2004 (Mikołajczyk, 2004: 146). The expressions from the model of *joining the EU* that the author uses are few; these are *accept*, *allow* and *let in*:

> (9) Bulgaria and Romania have been accepted into the club of countries. (Bułgaria i Rumunia zostają przyjęte do klubu państw. Ibid.)

(10) Initially both countries were going to join the EU along with ten other candidates. (Pierwotnie kraje te miały wstąpić do UE wraz z dziesiątką innych kandydatów. Ibid.)

The process of *expansion* was presented in a slightly different light in *Gość Niedzielny* compared to magazines and newspapers before 2004. In one commentary, Jacek Dziedzina speaks of the possible benefits after joining the EU, but at the same time of the contribution to the integration and construction of the EU. Thus, *completing Europe* (as mentioned in his title) has a bilateral character. *Integration*, which is the construction of a common home, implies co-creating Europe and calls for *expanding* its structures – and here we arrive at a fusion of the models developed by Mikołajczyk and Zinken. In the texts analyzed, the model of *integration* occasionally appears together with the model of *expansion*.

Passivity versus activity: *Container* and *road*

Coming back to conceptual metaphor and the *road* metaphor in particular, the article subtitle mentions defining the *direction of the road* after joining the European Union. The road to the EU does not finish at its threshold. After joining it, there are choices such as which further direction to take:

(11) Where, when, and who to go with? (Dokąd, z kim i kiedy iść dalej? *Gość Niedzielny*, 7 January 2007)

The metaphorical description of the *path* includes *crossroads*. Directly referred to as *traffic within the union*, this implies the existence of the metaphorical concept of the *road*, which is evident in lexical forms – *to be late*, *to accelerate* and so on. The continuation of the process enables measurable development, progress, economic increases and improvement of living standards. To be able to join the EU, Bulgaria and Romania had to comply with requirements and meet deadlines for domestic reforms. Having spent a long time on the *road*, they found themselves in a *waiting room* (poczekalnia). In this context, the verb *to aspire* (aspirować) appears, expressing attempts to be accepted and verbalizing expectations and endeavors to be allowed to *join* the EU. This verb is frequent in Polish discourse on the EU.

The text shows some sort of contrast between two metaphorical images, one of which concerns the metaphor of the *road*: *movement, dynamics* and *activity*. The other, the *waiting room*, is a representation of *waiting*, the synonym of stasis, passivity and weariness. The contrasting metaphors of the *waiting room* and *movement* emphasize the dissimilarity between two scopes of meaning with positive (i.e. activity) and negative coloring (i.e. passivity). Facts with a positive undertone can be associated with the future, development, the hope of joining the EU, dynamics and movement, which all imply the metaphor of the *road*.

Difficulties experienced by countries aspiring to join the EU manifest themselves in passivity, idleness and anticipation while encountering *obstacles* (przeszkody) on their road.

Human activity and performance are described positively within European discourse in other articles – for example, 'Wybór Serbii' (Serbia's Choice; *Polityka*, 10 February 2007). This is expressed in the same metaphors of the *road* and *dynamics*, which are carriers of the hope held out by the countries aspiring to join the EU. Here, the *obstacles* and *passivity* are associated with the memories of the past and unwillingness to introduce reforms. They concern both politics and economics. The description can also be found in the article 'Białoruś Bałkanów' (The Belarus of the Balkans):

> (12) Belgrade... is a sad city. Gloomy residential areas and the ruins of buildings damaged in the NATO air raids deepen the national trauma. The Serbian economy has begun to recover in the last few years... but it still lags far behind its neighbors. (Belgrad... to smutne miasto. Ponure blokowiska i pozostawione po natowskich nalotach ruiny pogłębiają narodową traumę. Gospodarka serbska w ostatnich latach zaczęła się rozwijać...., ale wciąż jest daleko w tyle za sąsiadami. *Newsweek*, 27 January 2008)

The troubles presented in the article 'Dokańczanie Europy' (Completing Europe) can be found in various fields, described by images based on the concepts of the *container* and the *path*. There are various political sympathies in Romania and Bulgaria. Similarly, there are political factions in the EU with their own pro- or anti-European preferences. Societies torn by internal differences and problems are absorbed – according to the logic of the mechanism of the metaphorical description of the world – by a larger and more spacious structure that also contains divisions and differences with relation to the future of Europe. The same applies to Serbia as shown in the *Newsweek* article 'Gorycz triumfu' (The Bitterness of Triumph):

> (13) The only element uniting all the Serbs is the Serbian character of Kosovo. Other issues have divided the Serbs into more groups than there are political parties. (Deklaracja serbskości Kosowa to jedyny element łączący właściwie wszystkich Serbów. Za to w innych kwestiach linii podziału jest więcej niż partii politycznych. *Newsweek*, 4 February 2007)

The metaphor of the *road* is determined by another concept. The phrases show a slightly more complex structure than the orientational or ontological metaphors. The metaphorical description corresponds to metaphorization models, the *source-journey/path/road-goal* scheme (typical for the model of *joining* the EU) and the model of *stretching* that refers to *expansion* of the EU. The combination of these metaphorical constructions is best illustrated in example (1).

Jacek Dziedzina finishes his reflection with a question about the future. In his opinion, the solution can serve as a foundation for a future Europe. The answer thus takes the form of the model of *EU integration* assuming joint responsibility of all the EU member countries.

Past versus future

In the article 'Wybór Serbii' (Serbia's Choice; *Polityka*, 10 February 2007), the key concepts presented are *past*, as a synonym for what belongs to the *former times*, and *future*, relating to the vision of EU membership.[4] Serbia's situation is presented in the text as an area between two extremes – *past* and *future* – similar to the situation of the country presented in the article 'Serbskie rozdroże' (Serbian Crossroads) in the weekly *Wprost*. Nothing in Serbia can be deemed simple. Since the dissolution of Yugoslavia, there has been no clear answer to the question of where Serbia is going:

> (14) Nothing is simple in Belgrade and the forecasts are completely discrepant. (W Belgradzie nic nie jest proste, a prognozy są całkowicie rozbieżne. *Wprost*, 1 January 2000)

The country is depicted as one situated between the positions of the radical nationalists and still weak European aspirations. These aspirations are mainly associated with younger Serbs. Hesitation between the two positions corresponds to the metaphorical *movement* between *past* (example 15) and *future* (example 16). The expression of *time* corresponds to the metaphor of the *road*. Heading for the future, which is the pro-European extreme, appears to be inevitable; however, it is not obvious in the article 'Serbia's Choice'.

> (15) In the last fifteen years, hundreds of thousands of people have left Serbia. Young and educated people fleeing from war, from joining the army, looking around the world for a better lot. (W ciągu minionych piętnastu lat z Serbii wyemigrowały setki tysięcy młodych, wykształconych ludzi, uciekających przed wojną, przed wcieleniem do armii, szukających lepszego losu w świecie. *Polityka*, 10 February 2007)

Despite the feeling of uncertainty, concepts connected with the future evoke positive implications:

> (16) When the decisions concerning the future of the province [Kosovo] have been clarified, investors will enter the Serbian market. (Kiedy decyzje w sprawie przyszłości prowincji [Kosowo] będą już klarowne, inwestorzy wkroczą na serbski rynek. Ibid.)

Optimistic metaphors are used in these contexts and they mainly concern the country's economy: for example, *healing economy* (uzdrawianie gospodarki), *modernizing* (modernizacja), *improving demand* (poprawa koniunktury) and *strengthening currency* (wzmocnienie pieniądza).

The Serbs still need to resolve issues in the future that have already become a reality in other countries, which are thus perceived as being *one step ahead* of Serbia. This is a subject of reflection in the article 'Nauka chodzenia' (Learning to Walk) by Jagienka Wilczak. Montenegro as depicted in the article is a country in a much better position than Serbia (even if much remains to be done) and the popularity of the country is on the increase. Montenegro has already made its choice, whereas Serbia still needs to decide where it is heading. A feasible challenge for Montenegro now is *learning to walk* – the article's title metaphor for the future, entailing hardship, education and activity:

> (17) There remains much to do and it is taking a long time. (Jest wiele do zrobienia i wolno to idzie. *Polityka*, 8 September 2007)

Solidarity with the Balkans

Reading the articles 'Serbia's Choice' and 'The Bitterness of Triumph', as well as other texts, gives the impression that the authors often attempt to put themselves in the Serbs' position. Even if the policy toward Kosovo exercised by the government in Belgrade creates a lot of controversy, Serbia is portrayed as a country that also suffered during the war:

> (18) The Serbs are probably the most divided European people. (Serbowie to dziś chyba najbardziej rozdarty naród Europy. *Polityka*, 10 February 2007)

> (19) ...Serbia [is] humiliated and impoverished after a series of wars. (...upokorzona i zbiedniała po serii wojen Serbia. *Newsweek*, 4 February 2007)

Journalists display even more fondness in the Balkan discourse on Croatia: for example, in the articles 'Szansa Chorwacji' (Croatia's Chance) or 'Dokańczanie Europy' (Completing Europe). The second article speaks about this war-torn area's chances of joining the EU (cf. example 8).

A slightly more critical judgment of Serbian politics is presented in the article 'Nauka chodzenia' (Learning to Walk) by the same author, Jagienka Wilczak. However, this only becomes clear after comparing it with the text already discussed (cf. example 17). 'Learning to Walk' deals with more pro-European Montenegro and its *justified divorce from Serbia* (uzasadniony rozwód z Serbią). Although not a single word of criticism is uttered about the government in Belgrade, the decision to say farewell to Serbia seems understandable. Incidentally, this text also contains words of solidarity with Montenegro expressed by the author, accusing the EU of failing to provide any aid or motivation to the country:

(20) It seems that after overthrowing the Milošević regime in 2000 the European Union has lost interest in supporting those aspirations. (Wydaje się, że po obaleniu reżimu Miloszewicia w 2000 r. Unia straciła swe poprzednie zainteresowanie wspieraniem tych aspiracji. *Polityka*, 8 September 2007)

Let us return to the article 'Wybór Serbii' (Serbia's Choice; *Polityka*, 10 February 2007). The picture of the past presented here may evoke negative associations; however, the text recalls them through indirect expressions and euphemisms. There is no mention here of past burdens; at most, only an embarrassing past. In comparison with the picture of the Balkans mentioned at the beginning in the daily *Rzeczpospolita* from the 1990s, the region is shown in a much brighter light. In the press published earlier, before 2000, Serbia appeared in the context of war and death, and the entire region was described as *a boiling cauldron*. This is shown not only in the articles published by *Rzeczpospolita* but also in other texts – for example, in the weekly *Wprost*: 'Serbski Titanic' (The Serbian Titanic; 25 October 1998), 'Wojna i pokój' (War and Peace; 28 February 1999), 'Prezydent wojny' (President of the War; 18 pril 1999), 'Pistolet w kolebce' (Gun in the Cradle; 25 April 1999) and 'Stan przedwojenny' (Prewar State; 29 August 1999) (cf. Bąk, in press).

In *Polityka*, Wilczak describes the fate of the young people who left the country in search of a better life (example 15). In the description of banishment, it is usually the Serbs who were the culprits, not the victims. In her more recent text 'Learning to Walk', the description of the Serbs is better articulated as those similarly aggrieved and as *people fleeing from war, from joining the army, looking around the world for a better lot* (example 15). Now, a few years after the war, the author presents the Serbs as weary. The cost of living is constantly increasing, although people do not earn much. In spite of no possibility of becoming part of the EU, the author emphasizes the hope that Europe without this part of the Balkans is *incomplete* (niepełna) (*Polityka*, 10 February 2007).

Here, the conflict concerning Kosovo is treated as the *Kosovo problem* (problem Kosowa). Over time, the author more readily uses euphemisms to refer to the ticklish question of the war. Albanians and minorities in Montenegro are depicted in a similar way in the article 'Nauka chodzenia' (Learning to Walk; *Polityka*, 8 September 2007) as those playing an important, positive role. The only innovation in the discourse on the Balkans is the solidarity with Serbia.

In addition, the previously cited weekly *Wprost*, which does not avoid controversial rhetorical figures or hesitate to express strong remarks, uses the euphemism *embarrassing past* (kłopotliwa przeszłość) when describing Serbia's past (*Wprost*, 16 November 2003).

The discussion of past difficulties matters in the new context of European integration, and the passing of time encourages the change in depiction and the creation of quasi-political correctness.

Other characteristics of metaphorism in Balkan discourse

In addition to orientational metaphors in the article 'Wybór Serbii' (Serbia's Choice), the closely related metaphors of *family* and *home* can also be found. Jagienka Wilczak gives a picture of the NATO as *home*: In a sense, Serbia has crossed the *threshold* of NATO structures, entering *the NATO atrium* (przedsionek do członkowstwa w pakcie) – a preface to joining NATO; *Polityka*, 10 February 2007).

Atrium can be considered as a blend of two metaphors, *heart* and *home*, due to the etymology of the word, shared in various European languages.[5] The metaphors of *home*, *heart* and *family* are omnipresent in the discourse on Europe (cf. Musolff, 2004: 437–452) and usually involve naming abstract concepts. These metaphors can be viewed in terms of the way they present feelings and emotions.

The metaphor of *home* can be linked with the metaphorical model of *EU integration* as shown by Mikołajczyk (2004). The same can be observed in the previously discussed article 'Dokańczanie Europy' (Completing Europe), which, while touching upon the foundations of common Europe, mentions Schuman, Adenauer and de Gasperi, calling them the *fathers of the EU* (ojcowie UE).

The article 'Nauka chodzenia' (Learning to Walk) describes international relationships by means of the *family* metaphor, in order to confirm the correctness of the government's decisions. This is the case in the account of the relationships between Montenegro and Serbia:

> (21) An old couple, but not getting along with each other so well. (Stare, nie najlepiej dogadujące się małżeństwo. *Polityka*, 8 September 2007)

> (22) Montenegro's pro-European plans accelerated the decision to divorce Serbia. (Proeuropejskie plany Czarnogóry przyspieszyły decyzję o rozwodzie z Serbią. Ibid.)

Apart from examining conceptual metaphors in different languages, the discourse shows explicit stylistic characteristics in the traditional sense of stylistics. What should be mentioned at this point is a reference to terms with historical meanings. When the author in *Polityka* talks of the *unshakable electorate* (żelazny elektorat) of the Serbian radicals and uses the term *mobilization* (mobilizacja), it still has a rather universal character. However, in the *Newsweek* article with the oxymoron title 'Gorycz triumfu' (The Bitterness of Triumph), the term used is a Polish one: namely, *levy en masse* (*pospolite ruszenie* – conscription of all able-bodied men for military service to defend the state; *Newsweek*, 4 February 2007). Using a historically motivated expression that is readily understood by Polish readers, Jarosław Giziński manages to set them thinking and encourages identification with the topic. A similar stylistic device can be found later on:

> (23) Yet another Serbian sorrow is not welcomed by anyone and this is the reason why words of encouragement are sent from the West. (Kolejna serbska smuta nikomu nie jest dziś na rękę, dlatego z Zachodu słychać słowa zachęty. *Newsweek*, 4 February 2007)

The expression *sorrow* (smuta) is a historicism of Slavic origin. However, the very lexeme might sound somewhat exotic to a Polish reader because it is associated with the history of Russia. Together with the determiner *Serbian* it recalls the subject of the article – Serbia is facing a choice between a future with Russia and a future with the Western world.[6]

Words of foreign origin (e.g. *doszlusować* 'to join' < Germ. *schließen* 'to shut') are employed to express distance from the issues discussed or to articulate a lack of identification with the opinions given. They can also be treated as those used to create the model of *joining* the EU. Nonetheless, they sound foreign to a Polish native speaker. The Polish discourse is more positively emotional and dominated by the *integrative* model.

Final Comments and Perspectives in Perceiving Discourse

In the analysis of strategies used by the press to depict the processes of European integration, general tendencies in the use of expressions within metaphorical models were taken into consideration. In the presentation of southeastern European countries that are not official candidates for EU membership, Polish journalists express a definite solidarity with the ambitions of these nations. This is revealed both at the lexical level and in the general application of metaphors. Identification with the situation in the region can be attributed to understanding the problems and common experience of being on the outskirts of Europe.

The Balkan countries are presented as actors on the European scene. Among them are Montenegro and Serbia. The press of Poland (as an EU member) has identified with Serbia's timid pro-EU aspirations.

The Balkans is a true mosaic of dissimilar cultures and identities. Bearing in mind the individual linguistic characteristics of media texts' authors and their own subjective attitude to the topics in question, one should never expect to discover complete homogeneity. The descriptions of individual countries contain dissimilarities. Nonetheless, a bird's-eye view of the issue reveals a stereotyped and generalized picture of the Balkan *melting pot*. The descriptions of the countries in the region are balanced, and any critical comments mainly concern the evaluation of politicians.

Considering the positions of the candidates seems to be vital when examining the account of integration. In addition to expressions such as *accept, let in* and *allow*, other common expressions include *attempts, volition* and *endeavors* of the candidates to join the EU, which is best demonstrated by the verb *aspire* (aspirować). This falls within the model of *EU integration*. Distinguishing the presence of descriptions falling within this model is possible by checking whether the candidates are *active* or *passive*. An expression similar to *accepting new countries* (i.e. presenting integration from the perspective of an EU member) is used here. However, this is not a typical expression of the perception of Europe in the Polish press, in spite of the fact that Poland has been a member of the EU for a few years.

In referencing positive or difficult issues, a certain uniformity can be observed concerning the *future*, which is combined with hope, the possibility of change and reforms, whereas the *past* is a euphemistic synonym for the haunting ghosts of the war – which is, however, not referred to directly. The metaphorical dimension of the future can even be identified in grammatical categories, where the use of future forms anticipates reforms, economic growth or hope for change. Morphological categories also play a role in shaping the significance of a text, its assessment and helping read between the lines.

Apart from conceptual metaphor, which has a universal character and is consistent with the means of expression in other languages, this chapter has discussed specific stylistic means. These are deeply rooted in culture, epoch characteristics and literary convention, which require reference to traditional styles of depiction; presentation of a complete stylistic specification in a discourse is only possible in a broad analysis. Lexemes with historical shades of meaning are used to express an attitude toward a community, solidarity and distance. Articulating identification with communities, bearing in mind existing differences, is an argument in favor of the idea of a united Europe. As portrayed by Jagienka Wilczak in one of her texts, such a Europe would be incomplete if deprived of this particular part of the Balkans.

Notes

1. In another analysis of the archives of *Rzeczpospolita* (Bąk, in press), some clear tendencies can be observed regarding the characteristics of a thematic range used to describe a particular region. Attributes and single lexical units in contexts involving the Balkans show an abundance of war-and-conflict associations. Weakening of the negative overtone is manifested in the less frequent use of pejorative terms referring to the Balkans.
2. Quotations 1–10 are cited from 'Dokańczanie Europy' (Completing Europe; *Gość Niedzielny*, 7 January 2007) because it is rich in examples for this survey.

3. Note that the Polish understanding of EU integration (= enlargement) differs from that which is characteristic for the West (= further intensification of political coordination).
4. For the metaphorical dimension of *time*, cf. Hudabiunigg (1999: 403–415).
5. 'Atrium – (1) the open main court of a Roman house; (2) a central often glass-roofed hall that extends through several storys in a building, such as a shopping center or hotel; (3) a court in front of an early Christian or medieval church, esp. one flanked by colonnades. (4) *Anatomy*: a cavity or chamber in the body, esp. the upper chamber of each half of the heart. History: from Latin...' (*Collins*, 2003: 103). Cf. the same etymology of *atrium* in German; Duden (2007: 103), and in Polish (Sobol, 2002: 89).
6. *Sorrow* in the history of Russia means the time of unrest and the crisis of the authorities in the 16th century.

References

Bąk, P. (in press) Südosteuropa in der polnischen Pressesprache. In J. Schiewe et al. (eds) *Kommunikation für Europa II. Sprache und Identität*. Frankfurt/M: Peter Lang.

Bilski, R. (2000) *Kocioł bałkański*. Warsaw: Politeja.

Collins (2003) *Collins. English Dictionary*. Glasgow: HarperCollins Publishers.

Duden (2007) *Das Fremdwörterbuch*. Duden Band 5. Mannheim: Bibliographisches Institut & F.A. Brockhaus AG.

Hudabiunigg, I. (1999) Ein Pole wie aus dem Bilderbuch: nobel, melancholisch und verwegen! Zur Metaphorik über Polen in deutschen Medien. *Kwartalnik Neofilologiczny* 41 (3–4), 403–415.

Lakoff, G. and Johnson, M. (1980) *Metaphors We Live By*. Chicago and London: The University of Chicago Press.

Mikołajczyk, B. (2004) *Sprachliche Mechanismen der Persuasion in der politischen Kommunikation: dargestellt an polnischen und deutschen Texten zum EU-Beitritt Polens*. Frankfurt/M: Peter Lang.

Mikołajczyk, B. and Zinken, J. (2003) Metaphern im politischen Diskurs: die Rolle der Metapher in Vorstellungswelt und Argumentation (Anhand von polnischen und deutschen Texten zum EU-Beitritt Polens). In L.N. Zybatow (ed.) *Europa der Sprachen: Sprachkompetenz – Mehrsprachigkeit – Translation* (pp. 369–378). Frankfurt/M: Peter Lang.

Musolff, A. (2004) The *heart* of the European *body politic*. British and German perspectives on Europe's central *organ*. *Multilingual & Multicultural Development* 25 (5–6), 437–452.

Olejnik, K. (2004) Co wydarzyło się w Jugosławii w marcu 1999 roku? – językowy obraz konfliktu serbsko-albańskiego w tekstach prasy codziennej. In P. Krzyżanowski et al. (eds) *Manipulacja w języku* (pp. 123–135). Lublin: Wydawnictwo Uniwersytetu Marii Curie-Skłodowskiej.

Šarić, Lj. (2004) Balkan identity. Changing self-images of the South Slavs. *Journal of Multilingual & Multicultural Development* 25 (5–6), 389–407.

Sobol, E. (ed.) (2002) *Słownik wyrazów obcych PWN*. Warsaw: Wydawnictwo Naukowe PWN.

Todorova, M. (2008) *Bałkany wyobrażone [Imagining the Balkans]*. Wołowiec: Wydawnictwo Czarne.

Chapter 10

The Eternal Outsider? Scenarios of Turkey's Ambitions to Join the European Union in the German Press

Andreas Musolff

Introduction

In 2004, a report by an independent commission of senior EU politicians, commissioners and academics that had been appointed by the EU to study the prospects of Turkey joining the Union endorsed opening formal accession negotiations, and also gave an explicit warning regarding the public perception of such negotiations: 'A considerable problem could develop in several European countries with the ratification of an accession treaty with Turkey, should public resistance persist and government policy continue to diverge from popular opinion' (Ahtisaari *et al.*, 2004: 44). In their follow-up report after five years, the same commission stated that 'negative reactions... from European political leaders and growing hesitation by the European public' had given Turkey the impression 'that it is not welcome', whereas 'Turkish Euro-skeptics' had 'attempted to delay the implementation of political and social reforms needed for EU membership' (Ahtisaari *et al.*, 2009: 6–7). As a result, support in Turkey had 'faded' and the 'lack of reforms' had 'triggered more European opposition' (Ahtisaari *et al.*, 2009: 7). The misgivings on both sides had created a 'vicious circle' that required renewed commitment and massive efforts on all sides to prevent a failure of the accession process (Ahtisaari *et al.*, 2009: 43–47). The two reports indicate a high degree of awareness on the part of the authors that politicians would have to overcome considerable obstacles not just at the legislative and administrative levels, but also in terms of public acceptance. Public opinion research on attitudes toward Turkish accession in existing EU member states over the last decade has consistently corroborated these warnings, especially with regard to countries that have witnessed mass immigration from Turkey, such as Germany and Austria (Jones & van der Bijl, 2004; Karp & Bowler, 2006; McLaren, 2006, 2007).

Such attitudes provide a practical challenge to politicians as well as a prime object of study for social, economic and political scientists interested in prejudices and public opinion. However, the main question pursued in this analysis concerns the possible influence that media coverage – in particular, press coverage – may have on the emergence and further development of such attitudes. One might suspect that any kind of strongly 'negative' reporting and commenting on Turkey-related issues by the media (and/or by populist politicians) that taps into xenophobic and Orientalist stereotypes reinforces latent hostility to Turkey's accession; however, such a general hypothesis begs too many questions to be amenable to operationalization for empirical research. Crucially, it assumes the pre-existence of prejudices and stereotypes that are then supposedly mirrored or reinforced by the media. However, where do these attitudes and opinions come from? Do the media play a role in their genesis? If yes, the concepts underlying such prejudices and attitudes must have an observable representation in the relevant media texts.

Metaphor and Public Debates about European Union Politics and Turkey's Accession

Modern cognitive research has established that social and political concepts are *not* conglomerations of atomistic pieces of (more or less correct) knowledge. On the contrary, concepts are essentially holistic and organized within 'frames' of knowledge that are shared within a given discourse community (Croft & Cruse, 2004: 14–21; Taylor, 1995: 87–90). Cognitively oriented metaphor analysis has shown that frame structures allow transfer between domains of knowledge: A known frame can thus be used as the source for a hitherto unknown or unfamiliar domain (Kövecses, 2002; Lakoff & Johnson, 1980, 1999). Whereas some of these metaphoric frame structures are extremely general and apply to all aspects of conceptualization, to a degree that they are hardly noticed by their users, others are ontologically richer and more specific, and it is the latter that inform discourses about contentious issues in the public domain. These 'discourse metaphors' (Zinken, 2007; Zinken *et al.*, 2008) not only transfer individual items and abstract (topo-)logical relations between source and target domains, but also transport evaluative and narrative elements that draw a seemingly self-explanatory conclusion from a mini-story or 'scenario' (Musolff, 2004, 2006). Evidence for the importance and ubiquity of such ethically, and often also emotionally, loaded metaphor scenarios has been found across various speech communities (Charteris-Black, 2004, 2005; Dirven *et al.*, 2001; Frank *et al.*, 2008; Musolff, 2004; Musolff & Zinken, 2009).

Among the major events and developments in international politics over the last two decades, the restructuring of the European political 'landscape' since the dissolution of the Eastern Bloc has attracted special attention as regards its metaphoric representation (Bachem & Battke,

1991; Chilton & Ilyin, 1993; Drulák, 2006; Luoma-aho, 2004; Musolff, 1996, 2000, 2004; Schäffner, 1993, 1995, 1996). The key issues that have been at the center of public debates and thus also of metaphoric reconceptualizations have been the economic, administrative and political integration of the European Union and its enlargement, which has involved several rounds of accession by new member states that transformed what had been a largely western European Confederation up until 1990 into a continent-wide political entity. In this historical context, the relationship between Turkey and the EC/EU is a singular one: Since the Association Treaty of 1963, Turkey has been officially acknowledged as a potential candidate for membership in the EU, but all attempts by Turkey to enter into official accession negotiations failed up until 2005 (Balkir & Williams, 1993; Müftüler-Baç, 1997; Tank, 2007). This contradictory (or, at the very least, complex) relationship has led to recent controversies and crises: for example, in 1997, when the Turkish government felt let down by the Luxembourg EU summit's failure to endorse formal accession negotiations, and in 2006 (i.e. after the official start of negotiations) due to the impasse over Turkey's relation to Cyprus (Ermagan, 2009; Merkel, 2006; Pamuk, 1997; Schmidt, 2004; Tank, 2007; Verheugen, 2004).

On the other hand, over the past four decades the EEC/EC/EU has witnessed mass immigration of Turkish citizens, especially into Germany and Austria, where they have formed stable migrant communities (Göktürk et al., 2007; Halm & Thränhardt, 2009; Jordan & Barker, 2000; Panayi, 2000, 2004). In this sense, Turkish citizens are already part of the EU, thus adding to the complexity and urgency of the Turkish accession project. The relations between the Turkish migrants (and their descendants) and the indigenous population in terms of mutual perceptions and attitudes, as well as the public debates about this relationship, have themselves been analyzed with a view to key categories and key metaphors – for instance, the imagery of FLOODING (*waves of migration*), FULL-UP/OVERFLOWING CONTAINERS (the EU as an overloaded *boat, house*) and OTHERNESS (Jung et al., 1997; Manz, 2004; Tibi, 2001). What then, are the metaphors and associated narrative/evaluative scenarios that are used in public debate to describe and explain Turkey's relationship with the EU?

To answer this question, it would be desirable to rely on a representative corpus of public discourse data that includes a range of text types and registers; for example, statements by political leaders, parties and governmental institutions; media texts; statements and discussion contributions by members of the public; and influential scholarly literature. So far, however, no such corpus is available; the existing EU-related metaphor studies rely either on politicians' statements and political science texts (Drulák, 2004, 2006) or on corpora of journalistic (mostly, press) texts (Musolff, 1996, 2004; Šarić, 2004; Schäffner, 1993, 1996). The following findings are based on a pilot corpus of press data from

German newspapers and magazines; these include *Bild, Berliner Zeitung, Der Spiegel, die tageszeitung, Die Welt, Die Zeit, Financial Times Deutschland, Frankfurter Allgemeine Zeitung, Frankfurter Rundschau, Mannheimer Morgen* and *Süddeutsche Zeitung*. The texts were compiled from an in-house databank at Durham University and material from the COSMAS corpus at the German Language Institute in Mannheim (http://www.ids-mannheim.de/cosmas2/uebersicht.html). They include reports, commentaries, background articles, interviews and letters to the editor. The corpus, which is still being developed, includes 132 text passages (31,000 words), which contain 232 tokens of semantically salient and transparent metaphors. In addition, we are in the process of building a parallel corpus from British press texts; so far only a very small sample exists, drawn from *The Economist, The Guardian, The Independent* and *The Times* (26 texts, 10,000 words). Neither sample is sufficiently large to allow us to draw detailed statistical conclusions. The following analyses are therefore intended to provide an indication of the conceptual range and main clusters of metaphors and associated scenarios.

Turkey-related metaphors in the German sample can be allocated to the following source domains: MOVEMENT–TRANSPORT, BUILDING–HOUSE, SOCIAL INSTITUTION, FAMILY, LOVE–RELATIONSHIP, BODY–LIFE–HEALTH, GAME–SPORT, WAR, PHYSICS–GEOMETRY, GEOGRAPHY AND NATURE–ANIMAL (cf. Appendix). All of these domains and most of the concepts are well established in German discourse about the EU, as larger studies have shown (Drulák, 2006; Luoma-aho, 2004; Musolff, 2004). The only genuinely idiosyncratic source concept of the Turkey-related corpus appears to be the depiction of Turkey as a *donkey that willingly follows the carrot in front of its nose* (held out by the European Union) as a negative model for another accession candidate, Romania – that is, as advice on how not to deal with the EU ('Die EU will Rumänien helfen, aber die Politiker zieren sich.... man wollte nicht das Schicksal der Türkei erleiden, die dem EU-Beitritt hinterherlief wie der Lastesel der Möhre, und stattdessen lieber das große landwirtschaftliche Potenzial ausbauen.' *Die Zeit*, 11 November 1999).

The Three Main Scenarios: OUTSIDER, PROGRESS and CONFLICT

With respect to the assessment of Turkish EU candidacy, the metaphors recorded in the corpus sample can be grouped into three main scenarios. The most frequently occurring scenario of Turkey's relationship with the EU is that of Turkey as an *outsider*, with little chance of *getting inside* the EU *house/guild/family*, as the following examples illustrate (with the relevant text passages italicized):

(1) Turkey would be ready for a takeover by the fundamentalists *if she were shown the door by Europe*. (Die Türkei wäre, falls Europa

ihr endgültig die Tür wiese, reif für die Fundamentalisten. *Die Zeit*, 20 January 1995)

(2) ... Turkey is being refused *access to the offices of the European guilds – like a customer without credit card she is being fobbed off and driven into frustration*. (... man verwehrt [der Türkei] den Zutritt zu den Kontoren der europäischen Kaufmannsgilde, wie ein Kunde ohne Kreditkarte wird sie im Vorzimmer immer wieder abgewimmelt und in die Verbitterung gedrängt. *Die Welt*, 19 March 1997; letter to the editor)

(3) As long as torture is being carried out in [Turkey], the country *cannot become a member of the European family*. (Solange in dem Land gefoltert wird, kann es nicht Mitglied der europäischen Familie werden. *Die Welt*, 15 December 1997)

(4) Is it not too easy now to invite Turkey in, after *having kept the door firmly shut* for many years? (Ist es nicht wohlfeil, jetzt mit der Tür nach Europa zu winken, nachdem man sie jahrelang für die Türkei zugehalten hat? *die tageszeitung*, 30 June 1999)

(5) [Turkish Prime Minister] Erdoğan has again found a *marriage metaphor* that captures the situation: All the new conditions put up by the EU just before the start of accession talks, especially the consolation prize of a 'privileged partnership' – *that's like a newlywed sitting at the wedding table and suddenly saying, 'let's just stay friends'*. (Und wieder hat Erdogan ein Ehegleichnis gefunden, das die Lage trefflich schildert: Die ständig neuen Auflagen der Europäer so kurz vor Beginn der Beitrittsgespräche, ja gar das Trostpflaster einer 'privilegierten Partnerschaft' – das alles sei, als "wenn man an der Hochzeitstafel sitzt und plötzlich sagt: 'Lass uns Freunde bleiben'". *Der Spiegel*, 31 January 2005)

(6) Europe urgently needs a pause before further enlargement – not just because *states such as Turkey and Serbia are knocking on its door*, which have far greater problems than Romania and Bulgaria. (Europa [braucht] dringend eine Pause im Erweiterungsprozess. Nicht nur, weil mit der Türkei und Serbien Staaten an die Tür klopfen, die Probleme noch ganz anderen Kalibers [als Rumänien und Bulgarien] mit sich herumschleppen. *Financial Times Deutschland*, 26 September 2006)

The OUTSIDER scenario accounts for about 47% of the German texts. It dominates the pre-2004 sample, but is still being used even after the start of official accession negotiations (see example 6). There are subtle differences between those scenario versions in which Turkish accession is presented as virtually impossible (examples 2, 3), as not opportune or timely (example 4, 6) or as conceivable for the future (examples 1, 5). The common features are: (a) The presupposition that the process of Turkey's accession to the EU is about to start or has started and (b) The conclusion that, at the time of this writing, some OBSTACLE (*closed door/shop/family, lukewarm solidarity/love*) is blocking or delaying further progress. This conclusion remains the same, irrespective of its explicit evaluation by the speaker as positive or negative – for the time being, Turkey is *outside* the EU entity. The Turkish prime minister quoted in example 6, for instance, strongly favors accession but still employs the OUTSIDER scenario (mainly for the purpose of complaining about alleged unfair treatment), whereas opponents use it to invoke reasons to halt/delay the process.

However, it is not always the case that Turkey is the 'snubbed' *outsider* that is *shut out*. The second main scenario, accounting for some 43% of the corpus, is usually signaled by vocabulary of PROGRESS and INCLUSION and depicts Turkey as *coming* or *about to come* into the fold of the union:

(7) After consultations with Chancellor Kohl, Turkish Prime Minister Mesut Yılmaz feels encouraged in his hopes for a turnaround in the relationship between his country and the European Union. First of all, Yılmaz said, *the Turkish train must be put back on the European track.* (Der türkische Ministerpräsident Mesut Yilmaz fühlt sich nach Beratungen mit Bundeskanzler Helmut Kohl in der Hoffnung auf eine 'Wende' im Verhältnis seines Landes zur Europäischen Union ermutigt.... Zuerst müsse der türkische Zug wieder aufs europäische Gleis gesetzt werden, sagte Yilmaz. *Süddeutsche Zeitung*, 1 October 1997)

(8) The positive decision by the EU in Helsinki provides the official confirmation that *Turkey is to be part of the European family. The door to Europe is now open.* (Der positive Bescheid aus Helsinki ist die offizielle Bestätigung des westlichen Europas, dass die Türkei zur Familie gehören soll.... Die Tür nach Europa steht jetzt offen. *Berliner Zeitung*, 11 December 1999)

(9) The EU commission has reprimanded Turkey because of her inflexibility in the conflict about Cyprus... but *Turkey's rapprochement to Europe* must not be put at risk, as EU Enlargement Commissioner Olli Rehn made clear. He said, '*The train will go more slowly but it won't be stopped.*'... Turkey would always have the chance *to score a 'golden goal' and kick-start the negotiations.* (Wegen der Unnachgiebigkeit der Türkei im Zypern-Konflikt hat die EU-Kommission das Land am Mittwoch verwarnt.... Die Annäherung der Türkei an Europa solle jedoch nicht aufs Spiel gesetzt werden, sagte Erweiterungskommissar Olli Rehn.... 'Der Zug wird langsamer fahren, aber er wird nicht anhalten', sagte Rehn. Die Türkei habe aber jederzeit die Chance, ein

'goldenes Tor' zu schießen und die Verhandlungen insgesamt wieder in Gang zu bringen. *Süddeutsche Zeitung*, 7 November 2006)

As example 9 shows, the PROGRESS/INCLUSION scenario is available even when actual political negotiations have been halted (in 2006, the EU commission froze ratification of accession treaty chapters until Turkey fully acknowledges Cyprus' status as an EU member). The PROGRESS scenario can also be applied to the internal development of the candidate. The magazine *Der Spiegel*, for instance, commended Turkey for being no longer the 'sick man on the Bosporus':

(10) It is now four and a half years that the Islamic-conservative AKP party of Prime Minister...Erdoğan has been in office – and with considerable success. No one speaks anymore of *the sick man on the Bosporus* .... The AKP has pushed through hundreds of reforms and led Turkey into accession negotiations with the EU. (Seit viereinhalb Jahren regiert die islamisch-konservative AKP von Premier Recep Tayyip Erdogan, durchaus mit Erfolg. Keiner spricht mehr vom 'kranken Mann am Bosporus' .... Die AKP hat Hunderte Reformen durchgeboxt und die Türkei in Beitrittsverhandlungen mit der EU geführt. *Der Spiegel*, 7 May 2007)

Although this special scenario version was probably intended as a compliment by the authors, Turkish readers might conceivably interpret it as patronizing and reinforcing stereotypes. The phrases *sick man on the Bosporus* and the closely related *sick man of Europe* are long-standing clichés that initially expressed a dismissive view of the Ottoman Empire. The phrases are often attributed to Tsar Nicholas I of Russia, who used them in the 1840s, but they can be traced back even further to the eighteenth century (*Brewer's Dictionary of Phrase and Fable*, 1999, 1983; Büchmann, 1898: 513–514; Soykut, 2007: 56). Nowadays, the phrase *sick man of Europe* is routinely applied to any country in the EU that experiences socioeconomic or political problems, in both the British and the German press, sometimes with explanations and comments regarding its Turkey-specific origin (Musolff, 2004: 97–101).

The metonymic reference to the Bosporus in example (10) leaves no uncertainty about the referent, and the quotation marks indicate even to historically uninterested or uninformed readers that this is a well-established phrase. The adverbial specification 'no longer' ('negation' + *mehr*) suggests that Turkey at some point in the past used to be called *the sick man on the Bosporus*. However, in the context of an article about a Turkish government that has only taken office in the 21st century, it seems unlikely that the average reader will easily associate the *sick man* verdict with the Ottoman Empire, which has been defunct for nearly a century; instead, post–World War II Turkey seems more likely as the historical frame of reference. Whatever the associations, the implied conclusion is clearly optimistic. The *recovery* of the former *sick man* is associated with favorably viewed reforms and accession negotiations, and the goal of this PROGRESS is the future FITNESS of Turkey for admission to the EU.

Between them, scenarios 1 and 2 demonstrate an ambivalent assessment of Turkish accession ambitions that varies between a static notion of the EU, which *excludes* Turkey, and a dynamic notion that provides some room for a *rapprochement*, with a reachable goal of *inclusion*, even when the immediate political context seems unfavorable. In some cases, the two scenarios are juxtaposed or mixed in the same text. Thus, after the disappointment of 1997, in an interview with *Die Zeit*, Prime Minister Ecevit first attempted a reversal of the *inside/outside* relationship by predicting that the EU might have to *knock on Turkey's door* in the future, only to fall back into the familiar pattern of blaming Europe for *shutting its door* to Turkey:

> (11) *Ecevit*: The time will come when *Europe will again be knocking on our door*, but first we concentrate on building closer relations with individual European countries.... We are ready to cooperate on a bilateral basis.... However, *as long as the EU's door remains closed to us* we shall not discuss political issues and only focus on economic and other issues. (*Ecevit*: Die Zeit wird kommen, da die Europäer wieder an unsere Tür klopfen. Zunächst einmal konzentrieren wir uns darauf, die Beziehungen zu einzelnen europäischen Ländern aufzubauen,... Solange uns jedoch die EU-Tür verschlossen bleibt, werden wir nicht über politische Probleme reden, sondern uns auf wirtschaftliche und andere Themen beschränken. *Die Zeit*, 25 March 1999)

This scenario mix lacked plausibility. As long as the relationship between Turkey and the EU is viewed as that of the latter *locking its door* to the former, any talk about a future reversal of roles is likely to be interpreted as a resentful complaint or threat by the rejected supplicant rather than as a realistic prediction. Turkey's current prime minister, Recep Tayyip Erdoğan, when faced with a comparable difficulty, tried a conceptually not dissimilar but more diplomatic and assertive tactic by combining DOOR/GATE and BRIDGE metaphors. Instead of simply reversing the bias of the DOOR/GATE concept – of one side *closing* it or the other having *to knock on* it – he depicted the GATE position as advantageous for all sides:

> (12) *Erdoğan*: Turkey is the *gate to the east for Europe and for the east it is the gate to Europe. We have a bridging role*, and Europe should not underestimate that (*Erdogan*: Die Türkei ist das Tor zum Osten für Europa und für den Osten das Tor nach Europa. Wir haben eine Brückenfunktion, und das sollte Europa nicht unterschätzen. *Der Spiegel*, 16 April 2007)

This is, strictly speaking, a 'mixed metaphor' because *Turkey-as-a-gate* is at the same time said to be a *bridge*, but this double image works successfully because in both cases the same target concept, Turkey's role as a mediator between East and West, is in the focus. In the logic of the metaphor, it would be stupid for anyone to neglect the chances that lie in this mediating function, let alone to opt in favor of *closing the gate*.

The remaining 10% of the corpus data contain CONFLICT scenarios, which conjure up the image of a *military confrontation* or *head-on collision* of the EU and Turkey:

(13) The diplomatic *collision* between the EU and Turkey *can be compared to an accident that initially seems to have merely caused damage to the bodywork. However, the serious and really expensive damage is only discovered on closer inspection – that to the chassis and the engine.* (Die diplomatische Kollision zwischen der Europäischen Union und der Türkei ähnelt einem Verkehrsunfall, der auf den ersten Blick nur Blechschaden verursachte. Die ernsten und teuren Schäden werden dann bei näherem Hinsehen erkannt – am Fahrwerk oder am Motor. *Die Welt*, 2 January 1998)

(14) During the important visit by Foreign Minister Fischer to Istanbul and Ankara *several torpedoes were fired with the intention of sinking Turkish-German relations for good. However, an initial damage check shows that this time the torpedoes have missed the target.* (Während des wichtigen Besuches von Bundesaußenminister Joschka Fischer in Istanbul und Ankara wurden einige...Geschosse gezündet, die das...deutsch-türkische Verhältnis gleich wieder auf den tiefsten Meeresboden versenken sollten. Eine erste Bestandsaufnahme zeigt aber, dass die Torpedos diesmal ihr Ziel verfehlt haben. *Süddeutsche Zeitung*, 23 July 1999)

(15) *'Two trains are racing towards each other, and no one is at the controls to apply the brakes'* – that is how EU-diplomats describe the current state of relations between the EU and the official accession candidate Turkey. ('Da rasen zwei Züge aufeinander zu, und keiner sitzt im Stellwerk, um die Bremse zu betätigen', beschreiben die EU-Diplomaten das gegenwärtige Verhältnis zwischen Europa und dem offiziellen Beitrittskandidaten Türkei. *Die Zeit*, 28 September 2006)

The explicit evaluations of the conflicting parties in these quotations are different but the common presupposition that underlies them is that a catastrophic outcome of the accession negotiations is conceivable. Example (13) expresses misgivings about the damage that may only be visible in the future. The image of WAR AT SEA in example (14) is invoked to emphasize the author's relief that *the torpedoes failed to hit the ship* (of Turkish-German relations). In example (15), on the other hand, the author's assessment of future developments in the accession process is grim: The collision of *trains racing toward each other* leaves almost no hope for a good ending. Like the PROGRESS scenario, the CONFLICT scenario implies a process aspect – but with the opposite outcome. It is thus not the case that a dynamic scenario would automatically imply a positive assessment of the process.

These three basic scenarios, which account for all the examples in the corpus sample, cover the following predictive options concerning Turkish accession to the EU: (1) That of Turkey as being excluded, or as being fearful of or being threatened with exclusion from the (static) European *house, family, club* or *company*; (2) An essentially optimistic prospect of inclusion in or partnership with the EU, which presupposes *movement*, including the chance of *opening up* new connections, as in examples (9) and (12); and, finally, (3) the confrontational prospect of mutual exclusion or *closing of doors, war*-like action or a *collision* ending in disaster. Although the distribution statistics for the relative strength of the scenarios in the corpus data cannot be regarded as valid, it seems safe to conclude that the more skeptical scenarios (1) and (3) at least match, if not outweigh, the more hopeful scenario (2) despite the fact that since 2005 the EU has conducted official accession negotiations with Turkey.

Implications for the Perception of Turkish Ambitions to Join the EU

When these findings about the press coverage of Turkey's ambitions for EU membership are compared with social science research results, some matching patterns appear to emerge. As is known from the 2004 report commissioned by the EU (Ahtisaari *et al.*, 2004), the perception of Turkey as an *outsider* is matched by widespread skepticism in public opinion about Turkish candidacy. According to the 'Eurobarometer' opinion polls, the EU average figures for popular opposition to Turkey's accession was 49% in 2002, and they have been at this high level since the late 1990s, having started around the 30% mark in 1986, when the official application for membership was lodged (Eurobarometer, 2008; McLaren, 2007: 252). Opposition is by far the highest in comparison with other accession countries (McLaren, 2007: 253; *Financial Times*, 27 September 2006). The Eurobarometer figures for opposition to Turkish EU membership in Germany are above average (i.e. 55%), but these are surpassed by the figures for other EU countries: Belgium and France (56%), Finland (57%), Austria (63%) and Luxembourg (66%). The least hostile countries are Spain, Ireland, Portugal and the United Kingdom (McLaren, 2007: 252–253).

On the basis of these and further statistical data on public attitudes toward EU enlargement in general and possible Turkish accession in particular, several factors have been identified that influence the marked hostility toward Turkish accession: economic self-interest (in terms of employment chances, income levels, etc.), perceived threats to in-groups regarding social benefits (school, welfare provision, etc.), cultural resources (religion, way of life, expected integration difficulties) and the sociohistorical context, which in the Turkish case is characterized by high mass migration into some EU member states, in particular France, Germany, Austria, Belgium and the Netherlands. Of these factors, context appears to be the strongest one, according to political scientist Lauren McLaren:

> Clearly, citizens are most worried about the potential effects of Turkish entry on the economic and social welfare benefits of their fellow citizens and on national culture and way of life, as they were with other candidates. The difference, however, is that large-scale migration from Turkey may have created an environment in which these fears are amplified to a much greater extent than was the case with the 2004 enlargement candidates. (McLaren, 2007: 273–274)

There is also historical evidence of the failure of successive German governments to implement political reforms that could improve further integration and multiculturalism – for example, concerning citizenship status, race relations legislation and the integration of minorities in the political process (Panayi, 2004). In the past, major agents in politics and public discourse in Germany have instrumentalized popular fears and prejudices about migration for party/political purposes, for instance, by attempting to define a German *Leitkultur* as a 'benchmark' for successful assimilation by cultural minorities (Jung et al., 1997; Manz, 2004; Tibi, 2001). Such statements by politicians and the one-sided framing of EU membership candidates in media reports have been shown to have 'priming effects' on public opinion (Maier & Rittberger, 2008; Nguyen, 2008), and in combination they create and reinforce hostility both toward Turkish migration and to Turkish EU accession.

It is here where the metaphor issue becomes important: The metaphorical scenarios provide the frames that members of the public use to categorize a complex and controversial issue, such as Turkish immigration and Turkish EU accession, and also to evaluate the political options relating to them. If the status quo of Turkey as the outsider vis-à-vis the EU as a homogeneous, self-contained entity is presented as a default condition, it is unlikely that people will be inclined to change their defensive stance toward either accession or immigration. Conflict-centered thematization of integration problems and exclusion-centered thematization of accession problems appear to mutually confirm each other and thus reinforce anti-Turkish prejudices.

The apparent predominance of the 'skeptical' OUTSIDER and COLLISION scenarios in our data therefore not only reflects existing opinions but also helps to shape the expectations of the general public and influence political decision making. Although the governing parties and politicians are not necessarily always at the beck and call of public opinion, they can hardly ignore it either, and they tend to adopt a cautious and accommodating stance, especially when their majorities are slim and consequently their hold on power is insecure (Nguyen, 2008: 285–288). However, the evidence of an alternative scenario that emphasizes the chances of EU–Turkey rapprochement shows that outcomes other than that epitomized by the image of the EU's *door remaining shut in the face* of Turkey are by no means inconceivable. If the public reflects on the presuppositions and implications of the metaphorical frames presented to it by the media and politicians, it can critically interpret and, if need be, question their biases.

References

Ahtisaari, M., Biedenkopf, K., Bonino, E., van den Broek, H., Geremek, B., Giddens, A., Oreja Aguirre, M., Rocard, M. and Rohan, A. (2004) *Turkey in Europe: More than a Promise?* Online document: http://www.independent commissiononturkey.org/pdfs/2004_english.pdf (accessed on 24 October 2009).

Ahtisaari, M., Biedenkopf, K., Bonino, E., van den Broek, H., Geremek, B., Giddens, A., Oreja Aguirre, M., Rocard, M. and Rohan, A. (2009) *Turkey in Europe: Breaking the vicious circle.* Online document: http://www.independent commissiononturkey.org/pdfs/2009_english.pdf (accessed on 24 October 2009).

Ahtisaari, M. *et al.* (2004) *Turkey in Europe: More than a promise?* Online document: http://www.independentcommissiononturkey.org/pdfs/English.pdf (accessed on 24 October 2009).

Bachem, R. and Battke, K. (1991) Strukturen und Funktionen der Metapher *Unser Gemeinsames Haus Europa* im aktuellen politischen Diskurs. In F. Liedtke, M. Wengeler and K. Böke (eds) *Begriffe Besetzen* (pp. 295–307). Opladen: Westdeutscher Verlag.

Balkir, C. and Williams, A.W. (eds) (1993) *Turkey and Europe.* London/New York: Pinter.

Brewer's Dictionary of Phrase and Fable (1999) (ed.) A. Room. London: Cassell.

Büchmann, G. (1898) *Geflügelte Worte. Der Citatenschatz des deutschen Volkes.* Ed. W. Robert-Tornow (19th ed.) Berlin: Haude & Spener'sche Buchhandlung.

Charteris-Black, J. (2004) *Corpus Approaches to Critical Metaphor Analysis.* Basingstoke: Palgrave-Macmillan.

Charteris-Black, J. (2005) *Politicians and Rhetoric. The Persuasive Power of Metaphor.* Basingstoke: Palgrave-Macmillan.

Chilton, P. and Ilyin, M. (1993) Metaphor in political discourse: The case of the "common European house". *Discourse and Society* 4 (1), 7–31.

Croft, W. and Cruse, A.D. (2004) *Cognitive Linguistics.* Cambridge: Cambridge University Press.

Dirven, R., Frank, R.M., and Ilie, C. (eds) (2001) *Language and Ideology. Volume II: Descriptive Cognitive Approaches*. Amsterdam/Philadelphia: John Benjamins.
Drulák, P. (2004) Metaphors Europe lives by: Language and institutional change of the European Union. SPS Working Papers EUI (14), Online document: http://www.arena.uio.no/events/documents/Paper_001.pdf (accessed on 24 October 2009).
Drulák, P. (2006) Motion, container and equilibrium: Metaphors in the discourse about European integration. *European Journal of International Relations* 12 (4), 499–531.
Ermagan, I. (2009) EU-Skeptizismus in der türkischen Politik. *Aus Politik und Zeitgeschichte* 39–40, 15–20.
Eurobarometer (2008) Online document: http://ec.europa.eu/public_opinion/index_en.htm (accessed on 24 October 2008).
Frank, R.M., Dirven, R., Ziemke, T. and Bernárdez, E. (eds) (2008) *Body, Language and Mind. Vol. 2: Sociocultural Situatedness*. Berlin: Mouton de Gruyter.
Göktürk, D., Gramling, D., and Kaes, A. (eds) (2007) *Germany in Transit: Nation and Migration, 1955–2005*. Berkeley/London: University of California Press.
Halm, D. and Thränhardt, D. (2009) Der transnationale Raum Deutschland – Türkei. *Aus Politik und Zeitgeschichte* 39–40, 33–38.
Jones, E. and van der Bijl, N. (2004) Public opinion and enlargement: A gravity approach. *European Union Politics* 5 (3), 331–351.
Jordan, J. and Barker, P. (eds) (2000) *Migrants in German-Speaking Countries: Aspects of Social and Cultural Experience*. London: Central Books.
Jung, M., Wengeler, M. and Böke, K. (eds) (1997) *Die Sprache des Migrationsdiskurses. Das Reden über "Ausländer" in Medien, Politik und Alltag*. Opladen: Westdeutscher Verlag.
Karp, J.A. and Bowler, S. (2006) Broadening and deepening or broadening versus deepening: The question of enlargement and Europe's "hesitant Europeans". *European Journal of Political Research* 45 (3), 369–390.
Kövecses, Z. (2002) *Metaphor: A Practical Introduction*. Oxford: Oxford University Press.
Lakoff, G. and Johnson, M. (1980) *Metaphors We Live By*. Chicago: University of Chicago Press.
Lakoff, G. and Johnson, M. (1999) *Philosophy in the Flesh: The Embodied Mind and Its Challenge to Western Thought*. New York: Basic Books.
Luoma-aho, M. (2004) "Arm" versus "pillar": The politics of metaphors of the Western European Union at the 1990–1 Intergovernmental Conference on Political Union. *Journal of European Public Policy* 11 (1), 1056–1127.
McLaren, L. (2006) *Identity, Interests and Attitudes to European Integration*. Basingstoke: Palgrave-Macmillan.
McLaren, L. (2007) Explaining opposition to Turkish membership of the EU. *European Union Politics* 8, 251–278.
Maier, J. and Rittberger, B. (2008) Shifting Europe's boundaries: Mass media, public opinion and the enlargement of the EU. *European Union Politics* 9, 243–267.
Manz, S. (2004) Constructing a normative national identity: The *Leitkultur* debate in Germany, 2000/2001. *Journal of Multilingual and Multicultural Development* 25 (5 & 6), 481–496.
Merkel, A. (2006) Für die Türkei kann eine sehr, sehr ernste Situation entstehen. *Süddeutsche Zeitung*, 6 November 2006.

Müftüler-Baç, M. (1997) *Turkey's Relations with a Changing Europe.* Manchester: Manchester University Press.

Musolff, A. (1996) False friends borrowing the right words? Common terms and metaphors in European communication. In A. Musolff, C. Schäffner and M. Townson (eds) *Conceiving of Europe – Unity in Diversity* (pp. 15–30). Aldershot: Dartmouth Publishers.

Musolff, A. (2000) Political imagery of Europe: A house without exit doors? *Journal of Multilingual and Multicultural Development* 21 (3), 216–229.

Musolff, A. (2001) The metaphorisation of European politics. *Movement* on the *road* to Europe. In A. Musolff *et al.* (eds) *Attitudes towards Europe. Language in the Unification Process* (pp. 179–200). Aldershot: Ashgate.

Musolff, A. (2004) *Metaphor and Political Discourse. Analogical Reasoning in Debates about Europe.* Basingstoke: Palgrave-Macmillan.

Musolff, A. (2006) Metaphor scenarios in public discourse. *Metaphor and Symbol* 21 (1), 23–38.

Musolff, A. and Zinken, J. (eds) (2009) *Metaphor and Discourse.* Basingstoke: Palgrave-Macmillan.

Nguyen, E.S. (2008) Drivers and brakemen. State decisions on the road to European integration. *European Union Politics* 9 (2), 269–293.

Pamuk, O. (1997) Verschmähte Liebhaber. *Der Spiegel,* 22 December 1997.

Panayi, P. (2000) *Ethnic Minorities in Nineteenth and Twentieth Century Germany: Jews, Gypsies, Poles, Turks and Others.* London: Longman.

Panayi, P. (2004) The evolution of multiculturalism in Britain and Germany: An historical survey. *Journal of Multilingual and Multicultural Development* 25 (5 & 6), 466–480.

Šarić, Lj. (2004) Balkan identity: Changing self-images of the South Slavs. *Journal of Multilingual and Multicultural Development* 25 (5 & 6), 389–407.

Schäffner, C. (1993) Die europäische Architektur – Metaphern der Einigung Europas in der deutschen, britischen und amerikanischen Presse. In A. Grewenig (ed.) *Inszenierte Kommunikation* (pp. 13–30). Opladen: Westdeutscher Verlag.

Schäffner, C. (1995) The "balance" metaphor in relation to peace. In C. Schäffner and A. Wenden (eds) *Language and Peace* (pp. 75–91). Dartmouth: Aldershot.

Schäffner, C. (1996) Building a European house? Or at two speeds into a dead end? Metaphors in the debate on the united Europe. In A. Musolff, C. Schäffner and M. Townson (eds) *Conceiving of Europe – Unity in Diversity* (pp. 31–59). Aldershot: Dartmouth Publishers.

Schmidt, H. (2004) Bitte keinen Größenwahn. *Die Zeit,* 25 November 2004.

Soykut, M. (2007) The genealogy of the "other": The Turks, Islam and Europe. In E. Benum, A. Johansson, J-E. Smilden and A. Storrud (eds) *Are We Captives of History? Historical Essays on Turkey and Europe* (*Tid og Tanke,* No. 11) (pp. 31–70). Oslo: Oslo Academic Press.

Tank, P. (2007) Turkey's ambiguous identity: The symbolic significance of EU membership. In E. Benum, A. Johansson, J-E. Smilden and A. Storrud (eds) *Are We Captives of History? Historical Essays on Turkey and Europe* (*Tid og Tanke,* No. 11) (pp. 129–148). Oslo: Oslo Academic Press.

Taylor, J. R. (1995) *Linguistic Categorization.* Oxford: Oxford University Press.

Tibi, B. (2001) Leitkultur als Wertekonsens. Bilanz einer missglückten Debatte. *Aus Politik und Zeitgeschichte* B1-2/2001, 23–26.

Verheugen, G. (2004) Das Kuschel-Europa ist von gestern. *Die Zeit,* 7 October 2004.

Zinken, J. (2007) Discourse metaphors: The link between figurative language and habitual analogies. *Cognitive Linguistics* 18 (3), 445–466.

Zinken, J., Hellsten, I. and Nerlich, B. (2008) Discourse metaphors. In R. M. Frank *et al.* (eds) *Body, Language and Mind. Vol. 2: Sociocultural Situatedness* (pp. 363–385). Berlin/New York: Mouton de Gruyter.

Appendix. Source domains, source concepts, German lexical tokens and share (%) of the German sample in the Turkey–EU corpus (descending order of frequency)

Source Domains	*Source Concepts*	*German Lexical Tokens*	*Share*
MOVEMENT–TRANSPORT	APPROACH	Annäherung, nähern, Heranführung, nicht im Weg stehen, bewegen, weiter sein, zurobben, überschreiten	41%
	ANCHORAGE	Ankergrund	
	SPEED	Geschwindigkeit	
	STEP(S)	step(s), Schritte	
	WAY	Weg, Marathon	
	TRAIN, TRACK, RAILWAY STATION	Zug, Züge, Gleis, Bahnhof, Weichenstellung	
	ROAD MAP	Roadmap, road map, Fahrplan	
- DELAY	OBSTACLES	Hürden, Stoppschild, Hindernis, Fallen, Minen, Fußangeln, blockieren	
	WAITING	Warteschleife	
- ACCIDENT	COLLISION	Verkehrsunfall, Kollision, Crash	
	DERAIL	Entgleisen	
BUILDING	BRIDGE	Brückenfunktion	24%
	PILLAR	Sicherheitspfeiler	
- HOUSE	HOUSE	Haus	
	BOLT	Riegel	
	DOOR	Tür	
	GATE	Tor	
	ROOM	Zimmer	
	THRESHOLD	Schwelle	
	WALL	Wand	
	WING	Flügel	

SOCIAL INSTITUTION	CLUB	Club, Klub, Christenclub	15%
	TRADES GUILD	Kaufmannsgilde	
	TABLE	Tisch	
	BENCH	Katzenbank	
– SCHOOL	TEACHER	Lehrmeister	
	HOMEWORK	Hausaufgaben	
	EXAM RESULTS	Zeugnis	
	CANE	Rohrstock	
FAMILY	FAMILY	Familie, Großfamilie	9%
	BROTHER	Bruder	
	CHILDREN	Kinder	
	COUSINS	Vettern	
LOVE–RELATIONSHIP	LOVER	Liebhaber	4%
	WEDDING	Hochzeit	
	DIVORCE	Scheidung	
BODY–LIFE–HEALTH	SICK MAN	kranker Mann	2%
	ALIEN BODY	Fremdkörper	
GAME–SPORT	GOLDEN GOAL	ein goldenes Tor	2%
	TRUMP CARD	Trumpfkarte	
WAR	TORPEDOES	Abfeuern politischer Torpedos, torpedieren	1%
PHYSICS–GEOMETRY	CORE	(magnetischer) Kern, Kerneuropa	1%
GEOGRAPHY	ISLAND	Insel	0.5%
NATURE – ANIMAL	DONKEY	Lastesel	0.5%
(TOTAL)			100%

Chapter 11
Contested Identities: Miroslav Krleža's Two Europes versus the Notion of Europe's Edge

Ingrid Hudabiunigg

Introduction

The controversial and highly charged issue of whether today's European Union of 27 states is based on a common European cultural tradition has been at the center of much debate between historians, politicians, political scientists, the media and representatives of wider public discourse. Hidden in this discourse is the assumption of an evolutionary and moral hierarchy of European nations that places the nations of the west in the leading positions and those in the east in the lower ranks.

On the basis of a large corpus of texts from British and German media, and from several separate analyses of German and British perspectives in the quality press about the Czech Republic, Poland, Russia and Slovenia (Hudabiunigg, 1996, 1999, 2000, 2003), I have developed the hypothesis of two specific cognitive models as underlying most news reporting (Hudabiunigg, 2004). There seem to be opposing frames of 'civilization' versus 'barbarism' as cognitive models that function as categories for the perception of Europe from the west European perspective, which includes the older members of the European Union. The eastern frame includes (to a greater or lesser extent) the central and east European countries and the Balkans. These frames are multielement cognitive models through which a society views and structures its own image and that of other societies, countries or nations. The function of the frame is to present a simplified, often manipulative schema of a complex social, political and cultural reality.

The widespread degradation of the eastern part of the continent is based on a very long tradition. This tradition started during the Enlightenment, which for the first time developed a secular idea of Europe with a set of political and cultural values, framing western centers as places of civilization in opposition to those in the east, which were seen as places of 'barbarism' devoid of western values (Bugge, 1999).

In this study, which focuses on Miroslav Krleža, a major 20th-century author from the edge of the current European Union, and on his views on this contested region, I focus my debate on Europe's cultural borders within the wider discourse on the construction of cultural entities, their centers and peripheries and their legitimacy. Toward the end of this analysis, I briefly discuss further texts by contemporary writers and journalists on the present state of the relationships between 'Europe' and the Balkans. Looking at different approaches to this problem shows whether such a synopsis can challenge the presentation of 'Europe's edge' in the western media.

Miroslav Krleža: A Short Biography

Miroslav Krleža (1893–1981) was a dominant figure in the cultural life of the two Yugoslav states of the 20th century, both monarchist and communist. His collected works number more than 50 volumes. His output covers all areas of imaginative literature and political texts. His enduring legacy is as one of the finest European modernist authors and independent intellectuals. Over long periods of his life, he was stigmatized for his unorthodox views in his own country (Baur, 1973a, 1973b; Lauer, 1984).

Krleža was born in Zagreb (German *Agram*) in the Hungarian half of the Austro-Hungarian Monarchy. He was educated in a Jesuit school in Zagreb, in a preparatory military school in Pécs (German *Fünfkirchen*) and at the Ludoviceum Military Academy in Budapest. At the age of 19, he changed sides and volunteered for the Serbian army to fight for the liberation of all South Slavs, but because the Serbs suspected him of being an Austrian spy, he was forced to return to Austria-Hungary. The Austrians stripped him of his officer's rank and at the outbreak of World War I, sent him to Galicia as a common soldier. Soon he started to write, expressing strong antiwar feelings by depicting the miserable conditions of the common soldiers on the front (Nilsson, 1990).

Like many young European intellectuals of this era, he was initially deeply impressed by the Russian revolution and joined the Communist Party in 1918. Opposing the newly established monarchist regime of Yugoslavia, he founded several left-wing journals. These were often censored or banned due to the nonconformist views expressed in them. He also worked for the stage, presenting plays that were a merciless revelation of social injustice in the unchanged class system of the society of the Kingdom of the Serbs, Croats and Slovenes. His attacks and comments on political, psychological, artistic and ethical issues frequently earned him the enmity of Yugoslavia's ruling class during the monarchy and, after the assassination of King Aleksandar, of the increasingly totalitarian government in the 1930s.

During World War II, he refused to collaborate with the Croatian Ustasha government. However, having been expelled by the Communist Party as early as 1939, he did not join the partisans either.

After the end of the war, in communist Yugoslavia under the leadership of Josip Broz Tito, Krleža became increasingly influential in cultural politics. In 1947, he was elected vice president of the Yugoslav Academy of Sciences and Arts. Being a determined opponent of 'socialist realism' and all kinds of dogma that limit artistic freedom, he became a driving force in liberalizing Yugoslav culture. From 1958 to 1961 he was the president of the Writers' Union of Yugoslavia. In addition to his literary activities, he was editor-in-chief of the *Enciklopedija Jugoslavije* and founded the Yugoslav Institute of Lexicography in Zagreb (Krležijana, 1993–1999). He proclaimed the aim of his many activities to be to analyze the historical and political facts that are the origin of the common culture of the peoples of this macro-region, to build up a shared cultural consciousness and to counteract nationalistic forces that might undermine these efforts.

In constant conflict with clerics, expelled by the Communist Party and harassed by members of the various governments, Krleža maintained his independence and fought for his country's independence. The biting criticism, often barely hidden, on political issues in his pseudo-fictitious settings also earned him the enmity of representatives of various Yugoslav elites. Furthermore, his Marxist views during the Cold War did not earn him much positive appraisal by the general public in the west either.

Nevertheless, there are critics who consider him to be one of the great intellectual forces in Yugoslavia and the Balkans of the 20th century. In this vein, he was, in an essay in the American journal *Modern Drama*, praised after his death as 'the dominant cultural, literary, and dramaturgic figure that bestrides 20th-century Yugoslav literature like a giant out of Rabelais' (Suvin, 1984: 81).

This analysis shows how Krleža's novels, essays and speeches analyze the complex economic, political and ideological forces in this region and how the protagonists and other characters often personified the forces in this power game. He highlights the divisions between the powerful political, economic and cultural centers in western Europe and the peoples in the east and southeast of the continent that are seen from these centers as being at the 'periphery', as inhabiting a poor 'backyard'. I focus on Krleža's social criticism, linked to the notion of the 'Two Europes', which he laid out in the novels *Banket u Blitvi* (Banquet in Blitva, 1964) and *Zastave* (Banners, 1976), the essays 'Šta je Evropa?' (What is Europe? 1963), 'Illyricum Sacrum' (Sacred Illyria, 1966a), 'Bogumilski mramorovi' (Bogumil Marbles, 1966b) and 'Hrvatska književna laž' (The Croatian Literary Lie, 1967b), and the speech 'Govor na kongresu književnika u Ljubljani' (Address at the Writer's Congress in Ljubljana, 1967a).

Parameters of Analysis

Krleža's writings contain frequent statements about the relationship of the centers of domination in Europe and the Balkans. In the following parameters of analysis, originally established by Foucault (1982) and adapted to my topic, I look at the following four kinds of resistance to exploitation and subjection by outside forces: (1) resistance to political oppression, (2) resistance to religious oppression, (3) resistance to economic exploitation and (4) resistance to the denial of one's cultural identity.

Resistance to political oppression

Throughout his writings, Krleža is deeply concerned that Croatia and the Balkans are treated as savage and primitive communities with no culture or history of their own (Dubravka, 1997: 48). This aspect is pronounced in the following defiant way by one of the characters in the novel *Banners*, commenting on the former glorious times of independence:

> (1) In the midst of Europe [is] one of the oldest European peoples, proud to have in its political past a seven-hundred-year-old parliamentary law-giving tradition, older than that of the English and one of the western European parliaments which, until the February Revolution of 1848, still passed its laws in Latin. (Usred Evrope, jedan od najstarijih evropskih naroda, koji se u svojoj političkoj prošlosti ponosi sedamstogodišnjim parlamentarnim zakonodavnim tradicijama, starijim od engleskih, jedan od zapadnoevropskih parlamenata, koji je do Februarske revolucije 1848 donosio zakone pisane latinskim jezikom. Krleža, 1982: 210)

It is significant that the parliament of Croatia is seen as being 'western European', linking this reference to the use of Latin, the old European 'lingua franca', as the official language of legislative administration.

Reflecting on Croatia's lost independence (its legislative body was moved to the capital of the Austro-Hungarian Empire until the end of World War I), the discourse among the novel's main characters is an appreciation of the accomplishment of self-government of past times and a complaint about the aggression of foreign powers. This aggression robbed the country of its independence and led to the subjugation of its people:

> (2) This parliament of the Croatian people today does not have its own voice in international legal forums because it is occupied by a foreign force against its people's will. This parliament has demonstrated its political independence so many times in the past that it does not acknowledge any other but its own people's law-giving government (... taj i takav Sabor hrvatskog naroda nema danas svoje riječi pred

međunarodnim pravnim forumima, jer je okupiran tuđinskom silom proti svoje, u historiji toliko puta manifestirane slobodarske političke volje, da ne priznaje nikakve zakonodavne vlasti osim svoje vlastite, narodne. Krleža, 1982: 210)

The later parts of *Banners* take place in the Kingdom of the Serbs, Croats and Slovenes, which did not bring democratic rights to the people either because it soon reverted to an oppressive monarchic dictatorship. The elites readily assumed the role of a *comprador bourgeoisie* in servicing western European finance in its exploitation of the natural and human resources in Yugoslavia (see Section 'Resistance to economic exploitation').

In the satirical novel *Banquet in Blitva*, the author depicts the brutal violation of human rights by a ruler of a semi-fictitious country, barely hiding its parallels to the historic Balkans. One of the main settings is the Hotel Blitvania. As a residence for the head of government, it hides its history as a torture prison:

(3) In the newspapers of that mythical period, when Barutanski ruled from that accursed hotel as the first Protector, some texts contained cleverly infiltrated hints that someone had been massacred in the Hotel Blitvania, that someone had given evidence in court from a stretcher, that someone had been blinded, ... but today it has all been forgotten, today the Hotel Blitvania has been renovated as a first-class hotel. Today rich foreigners and foreign diplomats of high rank stay there. Today, for whole nights, they dance the Tango-Milango. (U novinama onog mitskog vremena, kada je Barutanski vladao iz tog prokletog hotela kao prvi Protektor, čita se u tekstovima lukavo prokrijumčarenih redaka, između dvije-tri riječi plaho i oprezno, naslućuje se da su u hotelu 'Blitvanija' opet nekoga izmasakrirali, da je u sudnici netko odgovarao iz nosiljke, da su nekoga oslijepili, ... a danas je sve to zaboravljeno, danas je hotel 'Blitvanija' obnovljen kao prvorazredan Hotel ... danas u hotelu 'Blitvanija' odsjedaju otmjeni stranci i strani diplomatski dostojanstvenici, danas se tu čitave noći pleše 'Tango-Milango'. Krleža, 1964: 111)

In the author's view, foreigners coming from Europe's wealthier regions had the obligation to help the underprivileged and unhappy citizens of Blitva develop its economic and cultural potential. However, instead of dedicating their efforts to developing the region according to noble European values, they ruthlessly exploit the country:

(4) ... and that glorious Europe, instead of Europeanizing Blitva, was on the contrary itself becoming even more Blitvanized, and Blitvanized to a point of pure animalism; it played 'Tango-Milango' in the Hotel Blitvania and this today has become the sole role of its European

Blitvanization. (...i ta slavna Evropa, mjesto da je evropejizirala Blitvu, obratno od toga, poblitvinjuje se sama sve više i poblitvinivši se do potpunog poživinčenja ona svira 'Tango-Milango' u hotelu 'Blitvanija', i to je danas postalo jedinom svrhom njene evropske blitvinizacije. Krleža, 1964: 111)

Resistance to religious oppression

In *Illyricum Sacrum*, which can be seen as the cultural history of the region in the form of a long essay, Krleža goes far back into history to find more proof for his arguments about the uncompromising will for the independence of the peoples of this region and their own forms of expressing it.

Although missionaries to the Balkans from the large religious organizations in Constantinople and Rome Christianized the Balkans, there was soon resistance to their strict hierarchy, as can be seen from the emergence of the lay movements of the Bogumils as early as the 13th century. These were movements that consisted mostly of members of the lower and poorer classes of society. In the cultural history of all of Europe, the author maintains, they are deserving of special notice because these were movements against the institutionalized Churches long before John Wycliff in England, Jan Hus in Bohemia or Martin Luther in Germany. The Bogumils were pioneers and predecessors, and not the followers of religious leaders in the great centers. Against the strong opposition of Rome, they created their own totally independent church organizations. Their great sculptors left a legacy of thousands of stone monuments in honor of their dead, which were not imitations of any western or eastern styles, but unique forms of independent art. In their particular form of artistic expression, the author sees a stubborn and, at the same time, proud attitude against all claims of influence from outside.

(5) On these monuments there is not one figure of a human being bending his knees or clasping his hands in prayer before death. Nor is there a human figure honoring glorious gods or their regents from Byzantium or Rome. These hands signify a courageous challenge for dueling with all the moral authorities of their times. Much more radically than Wycliff, Hus, or Luther they accept no moral hierarchies – and two or three hundred years earlier. (Nema ni jedne ljudske pojave koja bi na ovim spomenicima klečala sklopljenih ruku u molitvi pred smrću, i nema ni jedne u proskinezi pred veličanstvom bizantinskih ili rimskih bogova i božanskih namjesnika. Ove ruke..., kao znamen smionog izazova na dvoboj sa svima moralnim autoritetima svoga vremena, ne priznavajući nikakve moralnev hijerarhije u

mnogo radikalnijoj formi od Wiclifa ili Husa ili Luthera dvjesta i trista godina ranije. Krleža, 1966b: 245–246)

In a very specific way, the 'national mentality' would assimilate and transform elements of religious expression from Byzantine, Greek, Latin, Carolingian and Gothic variants of art, and would thus produce something unique.

Resistance to economic exploitation

Krleža's importance as the leading voice of socially oriented writers grew steadily in the interwar period and after World War II. In his much-applauded programmatic speech at the Yugoslav Writers' Conference in Ljubljana, he analyzed and uncovered the hidden materialist interests of the west, which were covered by 'foul sympathies'. He dismissed the pretence of humanitarian motives by western representatives of the bourgeois class and the window-dressing in their rhetoric, charging that their actions were solely undertaken to ensure the exploitation of mineral resources and the human workforce. In Krleža's words,

> (6) Many of our western sympathizers are licking their lips for our political roast, when we are sizzling in the pan of our own illusions. The mouths of these diplomatic cooks are running from lusting for the profits from our copper, oil, aluminum, wood, and uranium, from thinking of our sausages and our plum brandy, our people as their work force and their cannon fodder. (Po mišljenju mnogobrojnih naših zapadnjačkih simpatizera mi tiho cvrčimo u taví vlastitih iluzija, i mnogi se taj diplomatski kogo već oblizuje nad ovom dragom političkom pečenkom, od pomisli na slatke dividende našega bakra i nafte, aluminijuma i hrastovine, uranija, kobasica i šljivovice, radne snage i topovskog mesa. Krleža, 1967a: 52)

Against this supposed exploitation, in the same speech, he supports a position of pride in the political sovereignty of the Socialist Federal Republic of Yugoslavia and its independent path:

> (7) The last decade of our history is not a plagiarism or a reflex of some western European movement. In the Balkans and on the Danube, we are the only socialist country that has fought for our own political form according to the laws of our own historical development. (Posljednji decenij naše historije ne javlja se kao plagijat ili kao odraz nekih pokreta zapadnoevropskih, pošto smo mi na Balkanu i na Dunavu jedina socijalistička zemlja koja se do svog vlastitog socijalističkog političkog oblika probila vlastitim snagama, po zakonu svog vlastitog historijskog razvoja. Krleža, 1967a: 55)

Resistance to the denial of one's cultural identity
Deconstructing the images of the Balkans as 'Other'

In his speech at the Writers' Union, Krleža argues that the problems of the regions of the South and East Slavs, of the Hungarians and Romanians as well, have to be analyzed and solved independently and not by falling back into past traps. The imperialist powers had built their empires and great cultures 'on the skeletons of defeated and crushed peoples' ('na kostima poraženih i zgaženih naroda' Krleža, 1967a: 56), to which unfortunately the people between Carinthia, Lake Balaton, Istria and Thessaloniki belonged. These powers had denied them the right not only to their own material identity but also to a cultural and moral identity of their own.

This point of view is taken up several times in Krleža's writings. In the essay 'What is Europe?' he scathingly ridicules western Europe's attempts to form an adequate image of the eastern part of the continent and its culture. According to Krleža, the images of the Balkans are nothing but ethnic clichés that have been transported over the centuries, sometimes even by writers of great fame:

> (8) In western Europe our country was always judged according to a ballad, translated by Goethe from our folk songs and edited by the Venetian Abbé Fortis: 'Viaggio in Dalmazia'... a picturesque ethnic image was constructed for the tourist. This was a folk image mixing Turkish coffee pots and billowing pants, veiled women, big drums, woolen caps in Albanian fashion, tamburitzas, and vendettas. It was a legend of Balkan people lagging behind the times in archaic primitivism consisting of blind gusla players, hajduks, and vampires – a thick mush of Oriental mysticism and melancholy passivity on the one hand, and brutal and bloody family feuds on the other. (...sve što [se] u Zapadnoj Evropi o nama znalo bilo je da je Goethe preveo jednu baladu iz naše narodne poezije, [u] poznatoj knjizi mletačkog abbéa Fortisa, 'Viaggio in Dalmazia',... Tako se rodila o našoj zemlji pitoreskna, turistička reklamna slika o narodu džezve, dimlija, feredže, goča, tupana, kečeta, tamburice i krvne osvete, legenda o arhajski zaostalom balkanskom narodu slijepih guslara, hajdučije i vampira, o nekoj vrsti melase orijentalne mistike i melankolične pasivnosti s jedne, a okrutne vendette s druge strane. Krleža, 1963: 8)

In 'Illyricum Sacrum', Krleža saw the other-image of the Balkans, held by the west, as a clear form of discrimination. His form of deconstructing this image is a basic attack on the underlying presuppositions of the 'grandeur' of rulers, in line with the egalitarian goals of the European revolutions. It also means questioning some of the basic assumptions of governance that have been taken for granted for centuries throughout Europe:

(9) It is correct that even today the critics of Western Europe show us their contempt. In their view we are 'barbarians' and, according to their logic, we are barbarians because we have never portrayed ourselves in a megalomaniac fashion. We are even ashamed somehow of our kings and saints. Their grandeur seems to us ephemeral. But this in fact holds true for most of the grandeur of European kings and saints. It is a delusion and nothing else. (Istina je da nas Zapadna Evropa i dan-današnji prezire, jer smo iz njene umišljene perspektive 'barbari', a barbari smo, po toj logici evropskih idealističkih predrasuda, jer nismo o sebi progovorili megalomanski, stideći se pomalo i sami svojih vlastitih kraljeva i svetaca, smatrajući ih efemeridama, kao što je velika većina tih evropskih kraljeva i svetaca samo to, doista, i ništa više. Krleža, 1966a: 31–32)

The importance that the southeast of the continent had for the defense of all of Europe, even being praised by the Pope as the 'bulwark of Christianity' (Žanić, 2005: 37ff.), had never been fully appreciated by the general public in the west. Here the poet acts as historical memory:

(10) For Byzantium, the Vatican, Venice, and Vienna, we had been for centuries the 'Antemurale', and this until the end of their power. And even the Habsburg Empire disappeared without ever acknowledging that it would have been the prey of the Kurdish devils in the sixteenth century, had we not been forced into that role of prey on its behalf and on its account. (Pa ipak, uprkos tome, mi smo Bizantu i Vatikanu i Mlecima i Beču bili 'Antemurale' vjekovima, sve do njihove propasti, a i habsburška Austrija nestala je sa pozornice nesvijesna do posljednjeg dana svoje egzistencije, da bi je kurdistanski đavao bio odnio već u šestnaestome stoljeću, da nije u njeno ime i za njen račun bio odnio nas. Krleža, 1966a: 32–33)

Closely corresponding to these other-stereotypes from literary critics and art historians of western Europe is the self-image constructed by nationalistic movements of the Balkans and their own writers. The movement called Illyrianism (or the *Hrvatski narodni preporod* 'Croatian national revival') aiming to create a Croatian national establishment had already been opposed by Krleža in his essay 'The Croatian Literary Lie', which he first published in the journal *Plamen* in 1919. This essay criticizes Croatian literature of the nineteenth century as poorly imitating the European romantic tradition without seeing the special conditions of its situation. In their works, these urban intellectuals addressed national and social problems, but the soft light in which they showed the poor falsified their actual suppression by the state, the church and their intellectual acolytes in a pseudo-harmonious way. The characters in this form of literature were not country people, but rather the authors in fake rural cover-ups:

(11) In this country one cultivates the motif of the peasant in literature in such a manner that our literature today walks one hundred percent in underpants and Balkan leather folk shoes as the romantic ideal of all ideologists. (U ovoj zemlji kultivira se seljački motiv u književnosti tako, da nam se danas književnost kreće sto posto u gaćama i u opancima kao romantičan ideal svih političkih ostvarenja. Krleža, 1967b: 104)

Reconstructing cultural identity

Most of Krleža's thoughts on the culture and art of the historical space of the macro-region between the Adriatic and the Black Sea can be found in the essays cited above: 'Illyricum Sacrum' and 'What is Europe?' In the latter essay, the author begins his account of the region by going back to the prehistoric and historical periods of the Illyrians, Greeks and Romans. He then shows that, from the times when Europe was being formed up until the twentieth century, the eastern parts of the continent always had more of a burden to bear than the western parts:

(12) When speaking of Europe today...we should not forget that there are two Europes. Alongside the classical, western, pantheistic, grandiose, historically pathetic Europe ...there lives a second one: modest, marginalized, and for centuries peripheral, the Europe of the eastern and southeastern peoples – peoples from the Baltic, Carpathians, Danube, and Balkans. Their destiny was to live not within the European walls, but 'antemurale', forming a sort of buffer and eastern border against the Ottoman and Mongolian danger and all other threats of a political and military nature. (...govoreći o Evropi...ne treba zaboraviti da i danas još uvijek postoje dvije Evrope. Uz klasičnu, zapadnjačku, panteonsku, grandioznu, historijski patetičnu Evropu živi druga, skromna, potisnuta, vjekovima osvajana periferična Evropa istočnih i jugoistočnih evropskih naroda, naroda iz pribaltičke, karpatske, dunavske, i balkanske perspektive, naroda kojima je sudbina odredila da ne žive unutar evropskih zidina (intra muros), nego da budu 'Antemurale' neka vrsta obrambenog tvrđavnog bedema: istočna Granica od osmanlijskih, mongolskih i raznih drugih vojničkih i političkih opasnosti. Krleža, 1963: 8)

Krleža views the inequality between the two parts of Europe as being caused predominantly by their different geographic (and therefore military) situations. Whereas the west could rely on relative protection from Asian aggressors, the eastern part of Europe was forced into continual fights due to its geographic exposure:

(13) The struggle for European values in the intellectual as well as material sense was much more dramatic in the eastern European countries than in the western provinces of Europe. The wealth of the

European heritage there could be taken forward in uninterrupted continuity from generation to generation. In the east, on the other hand, heritage could only be transferred under the desperate conditions of a brutal fight for existence. (Borba za evropske principe u idejnom i materijalnom smislu u istočnoevropskim zemljama nerazmjerno je tragičnija od one u zapadnim provincijama, jer dok su bogatstva kulturnog nasljedstva na Zapadu tekla u neprekinutom kontinuitetu od pokoljenja na pokoljenje, ovdje, na Istoku, ti se rezultati otimaju u očajnim uslovima okrutne, elementarne borbe za opstanak biološke supstancije. Krleža, 1963: 8)

Krleža argues that the achievements in the east in every form of political, philosophical or theological thought as well as in art and architecture are equal to those in the west and, in view of being constantly endangered by invasions from Asia, have to be evaluated in a fairer way in the future. He proudly names these achievements one by one:

(14) From Kant's burial place, and Gdańsk, the cradle of Schopenhauer, to Lithuania, the country of Chopin and Mickiewicz, the Wawel in Krakow, where Copernicus, Dürer, and Stoss left a legacy of their genius to future generations, to the Prague of Jan Hus and Comenius, the era of Matthias Corvinus, this unique variant of a South Slavic humanism and the inspiration of a Hungarian Quatrocento, the Dalmatian towns, testimonies to the spirit of the Renaissance of a symbiosis of Slavic and Romance features until the Baroque. (Od Kantova groba i Danziga, gdje je bila kolijevka Arthura Schopenhauera, do Litvanije, zemlje Chopina i Mickiewicza, do Wawela Krakovskog, gdje su Kopernik, Dürer i Stosz namrli pokoljenjima svjedočanstva svojih genija, preko Praga Jana Husa i Komenskoga do budimske Korvine, te jedinstvene varijante jugoslavenskog humanizma i madžarske kvatročentističke inspiracije, do dalmatinskih gradova, koji su u poetskoj varijanti slavenskog renesansnog duha varirali poetsku simbiozu talijansko-slavensku sve do baroka. Krleža, 1963: 8)

Krleža's main claim is that the west of Europe would lose immensely in many areas if the achievements in the east were not taken into account:

(15) All of these are glorious periods of European culture. Without them, the west would be amputated in philosophical and artistic, political, and scholarly areas. Europe is not only the west, but also the east! (Sve su to slavni datumi evropske civilizacije, bez kojih bi zapad ostao okrnjen i oštećen misaono i umjetnički, politički i naučno u mnogobrojnim predjelima duha i morala. Evropa podjednako je istočna kao i zapadna! Krleža, 1963: 8)

Krleža sees the acceptance of the equality of these two parts as a precondition for a future role of Europe in a global context. His vision of Europe's future based on its great past depends on overcoming this barrier dividing the continent:

> (16) When Europe, our glorious homeland, understands that it has two poles, then it will have the chance again to be what it has been for centuries, *lux in tenebris*, the only guarantee of a harmonious development of all continents, that it has discovered and civilized, from the days of ancient Greece until today. (Pa kad se naš slavni evropski zavičaj bude jednoga dana uzvisio do političke i kulturne svijesti o značenju svog bilateralnog raspona, postat će ponovno ono što je kroz vjekove i bio: lux in tenebris i jedini garant za harmoničan razvoj svih kontinenata koje je otkrio i civilizirao od starohelenskih dana do danas. Krleža, 1963: 8)

Conclusion

I conclude this condensed overview by postulating that Krleža's legacy is the deconstruction of the notion that Europe's sole cultural center is in the west, and his claim that there is, instead, a bipolarity in the continent. Eastern and southeastern Europe's great contributions to common European cultural heritage in philosophical and religious thought, literature and architecture need to be evaluated in the context of the extreme conditions under which they were produced.

Growing up under Habsburg rule and the often vain pomp and glory of the ruling classes, in his youth Miroslav Krleža was extremely receptive to the egalitarian ideals of European revolutions in the 18th and 19th centuries and, after the Russian revolution, also to Marxist ideas. From Croatia, a province of the Austro-Hungarian Empire, rankling mainly under the yoke of the Hungarian nobility, he soon became a major force in the Yugoslav movement for cultural, and eventually political, unification of the peoples of this region. The region was separated by historical circumstances under the Ottoman and Central European powers.

From his travels and long stays in western Europe and his extensive reading in several European languages, Krleža experienced the widespread degradation of the eastern part of the continent, a degradation based on a very long western European tradition.

It is a tragedy that, a decade after Krleža's death, the predominant frame for reports on southeast Europe is again that of 'barbarism' in contrast to the Enlightenment concept of 'civilization' for the self-approbation of the west. Yugoslavia, a country known for decades for its independent approach to communism, and economically and politically the most liberal country in eastern central Europe, fell apart. The Serbo-Croat speaking area became the scene of some of the worst atrocities since World War II, and language 'was readily drawn upon in bolstering up Our cause and satanising Their sides' (Bugarski, 2004: 29).

No other recent conflict in Europe has been more intensely studied and moralized over than the break-up of Yugoslavia. Western media almost unanimously focused on the tradition of feuds and vendettas in Balkan society, which Krleža had already criticized as unjustified other-stereotypes. The foreign policy of the leading NATO powers, according to the western press and their commentators, was driven by the highest moral concerns. Their forces were therefore trying to protect the population while Yugoslav forces were committing barbaric 'genocidal' acts (Hammond & Herman, 2000; Macdonald, 2002; Mappes-Niediek, 2005).

Eminent writers and scholars, such as Peter Handke (1996), Harold Pinter (2000) and Noam Chomsky (2006), on the other hand, have adopted perspectives differing widely from those of the most influential newspapers and television stations in the west. They targeted NATO governments and the western media as bearing their share of responsibility in the destruction of Yugoslavia. They argued that the proclaimed western ideals and high moral concerns were only the window-dressing for the pursuit of geostrategic and economic interests that promoted military intervention and eventually, the bombing campaign against Serbia in 1999. The *realpolitik* behind the rhetoric, according to them, was an unjustified abuse of military power and at the same time an exemption from international law and a calculated disregard for Serbian sovereignty in the name of 'human rights'. Handke's, Pinter's and Chomsky's defense of political and cultural autonomy against interference is linked to Krleža's dismissal of the pretence of humanitarian motives by western representatives (see Section 'Resistance to economic exploitation').

In a critical account of French and German war reports and a self-scrutinizing account of his postwar journey to the Balkans, Handke asked the following question: 'Who will ever rewrite this history differently, be it only in its nuances – something that nevertheless could help a lot to release the nations from their frozen stereotypes of each other?' (1996: 50).

It would be premature to assess the final outcomes of the acts of separation in the Balkans. The borders currently established and fortified by outside powers do not look likely to dissolve in the near future.

It is still an open question whether in the future a common cultural identity for all Europeans will evolve that successfully appeals to all citizens and will overcome foe-images for the east and particularly the Balkans in the southeast of the continent.

None of the critical authors cited above seems to be acquainted with Miroslav Krleža's writings. Nevertheless, they stand with him in a noble – and, as Krleža claimed, truly 'European' – tradition of thought, the fight against deception of peoples by governments and their propagandists.

Acknowledgments

The author would like to express her thanks to Dennis Beard and John B. Walmsley for their critical readings and useful comments on an earlier version of this chapter, to Anna Laggner and Barbara Sax for their help in exploring various archives to locate the works of Miroslav Krleža and last but not least to Ljiljana Šarić for her help with the translations.

References

Baur, R. (1973a) Miroslav Krleža und sein Werk. In R. Baur (ed.) *Miroslav Krleža zum 80. Geburtstag* (pp. 6–9). Munich: Südosteuropa-Gesellschaft.

Baur, R. (1973b) Krležas Kampf für eine freie Literatur und Kunst in Jugoslawien. In R. Baur (ed.) *Miroslav Krleža zum 80. Geburtstag* (pp. 9–29). Munich: Südosteuropa-Gesellschaft.

Bugarski, R. (2004) Language and boundaries in the Yugoslav context. In B. Busch and H. Kelly-Holmes (eds) *Language Discourse and Borders in the Yugoslav Successor States* (pp. 21–37). Clevedon: Multilingual Matters.

Bugge, P. (1999) The use of the middle: Mitteleuropa vs. Střední Evropa. *European Review of History* 6 (1), 15–35.

Chomsky, N. (2006) *Failed States*. London: Penguin.

Delanty, G. (1996) The resonance of Mitteleuropa: A Habsburg myth or antipolitics? *Theory, Culture & Society* 13 (4), 93–108.

Dubravka, J. (1997) Miroslav Krleža's "Zastave" 1962–1967: Socialism, Yugoslavia, and the historical novel. *South Atlantic Review* 62 (4), 32–56.

Foucault, M. (1982) *The Subject and Power*. Brighton: Harvester Press.

Hammond, P. and Herman, E.S. (eds) (2000) *Degraded Capability: The Media and the Kosovo Crisis*. London: Pluto Press.

Handke, P. (1996) *Eine winterliche Reise zu den Flüssen Donau, Save, Morawa und Drina*. Frankfurt a.M.: Suhrkamp.

Hudabiunigg, I. (1996) Nationale Gattungsbegriffe. Auto- und Heterostereotype von "Deutschen" und "Slawen". Eine textlinguistische Untersuchung. *Germanoslavica* 3 (8), 83–93.

Hudabiunigg, I. (1999) Ein Pole wie aus dem Bilderbuch: "nobel, melancholisch und verwegen". Zur Metaphorik über Polen in deutschen Medien. *Kwartalnik Neofilologiczny* 41 (3–4), 403–415.

Hudabiunigg, I. (2000) Der "Russische Bär"-redivivus. In E. Reichmann (ed.) *Narrative Konstruktion nationaler Identität* (pp. 251–281). St. Ingbert: Röhrig Universitätsverlag.

Hudabiunigg, I. (2003) Slowenien in der deutschen Presse. In K. Teržan Kopecky und T. Petrič (eds) *Germanistik im Kontaktraum Europa II. 1. Linguistik* (pp. 346–361). Maribor: Pedagoška fakulteta.

Hudabiunigg, I. (2004) The otherness of Eastern Europe. *Journal of Multilingual and Multicultural Development* 25 [5–6], 369–388.

Krleža, M. (1963) Šta je Evropa? *Borba* 28 (110), 8.

Krleža, M. (1964) *Banket u Blitvi. Roman u tri knjige. Knjiga prva.* (= *Sabrana Djela Miroslava Krleže*). Zagreb: Zora.
Krleža, M. (1966a) Illyricum Sacrum. In *Sabrana djela Miroslava Krleže 23. Eseji*, vol. 6 (pp. 2–235). Zagreb: Zora.
Krleža, M. (1966b) Bogumilski mramorovi. In *Sabrana djela Miroslava Krleže 23. Eseji*, vol. 5 (pp. 237–246). Zagreb: Zora.
Krleža, M. (1967a) Govor na Kongresu književnika u Ljubljani. (5 October 1952). In *Sabrana djela Miroslava Krleže 23. Eseji*, vol. 6 (pp. 9–57). Zagreb: Zora.
Krleža, M. (1967b) Hrvatska književna laž (originally published in *Plamen* 1, Zagreb, 1 January 1919). Reprinted in *Riječ u diskusiji na Drugom kongresu književnika Jugoslavije. Eseji*, vol. 6 (pp. 102–114). Zagreb: Zora.
Krleža, M. (1982) *Zastave*. Sarajevo: Mladost.
Krležijana (1993–1999) *Bibliografija*. Vol. 3. Zagreb: Leksikografski zavod.
Lauer, R. (1984) *Miroslav Krleža und der deutsche Expressionismus*. Göttingen: Vandenhoeck & Ruprecht.
Nilsson, N.Å. (1990) Miroslav Krleža als europäischer Dichter. In R. Lauer (ed.) *Künstlerische Dialektik und Identitätssuche* (= *Opera slavica*, new series, vol. 19) (pp. 215–222). Wiesbaden: Otto Harrassowitz.
Macdonald, D.B. (2002) *Balkan Holocausts? Serbian and Croatian Victim-Centred Propaganda and the War in Yugoslavia*. Manchester and New York: Manchester University Press.
Mappes-Niediek, N. (2005) *Die Ethno-Falle. Der Balkan-Konflikt und was Europa daraus lernen kann*. Berlin: Christoph Links.
Pinter, H. (2000) Foreword. In P. Hammond and E.S. Herman (eds) *Degraded Capability: The Media and the Kosovo Crisis* (pp. vii–x). London: Pluto Press.
Suvin, D. (1984) On dramaturgic agents and Krleža's agential structure: The types as a key level. *Modern Drama* 27 (1), 81–97.
Žanić, I. (2005) The symbolic identity of Croatia in the triangle *crossroads-bulwark-bridge*. In P. Kolstø (ed.) *Myths and Boundaries in South-Eastern Europe* (pp. 35–76). London: Hurst.

Chapter 12
Masculinity and the New Sensibility: Reading a Contemporary Montenegrin Novel

Biljana Jovanović Lauvstad

> That is *the new sensibility*, about which everybody likes to talk, but only the rare ones are able to articulate it.[1] (To je taj *novi senzibilitet* o kome svi vole da pričaju, a ipak samo rijetki i da ga artikulišu. Brković, 2002: 198)

Introduction

Balša Brković's novel *Privatna Galerija* (Private Gallery, hereinafter: *PG*) came out in 2002 in Podgorica, Montenegro, and became a best-seller.[2] *Everybody* wanted to read it. Even those who did not read it had an opinion about it. The very fact that a novel, rather than a polemical text, a new historical work or memoirs by some former army general, was mentioned so often is not usual in Montenegro. Furthermore, this was something as untraditional as a nonrealistic Montenegrin novel, as atypical as a Montenegrin urban novel and as different as postmodern literature in post-catastrophic everyday life.

PG was accepted as a 'novel of our time', narrating a change that happened in Montenegrin cultural practice. The very novel was a proof of this change. *PG* could hardly have been written or published some years before. Even if it could have seen the light of day, it is uncertain how it would have been accepted by Montenegrins (cf. Jovanović, 2002). Montenegrin writers of the 20th century wrote 'mainly in the shadow of the Internationale' (uglavnom u sijenci Internacionale; Jovanović, 2005). Through the past century, Montenegrin literature has for the most part been written in a traditional realistic manner, rather than in an avant-garde style. This literature has mostly been engaged in social topics and military topics (the Yugoslav front of World War II), and with the Montenegrin rural region as the main literary scene – primarily a Montenegrin village. Traditional Montenegrin literature has also often applied stylistic strategies from oral poetry (*epika*), including the use of the heroic mode of oral poetry. One important exception is the writer Mihailo Lalić.

For a literary historical overview of Montenegrin literature, see Deretić (1990: 288–360).

During the 1990s, while Yugoslavia disintegrated and wars raged in the Balkans, Montenegrin writers of various ages begin to produce literature that expressed a plurality of Montenegrin experiences. Jovanović (2005: 13–50) has created a bibliography of this new antitraditionalist literature containing the names of 40 writers and 157 titles of prose, drama and poetry from 1990 to 2005.[3] So far he is the only Montenegrin critic to have written systematically about (post)modern Montenegrin literature.

Speaking in Wachtel's terms of the development and dissolution of the idea of the Yugoslav nation (cf. Wachtel, 1998), one can outline a historical process of political and cultural connection of the Montenegrin notion of the nation to the broader Yugoslav and/or Serbian context. Later critics have argued that institutionalized ideology has helped provincialize Montenegrins' minds by cultivating utopias (such as Yugoslavism, Serbism and communism; cf. Jovanović, 2005; Popović, 1999):

> Montenegrin literature of postmodernity means the end of the grand narratives, first of all the end of the great Montenegrin utopias. (Crnogorska postmoderna jeste kraj velikih priča i posebno velikih crnogorskih utopija. Jovanović, 2005: 20)

By breaking the old literary forms, modern Montenegrin writers are breaking with the old understanding of reality. The main subject of Montenegrin literary discourse in the post-communist era is the new critical approach to Montenegro's own cultural and ideological tradition. This critical turn inwards toward the nation's own political, cultural and esthetic heritage in Montenegrin postcommunist literature can introduce an additional dimension to analyses of postcommunist literature in Eastern Europe (cf. Wachtel, 2006).

The innovation in Montenegrin literature lies both in its new topics and in its avant-garde occupation with esthetics. Because textual focus in this literature is often on the individual, rather than on collective experience, a new practice of self-representation opens for negotiation of new masculinities, first of all in narratives of new intimacy by a male narrator, as in Brković's novel.

This chapter discusses some elements in self-representation of the dominant masculinity in Brković's novel, as constructed at both the explicit and implicit level of the text. The theoretical framework for this approach is a critical feminist reading, and the method applied is close reading. Critical theory is chosen because it 'suits' a metafictive strategy of textual construction and deconstruction of this novel. The analytical term *masculinity* is understood as relational. An introduction to masculinity as an analytical term is given by Lorentzen and Mühleisen (2006).

I focus on how the new sensibility is articulated in new forms of intimacy, particularly in the sphere of love and Eros. The analysis shows that, in the case of this novel, the unstereotyped image of woman is left outside of the discourse. I argue that not only what is in the discourse, but also what is left outside of it, appears as the constitutional element of the dominant masculinity in this text.

An Urban Writer

PG is an intimate story told by the writer and journalist Bartolomej Braunović. It is a story about himself and his times, written in the first-person singular from the perspective (focalization) of a 35-year-old man. Baki – or BB, as he also refers to himself – lives in the Montenegrin capital Podgorica and works as editor at the daily *Vijesti*. He is divorced and has a 7-year-old son who lives with his mother in Serbia. The novel takes place during a Podgorica summer. The span of the summer overlaps with BB's entering and leaving a sexual relationship, and partly with his son's visit. The text is divided into 11 chapters: 10 stories and the epilogue.

PG starts with a visit to a literature seminar in Russia and ends with an opening of an art gallery. BB's daily life is, as during any other time of peace, filled with work, socializing, habits, Sunday family dinners, free activities and some very private projects. BB gives the impression of being a competent consumer of high culture and critical observer of social and political events. The social frame of the novel has 'post-period' characteristics – from a postwar atmosphere of nationalistic rampage whose consequences are still felt to new power constellations and characters that emerged as a result of wartime chaos and decay; *an unbelievable and above all picturesque nouveau rich–police-political-economic or cultural establishment* (nevjerovatni, ali nadasve slikoviti novobogataško-policijsko-političko-ekonomski ili kulturni establišment; Brković, 2002: 84). BB's project, as a journalist and as a writer, is to articulate and make visible an alternate attitude and experience.

As a literary project, BB's novel aims to conquer literary territory for a new intimacy. This new intimacy is being connected with new space: that is, city space. This space is first meant to be constructed. The city takes form through particular meeting places, buildings, the theater and other institutions, coffee shops and restaurants, food and drink, climate and the Mediterranean city atmosphere. Taking over the city space happens through a recognizable jargon of the capital, as well as a particular way of socializing and a specific humor. It happens through the introduction of personal habits and personal rhythm into the rhythm of the city. BB's elitism, intellectualism and bohemianism are the inheritance of urban literature from the time of Baudelaire. Thus, it is possible to talk about a simulacrum of the urban. The 'territorial belonging' of the project is highlighted at the very beginning of the novel, as well as at its end through the recognizable geography of Podgorica. BB's urban identity is thus first of all his literary identity as an urban writer.

In Opposition to Traditionalism

A significant element of BB's poetic practice of self-representation is to situate himself in opposition to traditionalism. He does so by dethroning what he understands as the dominant practices in this particular society. For BB, heroic literature (*epika*) is an old-fashioned literary concept as well as an old-fashioned way of understanding history. In times of great social changes, these cultural practices can function as a petrifying and directly reactionary force. *PG* expresses this in a humorous way. The novel suggests that wearing a mustache is an old-fashioned style of being a man, connected to an outworn patriarchal-heroic codex. A local underground multiartist in the novel was thus very disappointed that the president of the country had a moustache. Once he arrived naked at the presidential palace. When arrested, he answered,

(1) 'Why don't you arrest him, he's wearing a mustache.' ('Što ne uhapsite njega, on nosi brkove.' Brković, 2002: 60)

In other words, the degree of shame should be the same for wearing a mustache as for going naked.

At the very beginning of the novel, and in the same carnivalistic way, BB introduces a topic of outworn poetics – that of large novels and big narratives:

(2) Kouchumov [the writer] took really, without any metaphoric meaning – a mega shit... Monstrous. And compatible with the theory about the connection between artistic expression and bullshit. (Kouchumov je posrao, ali odista, i to bez ikakve metaforike – gigantsko govno.... Monstruozno. I kompatibilno sa onom teorijom o povezanosti umjetničke ekspresije i sranja. Brković, 2002: 27)

The metaphorical aspect of this passage is based on a colloquial denotation of artistic verbalism. BB's mocking concerns the traditional institutional favoring of large literary forms. The metaphorical connotations of verbalism also concern the ideologized language of (some) Montenegrin communists, whom BB denotes as 'masters of mega-narrations' (majstori mega-naracije; Brković, 2002: 26).

Wax is one of the central metaphors in the novel. It is related to the topic of integrity. BB's father says,

(3) People are made of wax, you can shape them as you want. (Ljudi su od voska, možeš ih oblikovati kako god hoćeš. Brković, 2002: 47)

BB observes how political power functions as the 'modeling force'. Two episodes with women that BB has been involved with are significant. Both of them give up their artistic integrity. Placing the episodes at the beginning and at the end of the novel – in the same context as the final scene in the theater with the president who lords over the audience of a humble anonymous assembly – situates BB in relation to the world.

The metaphor that connects episodes comes out openly in a scene with a performance artist creating a man of wax that melts in front of the audience. The audience themselves get the drops of melting wax all over them, and have to clean it from their hair and clothes. This action of cleaning is thus needed to avoid contamination. The following words by BB's father are also to be understood as a duty to be active:

> (4) My son, the whole of life in some way is defining of your own position. You should never stop doing this, he told me on innumerable occasions. (Sine, čitav život je na neki način utvrđivanje sopstvene pozicije. Nikada ne smiješ prestati to da činiš, rekao mi je nebrojeno puta. Brković, 2002: 54)

BB chooses the position of a minority, and he thereby both defines his attitude and identifies himself as different.

> (5) To be a minority is a question of style, not destiny. (Biti u manjini je pitanje stila, a ne sudbine. Brković, 2002: 9)

In other words, it is a difference between a minority identity given (destiny) and chosen (style). This elitist attitude is a step in an attempt to maintain control of one's own biography, speaking in the terms of Boris Davidovič (Kiš, 1990); that is, having in mind what 'destiny' did to the people in the previous war in the Balkans.

A Modern Man

BB expresses a modern, antipatriarchal attitude to the relationship between men and women. He and his friends used to *parody traditional Montenegrin discourse on women* (parodirajući klasični crnogorski diskurs o ženama; Brković, 2002: 29), focusing on their honor and virtue (*poštenje*). BB's comment that the girl from the following passage is 'from the periphery' places this still old-fashioned patriarchal world outside of the urban territory. Late one night, BB and his friends are witnessing a scene in a fast-food restaurant, involving a girl who works in the shop and her friend:

> (6) – I noticed that the girl that was working here had company. A guy around 30 years old, probably her fiancé (she's from the periphery, where girls don't have boyfriends, only fiancées) . . .

– You always keep me locked up, she said.
– You have no idea what this world is like, he said convincingly (probably a trait of some bitter experience).
(– Opažam da djevojci koja ovdje radi neko pravi društvo. Muškarac oko trideset godina, sigurno je njen vjerenik. (Ona je sa periferije, a tamo djevojke nemaju momke, nego vjerenike.) ...
– Vazda me držiš zatvorenu, kaže ona.
– Nemaš ti pojma kakav je ovaj svijet, prilično uvjerljivo (neki gorki talog iskustva, možda), veli on. Brković, 2002: 137)

This conversation echoes a conflict based on the man's and the woman's different understanding of *her* needs. His understanding is based on the traditional practice of controlling female sexuality.

In traditional Montenegrin narratives on woman, a woman is a compatriot, mother or sister. As a compatriot, she is present in popular culture, as in an anthology titled 'Famous Montenegrin Women' that gives examples of 34 women's self-sacrifices as compatriots in the 19th-century Ottoman period (cf. Vujačić, 1961). In the sphere of home and family, a woman is a mother and a sister. In her anthropological work on Montenegrin women, Milić (2003) illuminates the double sexual standards for men and women in traditional Montenegro. Although the control of sexual life was important for both men and women, patriarchal society is based foremost on controlling female sexuality. Furthermore, in the private sphere of his home, a traditional man never shows tenderness for his wife, not because he does not love her, but because of the fear that society would lay blame on him. Traditional Montenegrin women lived in line with very strict laws of an androcentric milieu, adhering to the cult of man's superiority.

Yet another woman who spends lot of time in the kitchen is BB's mother. BB is bothered by his mother's only preoccupation: what his father Josif thinks.

(7) She does not see things the way they are, but she always tries to find out how Josif sees them. (Ona ne gleda na stvari kakve jesu, nego uvijek grozničavo pokušava odgonetnuti kako ih Josif vidi. Brković, 2002: 48)

He is bothered because his mother is an educated woman; she teaches at a school and *she hasn't always been like that*. Her husband's superiority is something she has excepted voluntarily, and to the degree that she *does not have her own opinion* any more. It seems that his father's superiority is the marriage's condition (he has had three marriages before this one): 'This is truly the only functional mode for J.B.' (To je vjerovatno jedini funkcionalni modus kada je o J.B. riječ; Brković, 2002: 48).

Construction and Deconstruction

The core story in the novel is about an unusual forgery. BB and his brother Kuzma, an art student, dream about opening an art gallery, and they need money for it. They begin to produce works of art mentioned in literature that never actually existed in real life. They sell these paintings as authentic works of art to random foreigners looking for adventures in the wartime Balkans, to army officers 'interested in literature', to the nouveau riche and so on. The brothers instruct their 'clients' about the text sources first. Then, through the old canvases they paint over, and fiction becomes reality. With the money earned in this business they can open an art gallery, and the dream can become reality.

The motif of forgery also functions at the tropological level, as the (postmodern) condition of the text. As the central element in the poetics of this novel, forgery functions as an allegory of narration. *PG* contains numerous variations on the topic of camouflage and forgery because *nothing is what it seems to be* (ništa nije ono što izgleda da jest; Brković, 2002: 42). The hide-and-seek game of *PG*, construction and deconstruction of textual reality, points to the metafictive nature of the poetic concept of *PG*. 'Metafiction is a term given to fictional writing which self-consciously and systematically draws attention to its status as an artifact in order to pose questions about the relationship between fiction and reality' (Waugh, 1984: 2). The subversion of metafiction lies in the manner in which it brings out the contemporary experience of the world as a construction (Waugh, 1984).

Every story contains a number of other stories (sve priče sadrže u sebi mnoštvo drugih priča; Brković, 2002: 119). This implies that the story can never be told. The storytelling is forgery per se, and so is the possibility of telling a story about oneself without falsifying it. Here, the narrating subject advertises the constructive nature of his self-representation:

> (8) I will write a mystifying story about Baki.... I say mystifying because, no matter how one talks about oneself, it means exactly that – making things somewhat different. (Napisaću jednu mistifikatorsku povijest o Bakiju.... Kažem mistifikatorsku – jer, bilo kako govoriti o sebi, znači upravo to – stvari činiti unekoliko drugačijima. Brković, 2002: 162)

Characters

Saša

In the passages that follow, I try to outline a significant inconsequence in the textual practice of self-representation.

Three women assume a central position in the novel. First, there is BB's ex wife, Saša. The first thing noticed about her is her physical absence. Her distance is geographical and referential: She lives in another country

(Serbia), and she comes from a different cultural-referential frame, being a Central European. The only contact between her and BB is via telephone, and the reason they sometimes communicate is their son. Furthermore, her absence in the text is almost absolute because she utters only two sentences in the novel, in a phone conversation. Saša's physical absence and the absence of contact between her and BB are disproportionate to her presence in his memory. In the story's time frame, there is a constant feeling of missing. Thus, while he is looking at his sleeping son, BB is thinking:

> (9) A thought emerges – that I terribly miss his mother. (Iza toga mi se jasno ukazuje misao da mi užasno nedostaje njegova majka. Brković, 2002: 100)

This (past) love meanwhile seems to be the ultimate love story:

> (10) I don't know if you will ever be able to understand what kind of love that was. I mean, how much I loved your mother. Honestly: I haven't even met that type of love in books. Everything is, believe me, ridiculous in comparison to that. (Ne znam hoćeš li ikada moći da shvatiš kakva je to ljubav bila. Mislim, koliko sam volio tvoju majku. Najiskrenije: ja nisam čak ni u knjigama sreo baš takvu ljubav. Sve je smiješno, vjeruj mi, pri tome. Brković, 2002: 101)

Even though BB regrets the past, nothing in the text implies that a new contact can be made. From BB's relation to Saša, it could be concluded that absence is the only way for love to exist.

Milva

The dominant female character in the novel is Milva. At the same time, she is the most charming character in *PG*. Milva has a very special place in BB's life. First of all Milva is an artist, whose large canvases hang in BB's apartment. BB is an aficionado and connoisseur of Montenegrin painting and a passionate art collector. When BB says that Milva is his favorite painter, a significant closeness is formed. However, she is more than just a good artist. Milva is BB's friend, perhaps his closest friend, somebody who knows him well, is there when he needs her, is like a member of his family, can save him from unwanted company and is good to his son. BB sees her as somebody whose originality is astonishing, and as a woman different from other women and everybody else:

> (11) Again that unique expression. The face that is as unreachable as the very world. (Opet taj jedinstveni izraz. Lice koje je nedokučivo kao svijet. Brković, 2002: 81)

(12) She is undoubtedly dark: restless eyes and hair the color of half of the chess figures. Her somewhat large nose, unusually elongated, could make any Earthling bound by esthetic frustration go into despair. On her face, the nose was something like a noble contempt, a slap directed towards all other women, the whole ocean of women. (Nedvosmisleno je crna: oči za nespokoj i kosa koja ima boju polovine šahovskih figura. Njen poveći nos, neobično izdužen, mnogu bi Zemljanku dovodio do očajanja, sapetu sopstvenim estetskim frustracijama. Na njenom licu, taj nos je nešto poput otmjenog prezira, packe upućene svim drugim ženama, čitavom okeanu žena. Brković, 2002: 117)

In BB's friendship with Milva there is something that resembles the traditional Montenegrin ethos of closeness between brother and sister. Milva is something between a hero's friend from the heroic literary tradition and a sister surrogate. Milva represents loyalty, then closeness: *my favorite witch* (moja omiljena vještica; Brković, 2002: 83) and tenderness: *he kisses her hair* (ljubi [je] u kosu; Brković, 2002: 79). He is proud of Milva as one is proud of one's own sister. Sometimes she turns into an Amazon that challenges the borders of masculinity, as in the street scene when she defeats a traditional macho Montenegrin man in car driving, who then flees, perceiving her as a danger.

The relationship between BB and Milva is asexual. An erotic relationship with a sister is unimaginable. That gives a certain freedom to their relationship, which is not seen in his relationship with other women:

(13) – Baki, stand guard for me in case somebody attacks me. I have to write a graffito here, she said.

– Is that why you dragged me all the way here? You could have gotten somebody else to do that, I replied.
– But I want you to be the one, she said in a cuddly way and stepped out of the car.
(– Baki, čuvaj me. Brani me ako me neko napadne. Moram ovdje da napišem jedan grafit, ona će.
– Pa si me zbog toga potegla. Mogao je neko drugi poći sa tobom, odvraćam.
– Ali ja hoću da si to ti, veli ona mazno i izlazi iz kola. Brković, 2002: 80)

Lidija

Cuddly behavior without sexual connotations is an exclusive privilege of a sister. The other woman that uses cuddly tones is Lidija, but in this case it has a totally different connotation.

Lidija is BB's favorite film critic. He enters into a relationship with her at the beginning and leaves her at the end of the novel. Entering the relationship is described in the following way:

> (14) I feel her naked hand leaning on the painted canvas, as we construct our first kiss under Milva's painting called 'Nothing is what it seems to be.' (Osjećam kako se njena gola ruka oslanja na islikano platno, dok konstruišemo prvi poljubac ispod Milvine slike koja se zove 'Ništa nije ono što izgleda da jest'. Brković, 2002: 42)

BB's relationship with Lidija is exclusively sexual. Lidija's strong attraction from the very beginning is an erotic one. The fact that the kiss is not *what it seems to be* (i.e. that it does not have anything to do with love) will be obvious in the following scene, a totally conventionally erotic sex scene that starts in the following manner:

> (15) Lidija, totally unexpected, puts her hand on my crotch. Like all blonde women, she looks erotic in the space of a clear game. She starts, with cuddly gesticulation, to call me into her hug. (Lidija sada, sasvim neočekivano, polaže ruku na moje međunožje. Kao i sve plavokose žene, djeluje dosta erotično u prostoru jasne igre. Počinje, uz maznu gestikulaciju, da me zaziva u zagrljaj. Brković, 2002: 58)

The relationship with Lidija confirms the dichotomy also present in BB's relation to his ex-wife; that is, the impossibility of the coexistence of love and sex.

The final scene with Lidija gives an additional dimension to these relations. The scene happens on the beach, the story is next to last in the novel. A presentation of Lidija's short promotional film for the Ministry of Tourism is being completed. The film is bad, kitschy and cliché, but the audience is very positive about it. BB is disappointed and he waits for Lidija to approach him and ask for his opinion.

> (16) – I realize that she is whispering something and I make some effort in order to understand what she is telling me.
>
> – How did the president react? Did you see how the president reacted? she asks me for the third time, my darling...
> (– Tada shvatam da mi ona nešto šapuće, i ulažem izvjestan napor ne bih li razabrao o čemu govori.
> – Kako je reagovao Predsjednik? Jesi li snimio kako je reagovao Predsjednik?, pita me, treći put zaredom, moja draga... Brković, 2002: 175)

Lidija is more occupied by the president's opinion than by BB's. What follows is the kiss that *is not what it seems to be*:

> (17) When I realized what she was asking, I felt, for the second time today, an incredible rage coming over me. What a bimbo, I think and I put my hands around her cheeks as if I wanted to kiss her lips, but instead, I put my lips next to her right ear, and very clearly I say:
>
> – You are – nothing.
>
> Then I kiss her lips and move away from her, several steps.
>
> (Kada shvatam šta me pita, osjećam, drugi put danas, nevjerovatan priliv bijesa. Kakva ćurka, mislim i uzimam šakama njenu glavu kao da je kanim poljubiti u usta, ali svojim se ustima primičem njenom desnom uvu, i, veoma razgovijetno izgovaram:
>
> – Ti si – ništa.
>
> Onda je ljubim u usta, i pomjeram se nekoliko koraka unazad. Brković, 2002: 176)

This scene of BB's break-up with Lidija, as suggested by Matanović (2002), intensifies the narrator's moral framework and additionally crystallizes his own clean position. What still remains unexplained is the brutality of BB's reaction. Lidija's action cannot be surprising for BB because it was prepared in her dressing up and the importance she already gave to the event. The explanation is given by BB in the scene that follows. When Milva asks him what happened, he explains it in a way that associates him with his father:

> (18) Actually, that is very simple, I don't want to be with a woman who considers a president's, pope's, or prince's opinion more important than mine. For me that seems very understandable. (Zapravo, to je jednostavno: ni po koju cijenu ne želim da budem sa ženom kojoj je o bilo čemu važnije mišljenje Predsjednika, ili Pape, ili Princa, od onoga što ja mislim. Meni se to čini tako shvatljivim. Brković, 2002: 177)

Because the Montenegrin ethos is one of the topics in the positioning of the narrator, it is interesting to connect this scene in the novel with the psychological literature about Montenegrin man:

> The combination of narcissism and aggression strengthened his [the Montenegrin man's] solipsistic attitude towards a woman, particularly towards his own wife. As a consequence of this attitude there is no worse situation for a Montenegrin [man] than when his wife does not ask him for his opinion, when she neglects him or 'runs over him'. (Baković, 1997: 153)

The explanation given (to Milva) for breaking up is thus the anger caused by her neglecting of his opinion, simultaneously subordinating him to other men (the president, etc.). Lidija is less a woman and more a function in the self-representation of BB, an instrument of positioning of masculinity in relation to the competitors. The clear game between BB and Lidija became even clearer (nothing is what it seems to be) in the moment of recognizing the competing masculinity. The number of players in this game is thus greater than two and, although invisible, other males are present in it.

The manner of breaking up with Lidija is a gesture of giving to other men (the president, etc.) what he does not want any more. In doing so, he is continuing understandable communication with competing masculinity, confirming togetherness in competition. Through the brutality of the way BB breaks up with Lidija, BB confirms his togetherness with the macho world he despises. Milva appears as a savior and consoler, to confirm the existence of the only thing he can trust – sisterly love that understands him and love that will always put him before everybody else.

> (19) – Baki, let's disappear from here.
>
> – Without telling anybody. Let's disappear like a good opportunity disappears, unnoticed, so that everybody thinks that we are still somewhere around.
>
> (– Baki, hajde da nestanemo odavde.
>
> – Ali da se nikom ne javljamo. Nestanimo kao što nestaje dobra prilika – neosjetno, a da svi misle da smo još tu negdje. (Brković, 2002: 179)

It can be concluded that the intimacy of the dominate masculinity is built upon a dichotomy of love and Eros.

In articulating the dichotomies in the game played in the novel, called 'right-left jazzing', the dichotomy of love and Eros is missing. The system BB and his friends use in this game for classifying the opposite parts of the same level of phenomena follows the European tradition of right and left:

> (20) Left is signs and money / Right is the territory and the community; Left is sex / Right is family; Left is metaphor / Right is metonymy. (Lijevo su znakovi i novac / Desno je teritorija i zajednica; Lijevo je seks / Desno je porodica; Lijevo je metafora / Desno je metonimija. Brković, 2002: 73)

Metonymy is thus placed on the right side (as the trope for closeness) and metaphor on the left (as a trope for universalism). It is interesting that dichotomy of sex (left) and family (right) in this schematic classification also survives in the textual reality of self-representation in the same stereotypical way. However, what is more interesting (in the text) is the unarticulated dichotomy between love and sex.

The narrator says that Saša is/was talented and intelligent, and that BB was both intellectually and emotionally very close to her. He says very little about why they broke up; he talks in general terms about *a fatiguing transformation* (zamarajuća transformacija, Brković, 2002: 102) and quarrels that ended in divorce. Moreover, it was he himself that 'fucked it all up' (sve to uspio da zajebem; Brković, 2002: 103). This explanation seems inadequate and superfluous. Another explanation can be found in the latent danger to his masculinity. That is a possible neglect that he could not accept (as easily as Lidija's neglect), and this is why he chooses (and nourishes) a memory instead of a real woman.

The analysis shows that the dichotomy between love and sex survives because of the fear of being annihilated by competing masculinity. The conclusion is disappointing because of the proclaimed *difference* of BB's project. BB's construction is still the world of intimacy in which the construction of dominant masculinity is based on a stereotyped image of woman: blonde Lidija (Eros), dark Milva (a female android) and remote Saša (memory) – none of them a real woman.

Brajan

Before concluding this discussion, attention should be given to one additional type of love. The only realizable and dominant love in *PG* is not love toward a woman, but love toward a son. The only sequences in which lyrical pathos is present in the novel are in the relation to the son, Brajan (alongside the sequences about Saša). Consequently, it is interesting that BB channels the element of nostalgia through his son's mythological experience of the world, and that it is the boy who gets the role of being the connection between the old and the new. All the pathos and conventions of heroic literature – inheritance and ancestors, famous battles, bravery and patriotism – are channeled through the experience of a sensitive and gifted boy. This represents the entrance of heroic literature through 'the small door', under grandfather Josif's guidance.

The very fact that the only child in the novel is a boy, not a girl, is moreover epical: Montenegrin men's obsession with having a son is legendary.

The entrance of tradition into the new through a son is surprising because the son is the youngest and most distant from the old, and according to literary conventions he symbolizes the future. One of the possible answers is that son's 'journey' in the epic past is an obligatory part of the sentimental upbringing of a Montenegrin boy. Later, when he becomes a man, he will rise against BB's world and write a novel about the new.

Conclusion

The beginning of the 1990s marked a visible change in Montenegrin literature. The prose published during that period placed the writers in opposition to the dominant literary tradition. As the number of published texts increased, it became possible to talk about this literature as a cultural phenomenon. The writers born in the 1960s and 1970s write prose that introduces a private and fragmented mini- and intimate story into the contemporary Montenegrin narrative.

Brković's novel aims to contest a literary territory for new identities, in order to articulate new Montenegrin experiences. The narrator's self-definition as a minority by style indicates the exclusiveness of his project. This literature offers an alternative to the traditional cultural discourse on masculinity. One of the discursive strategies is to dethrone what the dominant masculinity in the novel experiences as institutionalized models of stereotyped cultural expression and ideologized language.

In this highly 'conscious' metafictive text, there is also an inconsequence, 'the blind spot' or the 'space off' ('the space not visible in the frame but inferable from what the frame makes visible' deLauretis, 1987: 26). The essentially patriarchal dichotomy of Self and Other in the sex/gender relations remains. It is the absent woman, the one pursued in dreams and found only in memory, that serves as the guarantee of masculinity (deLauretis, 1987: 82).

It is not easy to write a mystifying story about BB. As fiction, BB and his world are transformed (made different), not only by the narrator (BB), but by the 'subversive affect' of literary conventions as well. Because of this, there is a danger that 'the mystification' unwillingly becomes stereotypical, which is obvious in the intimate sphere of the dominant masculinity in the novel.

PG does not threaten the status quo of the patriarchal sex/gender relations. However, it is clear that Montenegrin literature is at the beginning of creating new masculinities that are trying to break out from the patriarchal masculine ideal and, in doing so, making room for men's practice of change.

Notes

1. The translations of the text excerpts are not literary translations. They follow the original closely in order to facilitate comparison with the original text.
2. Balša Brković was born in 1966. *PG* is his first novel. He has written poetry since 1985. He also writes stories, essays and literary and theater criticism. He lives in Podgorica and works as an editor for the daily newspaper *Vijesti*.
3. Jovanović points out that this bibliography is not complete, neither in the number of writers nor titles.

References

Baković, T. (1997) *Depresivni optimizam Crnogoraca*. Belgrade: Elit–Medica.
Brković, B. (2002) *Privatna galerija*. Zagreb: Durieux, Sarajevo: Buybook, Cetinje: Otvoreni kulturni forum.
deLauretis, T. (1987) *Technologies of Gender*. Bloomington and Indianapolis: Indiana University Press.
Deretić, J. (1990) *Kratka istorija srpske književnosti*. Belgrade: BIGZ.
Jovanović, B. (2002) *Libroskopija*. Cetinje: Centralna narodna biblioteka.
Jovanović, B. (2005) *Crnogorski književni urbanitet*. Cetinje: Centralna narodna biblioteka.
Kiš, D. (1990) *Grobnica za Borisa Davidoviča*. Belgrade: BIGZ.
Lorentzen, J. and Mühleisen, W. (eds) (2006) *Kjønnsforskning*. Oslo: Universitetsforlaget.
Matanović, J. (2002) *Pisanje na tuđem nacrtu*. – Online document: http://www.diwanmag.com.ba/arhiva/diwan11_12/sadrzaj/sadrzaj8.htm. Accessed 12 May 2009.
Milić, Z. (2003) (transl.) *Tudja večera*. Podgorica: CID.
Popović, M. (1999) *Crnogorsko pitanje*. Cetinje: Dignitas, Ulcinj: Plima.
Vujačić, M. (1961) *Znamenite Crnogorke*. Titograd [Podgorica]: Grafički zavod.
Wachtel, A.B. (1998) *Making a Nation, Breaking a Nation: Literature and Cultural Politics in Yugoslavia*. Stanford, CA: Stanford University Press.
Wachtel, A.B. (2006) *Remaining Relevant After Communism: The Role of the Writer in Eastern Europe*. Chicago: University of Chicago Press.
Waugh, P. (1984) *Metafiction*. London: Routledge.

Chapter 13
The Rhetoric of Present Absence: Representing Jewishness in Post-Totalitarian Poland

Knut Andreas Grimstad

Introduction

More than half a century after the Holocaust and a decade after the fall of communism, Europeans are grappling with the legacies of their past as they seek to redefine who they are. This is certainly the case with Poland, where the thematization of 'the Jews' in the public domain since the late 1980s is, to put it mildly, complex and controversial. As regards Poland's transition from a totalitarian to a post-totalitarian society – especially, perhaps, the process of handling and handing down multicultural history – it is difficult to draw a clear line between before and after, that is, between total censorship and freedom of expression. Instead, there seems to be a gradually increasing urge to be open, to discuss and even transgress tabooized topics. The writer-cum-sociologist Kinga Dunin asks, 'Can we be a homogeneic, Catholic, Polish nation adhering to traditional values and, simultaneously, a liberal, tolerant, modern society?' (Dunin, 2009: 270). The public discourse is fraught with a multifaceted yearning to understand national belonging, identity and 'brotherhood'[1] (cf. Czapliński, 2009: 15), as witnessed, above all, by the many contemporary writers who deal specifically with Polish-Jewish relations.

By the same token, the field of Polish-Jewish studies has developed into a significant area of study in its own right, thanks in no small part to the Poles' own 'voyage of self-exploration'; as put by Mieczysław Dąbrowski, coeditor of the book *Pisarze polsko-żydowscy XX wieku. Przybliżenie*: 'The Jews. For the Polish consciousness, they are a constantly annoying question mark, evoking anxiety and distress. Aliens? Ours? Surely, they are different' (Dąbrowski, 2009: 7).[2] As most Poles try to cope with history's monstrosities (the extermination of the Jews on Polish soil, the pogroms in some Polish towns in the wake of World War II, the culmination of state anti-Semitism in March 1968, the later discovery of the murder of Jews in Jedwabne, etc.), the nonexistent Jew has become a rhetorical figure that dominates not only much of post-totalitarian literature but also much of the public domain as a whole. In elucidating the contours of what might be called 'the virtual Jew'[3] – that is, a phantom-like, empty figure that can be filled with various, often provocative content – I propose examining the representation of Jewishness by well-known writers, a representation that is about processing collective and individual traumas through affirmation, empathy and multiperspectivity – or, as expressed by Dunin, about 'taking responsibility for reality' (cf. Dunin, 2004: 296–298). By pretending to deny a Jewish presence while really affirming it, the texts discussed here can thus be viewed largely as an 'apophatic' corrective: when they speak of absence, when societal conditions of a not-too-distant past are evoked, this means that a presence is upheld – images of a pronounced ethnic minority are retrieved, so to speak, from Poland's multicultural memory. In an increasingly pluralistic Europe, such texts seem to be less about consolidating any one national or ethnic identity, and more about providing boundary encounters between two kinds of identity – as well as promoting greater tolerance of difference.

At the most general level, boundary encounters occur between social worlds that are limited by obstacles to effective communication or, to be more precise, boundary encounters can be found where people interact in some way across these boundaries. Such dialogic encounters may be directly interpersonal and/or mediated by artifacts: for example, literature.[4] My main concern here is with novels, stories and essays from the late 1980s onwards in which the following devices are used: nostalgic idyllization, autobiographical recollection and uncompromising critique. Although these devices, or strategies, may overlap and have different aims in any individual text, the authors may be read jointly as a response to retrospective ethno-nationalist impulses, thus constituting a potent foreshadowing: away from the oppressive historical 'legacy' with which all post-totalitarian governments in Poland have been forced to deal and toward a future civil national society, based on a more inclusive culture.

Rethinking Poles and Jews

In today's Poland, where Jews make up just a tiny fraction of the population, products of Jewish culture, or what is perceived as Jewish culture, have become viable components of the public domain. Notably, Polish literature is still rich in Jewish content: This is small wonder because Poland has perhaps the richest, most varied Jewish history of any country in Europe. Jewish habitation, which can be traced back on Polish soil to as early as the tenth century, grew gradually until 1939 and the Nazi invasion, when this ethnic minority made up 10% of the total population.[5] Generally speaking, the centuries-old tradition of describing Jews and their characteristics in literature fell under the rubric of 'the Jewish issue' (*kwestia żydowska*); that is, the question of whether, how and to what extent this minority should be integrated into the multiethnic and multicultural

Polish state. Contrary to the period after 1945, when Polish-Jewish relations started to be represented as 'absent' and gradually became virtual, the pre–Second World War period was characterized by a 'rhetoric of presence'. In the context of this rhetoric, the strategies of almost all of these writers to varying degrees reflect either anti-Jewish/anti-Semitic or pro-Jewish/pro-Semitic tendencies, or something in between. According to Segel (1996), Polish literature is the richest of all European national literatures when it comes to representing the Jewish experience, whether autobiographical or imaginary on the part of the writer. However, for many, he says, such a statement may appear absurd: 'Widely regarded as notoriously anti-Semitic, the Poles seem hardly likely to have encompassed Jewish experience in their literature in any but the most negative terms. But this is not the case' (Segel, 1996: xi).

That said, the representation of Polish-Jewish relations has also always had a darker side. With the Jew perceived as Poland's foremost domestic 'threatening Other', who is damaging to the Polish people and to all aspects of the nation's life, the anti-Jewish formation of myths yielded enormous influence on the development of national identity in post-totalitarian Poland (cf. Michlic, 2006: 109–131). The Polish discourse about the Jews has, in this connection, been described as 'replete with strange testimonies – now popular formulas, now dead metaphors, or fossilized notions. It is a children's language, but threatening at the same time... at any moment, the word may explode' (Tokarska-Bakir, 2008: 39). I am interested here in contemporary writers whose texts may be said to rethink Poles and Jews in the sense that they form part of a deconstructing project of comprehension. My material has been assembled on the basis of two criteria: (a) The text must deal, essentially and explicitly, with the Polish-Jewish theme; and (b) it must have played a significant role in the production of meaning in the public domain by being adapted, for example, into a film or a theater play, or by having made a difference in some other way in general discussions. Due to limitations of space, I must refrain here from discussing the extent to which the individual author informs public discourse. Suffice it to say that almost all the writers examined in this chapter have received or been nominated for prestigious literary prizes (notably the NIKE, Stanisław Wyspiański and Stanisław Piętak awards); also, they regularly appear or are cited in influential newspapers (e.g. *Gazeta Wyborcza*, *Rzeczpospolita* and *Nasz Dziennik*), as well as in other forms of mass media.

Significant Strategies of Representation

The themes and narratives of any myth, including the myth of 'the Jew' as the threatening Other, can be expressed in more or less detailed and intensified forms; they can be the object of addition and expansion as well as deletion and substitution. The narratives that are linked to a single myth may also be mutually contradictory or overlap with one another, without this necessarily affecting the myth in terms of its persistence and emotive power. As Michlic (2006) indicates, this is exactly the case with the representation of 'the Jew' as a threat to the Polish nation, in which 'the narrative of the Jew as communist comfortably coexists with the narrative of the Jew as Western capitalist and carrier of Western liberalism – two narratives that constantly appeared in ethnonationalist discourse in interwar Poland' (Michlic, 2006: 17). Much the same applies to today's public discourse, in which it still appears to be fairly easy to use 'the Jew' as an abstract enemy image and, indeed, to try to project the problems of Poland as a modern, European state onto this abstract enemy.

It is one thing to claim that the narratives mentioned above are still operative; it is quite another to suggest that such *hate thought* may be directed at any of society's minorities, which are perceived as a threat to Polish societal values. To a large extent, here we are dealing with what might be called a 'nationalism of decency' that always, in the name of the public good, mistrusts 'the Other'. Nonetheless, after the literary historian Jan Błoński published his seminal essay 'The Poor Poles Look at the Ghetto' (Biedni Polacy patrzą na getto, 1987) – admitting, among other things, that prewar Polish anti-Semitism was influential for the Poles' attitudes toward the Jews during World War II (Błoński, 1990) – several writers have placed themselves outside the negative, ethnocentric nationalist way of thinking, irrespective of whether they are of Jewish descent or not. What these writers have in common is their attempt to comprehend Poland, its past and present, not as a totality of things nor as a background to events, but as itself an ongoing event. To be able to thus 'see' time, Bakhtin would have argued, is to see evidence of multitemporality or 'heterochrony' – the many different rhythms of time – in the present, and to feel everything that pulsates in the present.[6] Bearing in mind these considerations, let us take a closer look at certain texts in which the main tendency is to evoke and, more often than not, destabilize if not deconstruct the traditional image of the Jew as being the threatening, harmful Other.[7] As mentioned above, the authors of these texts use three distinct rhetorical-discursive devices that indicate multidirectional and also shared aspirations to recover a Polish-Jewish cultural legacy.

Idyllizing the multicultural past

In the same year as Błoński's text appeared, a young writer called Piotr Szewc caused a sensation with his debut novel *Annihilation* (*Zagłada*, 1987). The book is about a day in the life of an eastern Polish-Jewish town, Zamość, shortly before World War II, a town that would soon be ravaged by Nazi atrocities. The style is laidback and subdued throughout; the narrator proceeds with grace, wit and love for the people and place that will be destroyed, with an almost photographic gaze, for exquisite everyday poetry and also for more mundane activities:

> We are on Listopadowa, the second street crossing Lwowska. In one of the tiny backyards close to the intersection, Mr. Hershe Baum is standing near the house and feeding pigeons perched on his arm. Here they are called Persian butterflies. Isn't that a beautiful name? In all likelihood they were brought from Persia. But is that certain? We won't be able to verify it. Data, documents, and credible explanations are unavailable. (Szewc, 1999: 3)

In Szewc's multiethnic universe, it is as if a time- and motion-denying atmosphere rules; everything in time and space develops at a slow pace, the world is observed, as it were, by the dead eye of a herring in a glass jar. However, we could also say here that the 'chronotope' of the Polish-Jewish community assumes that space and time are fundamentally interconnected; they can be separated for the purpose of analysis but, as lived experience, space and time are fused:

> The Eye of the Town, the dome of the Town Hall, sees everything. We would like to see a fraction of what it sees. We would know where the droshky has gone. And where the dog with a cut-off tail is. We would see what Kazimiera M. [a prostitute] is doing right at this moment. And Mr. Rozenzweig and Mr. Baum. We would learn where the Baums' sons are. Who enters and leaves Rozenzweig's tavern. Whether the Hasidim have reached the Jewish cemetery. What is happening in the linden trees in front of the attorney's office... we would have to ask the dome of the Town Hall, which sees everything. The Eye of the Town. (Szewc, 1999: 72–73)

As a contrast to Szewc's balanced, easy-going depiction of Polish-Jewish relations, one should mention Teresa Lubkiewicz-Urbanowicz's bestselling novel *Living near God* (*Boża podszewka*, 1997), which became even more popular when it was made into a TV series (1997). The action is set during the first half of the 20th century in eastern Poland, in the *Kresy* region (today's Ukraine and Belarus). Although this society was overwhelmingly multiethnic right up until World War II and the Jewish population was integrated to a large degree, the narrator pays little attention to how Poles and Jews actually interact. When such interaction occurs, the reader is always offered stereotypical descriptions of industrious (= crafty) Jews such as the peddler, the pawnbroker, the innkeeper, the milkman and so on – characters that exploit the 'naive Poles' within the colorful framework of a Polish-Catholic utopian paradise.

A very different *Kresy*-paradise emerges in Anna Bolecka's *The White Stone* (*Biały kamień*, 1994). The very premise for her retrospective novel is the fact that pre-1918 Poland's multiethnic world, so rich in traditions, no longer exists; moreover, that the new world is fraught with national conflicts on a local level, with the nationalistic powers already bent on the total breakdown of the community. At many points in the narrative, the storyteller's imaginative powers take over where ethnography and folk culture leave off; thus the novel is largely dependent on images created out of empathy and emotional identification with the world being described:

> The inhabitants of Kuromęki harbored no feelings of resentment towards strangers because nobody actually knew who the strangers were. This world was situated on the border between the Russian and the Austrian partitions. Catholics, Lutherans, and Calvinists came from the west – Orthodox, Uniates, and Muslims from the east.[8] The Jews were in the middle, separated by their customs, but too poor to be the cause of envy. Each had his place in a society that was founded on the mutual exchange of goods and services.... People knew that the Orthodox had a faith that allowed the priests to marry and have long hair; that the Lutherans did not observe the fast or venerate the Holy Virgin; that the Calvinists ate meat on Good Friday; and that the Jews slaughtered animals kosher style, in order to preserve the mystic power that was still in the living muscle. (Bolecka, 1994: 36–37)

Whereas Lubkiewicz-Urbanowicz's nostalgic idyllization of Polishness – tendentious or oversimplified at best – is carried out at the cost of what was historically the largest ethnic minority living in those areas, the novels of Szewc and Bolecka may be said to relate, or attempt to encompass, Polish multicultural society in its entirety, the 'little homeland' of bygone years that disintegrated when History, as it were, drove the Jews to flee from eastern Poland, annihilating or dispelling them. Implicit in this type of 'homeland' would be the fact that it is no longer threatened by History as an all-powerful, external power, but by intolerance, which resides latently within the individual, modern Pole. Here Bakhtin might have said that contemporaneity – both in nature and in human life – is revealed as an essential multitemporality: as remnants or relics of various stages and formations of the past and as rudiments of stages of the more or less distant future.

Autobiographical recollection and the experience of the Holocaust

Another writer who recreates an absent Jewishness but links it more directly to the suffering connected with the Holocaust is Jarosław Marek Rymkiewicz. In his documentary novel *The Final Station: Umschlagplatz* (*Umschlagplatz*, 1988) – the title refers to the collection point in the Warsaw ghetto where the Jews were assembled before being sent to

Figure 13.1 Symbols used on Jewish tombstones in Poland
Source: Link: http://www.polishjews.org/photos/phsymb1.htm. Copyright by Polish-Jews.org.

the concentration camps – he immerses himself in the intricate web of Polish-Jewish relations during the war and the following years. Especially striking is his bold and straightforward evaluation of the communists' political line in relation to the Jews in the postwar years, as well as the amplification of Polish-Jewish tensions, which culminated in the anti-Semitic mass expulsions of 'Zionists' in March 1968.[9] Rymkiewicz explores 'the Jew' and 'Jewishness', describing the situation from the perspective of the Other – that is, his own. Rymkiewicz's narrator bases his utterances on episodes from World War II experienced by himself as an 'ethnic' Pole – as opposed to the narrator in Michał Głowiński's autobiographical book *The Black Seasons* (*Czarne sezony*, 1998).

A well-known literary theorist of Jewish origin, for a long time Głowiński was incapable of directing his gaze backwards at his own, personal past. Apparently fully aware of the complex subject matter at hand, he takes care, initially, to emphasize the subjective nature of his recollections:

> Flashes of memory possess their own rules; they dissolve concerns about consistency and justify fragmentariness – indeed, they assume this from the outset. And they give impetus to heterogeneity. I write of what I have remembered, and when I am not certain of something, I say so openly. Readers should not wonder when from time to time they encounter the phrase 'I don't know.' (Głowiński, 2005: 3)

We learn that little Michał's childhood years were spent in harmonious, well-integrated Polish-Jewish surroundings, and that during the war he was hidden by Catholic nuns. However, Głowiński's narrator never abandons his enquiring attitude toward 'good' and 'evil', values that do not depend on ethnic belonging. On the other hand, he reveals how the Jewish boy and his family were living at the mercy of Polish blackmailers (*szmalcownicy*) that helped save their lives but stripped them of money. A highly critical description of Polish xenophobia appears in the chapter 'A Quarter Hour Passed in a Pastry Shop'. Left on his own for a moment, the boy feels uncomfortable when he is stared at by some Polish women:

> As usual in such situations, I would have most preferred to melt into the ground. I heard 'A Jew, there's no question, a Jew'.... The women deliberated: what should they do with me? The shop owner opened the door leading to the back room where the oven must have been, and called out 'Hela! Hela, come look.' And after some time Hela appeared in a flour-covered apron, obviously interrupted from her work. The women awaited her judgment; clearly they valued her opinion. Perhaps she was an authority on various matters, or even an expert in racial questions, within the context of the pastry shop. One more pair of piercing eyes came forward to examine me. I tried not to think of how it would end. (Głowiński, 2005: 93–94)

Głowiński gives a nuanced description not only of the widespread anti-Semitism to which he was exposed but also of his experience of a fluid, crossover identity – the very 'sum', as it were, of the Jewish elements of his early integrated life and later Polish-Jewish connections. Thus the narrator's unequivocal fear is not directed primarily at the Poles. The last chapter is titled 'Germans Are People, Too'. It ought perhaps to have a question mark in the title: in spite of many positive experiences with Germanness throughout his adult life, Głowiński never quite manages to free himself of the feeling that there is something profoundly unsettling about the Germans as a people (Głowiński, 2005: 169–186).

Seen through the lens of a rhetoric of presence and/or absence, another intriguing text is Hanna Krall's 'Dybbuk' (Dybuk, 1995). The title of this story creates immediate associations in the reader with the play *The Dybbuk* (*Dybuk*, 1920, in Ansky, 2002), written in Yiddish by the Polish-born writer Szymon Ansky (1863–1920). Both texts focus on the dybbuk; that is, a beloved person that has passed away and that, according to folkloric Jewish mysticism, comes back to haunt and accompany a living person for the rest of his or her life. In Ansky's play, a young Hasidic woman is haunted by her deceased lover's spirit, whereas the dybbuk in Krall's story is a little boy that was murdered in the Warsaw ghetto. The father, who is a Holocaust survivor, has emigrated to the United States and had a second son, Adam S., who teaches architectural history at an American college. Adam S. has visited his father's homeland many times because he is interested, among other things, in the wooden synagogues that were burned down during World War II. The young man is now haunted by his brother:

> Quite early in his life Adam S. realized he wasn't alone. He was possessed by outbursts of unexplicable rage; someone else's rage. At other times he was swept up in sudden, alien laughter. He learned to identify these moods, controlling them well enough and not revealing them in the presence of others. From time to time this tenant would say something. Adam S. had no idea what, because the dybbuk talked in Polish. He started studying the language: he wanted to understand what his younger brother was saying to him. When he had learned enough, he visited Poland.... Maybe he hoped that this time in Grójec he would see the rivers of Babylon in a synagogue, and the willows, on which 'we hung up our harps...' Perhaps in Zabłudów he wanted to find gryphons, bears, peacocks, winged dragons, unicorns and fish-serpents.... As was to be predicted he found only grass and a few sad trees. (Krall, 2007: 1–2)

With his sensational theatre production *Dybbuk* (*Dybuk*, 2003), the Polish director Krzysztof Warlikowski made use of an ingenious device when he combined Krall and Ansky's texts: more precisely, he effectively juxtaposed the Polish Hasidic Jews, their world and their faith and superstitions, with topical events from Polish contemporary life. In letting the tragic love story between two young Jews from the interwar years resonate in the story with the people from the contemporary text and vice versa, the director gave his audiences the experience not only of being led over a boundary and into a borderland 'between two worlds', but also of being confronted with a series of worlds that they believed were directly opposed to one another. Judging from the tone of the critics' reviews and the comments in the theater foyers, Warlikowski's production caused everything from excitement to hurt and fury (Tokarska-Bakir, 2003). 'If

Figure 13.2 Scene from Krzysztof Warlikowski's production *Dybbuk* (2008)
Source: Link: http://www.poland-israel.org/event/?lang=en&wid=41. Copyright by poland-israel.org.

Poles don't adopt a new way of thinking about Jews, we will never be at peace with ourselves. Anything we say will be dishonest. Theater will be dishonest' (Warlikowski, 2003). The director's 'multitemporal' statement says a lot, I think, about how sensitive Polish-Jewish matters continue to be in the popular public domain.[10]

Critique of xenophobic and nationalist tendencies

It seems fitting, at this stage, to bring in the writings of Henryk Grynberg, another powerful and consistently critical voice. A 'Holocaust child', he too was kept hidden as a Jew during the war and provided with 'Aryan' identity papers. In his autobiographical prose, he expresses a view of Polish-Jewish connections that deviates in many ways from his contemporaries' treatment of the same theme. Take, for example, *A Polish-Jewish Monologue* (*Polsko-żydowski monolog*, 2003), in which the self-styled narrator describes his own relationship to Poles and Polishness; having stayed behind in the United States after touring with a Polish theater company in 1967, he has just paid a visit to his old fatherland but is overjoyed to be able to leave again:

> And I did not feel any nostalgia. On the contrary, I awoke every morning with a feeling of relief and thanked God for not having let me awake in Poland. This was an *anti-nostalgia* (which I have accumulated and also called one of my poetry collections). It has never deceived me, always helped me when things were bad. It was enough for me to think: but at least you are not in Poland. For the Poles, this is unforgivable. Even those who deny the Jew everything Polish,

would like him to love Poland. And to suffer like a perfect lover [*rasowy* 'perfect'/'race-' ≈ 'a lover burdened with race'; the ambiguity is deliberate; K.A.G.]. (Grynberg, 2003: 94)

Grynberg simply cannot forgive Poland, nor Europe, its anti-Semitism. In his narrative, the Poles are inveterate xenophobes that fundamentally regard the Jews as expressions for 'the alien' and 'the enemy'. Instead of allowing Jewishness to be a source of new thinking, improvement, wisdom and everything worth acquiring, or at least respecting, the Poles have begun to treat 'the Other' as a mythic threat, as something dangerous. In his essay 'The Polish-Jewish War' (Wojna polsko-żydowska, 2004), the author sharpens his argumentation: "Poland could have had friends all over the world, had she wanted to. But she did not want to, just as she did not want her 'colony' in Israel. On the contrary, Poland did everything in order to frighten, to reject. It was like this before the war and it is like this now" (Grynberg, 2004: 145). Although both Grynberg and Głowiński participate in a process of representation that involves testimony, trauma and voice (cf. Ubertowska, 2007), Grynberg constitutes a monomanic contrast to his more dialogically inclined co-discussant, Głowiński. The former emerges almost as a 'Jewish ethnonationalist'. As a member of the international Jewish community, he projects his problems associated with the Holocaust, 'homelessness' and Polish-Jewish ambivalence onto the abstract enemy, which, in the universe of the self-professed American Grynberg, remains, above all, the Pole and Poland.

Finally, a word on Kinga Dunin and her penetrating book *Reading Poland: Polish Literature after 1989 in Relation to the Dilemmas of Modernity* (*Czytając Polskę. Literatura polska po roku 1989 wobec dylematów nowoczesności*, 2003). In combining literary criticism, philosophy, and sociology, this writer creates her own essayistic metanarrative about Poland, while also countering one of the accusations that is often directed at Polish contemporary prose; namely, that it says very little about reality. 'But it does', replies Dunin, 'for those who listen' (Dunin, 2004: 6), and here she implies texts from both before and after the fall of communism. Uncompromisingly, she challenges all Poles, private individuals as well as politicians and religious leaders who let themselves be governed by narcissistic Polonocentrism, or by smug compliance at best:

> What renders a Pole a Pole? Language, culture, and tradition – to resort to the most banal answers – form, partially at least, our human nature. My son had just turned five when he suddenly acknowledged that not for anything in the whole world would he wish to be a Jew. When I asked him why, he answered without hesitating: 'because it's an ugly word'. In Poland, even a preschool child knows, or perhaps

feels, that 'Jew' is an ugly word. And here we cannot pretend that it is not about our language. Or our culture. And he or she that admires our culture – commits a sin. (Dunin, 2004: 74)

In this way, Dunin highlights the ethical dimension of her and her fellow writers' literary work: to be aware of one's responsibility for reality, to read and write for the purpose of building modern Polish society. More precisely, 'to see Poland as it may become – the country that after half a century in the communist waiting room is confronted at last with the symptoms of classic modernity, but also, at the same time, with the revision of high modernism.' This is the country 'that has not yet finished its play with tradition' (Dunin, 2004: 6).

Quo vadis Polonia, or the Rebuilding of a New State?

In Poland after the fall of communism, it is easier to process the various traumas tied up with the country's Polish-Jewish history. However, here the attitude toward Jewishness becomes a litmus test for modern Polish democracy. Insofar as the writers discussed here aspire – regardless of their ethnic descent – to something more than saving old-time Judaica from oblivion, I believe they reflect the tension in the Polish population between cultural pluralism on the one hand, and a feeling of uniform national identity on the other. In this connection, 'absent' and 'virtual' Jewishness are two sides of the same coin. More importantly, the writers' *boundary encounters* amount to *boundary crossings*, which, in turn, indicate an increased knowledge about how 'others' think and react when faced with questions of identity; their pluralistic orientation points to the significance of facilitating forums and meeting places where one can converse about identity and the formation of identity across differences without being afraid that one's 'otherness' shall disqualify one from having a point of view. In a word, the boundary encounters and crossings are meaningful because they are dialogic.

As a 'literary' response to the antidemocratic trends in late communist and post-totalitarian Poland, writers such as Szewc, Bolecka, Lubkiewicz-Urbanonowicz, Rymkiewicz, Głowiński, Krall, Grynberg and Dunin contribute – each in his or her own way – to a deconstruction of Jewish as well as other well-established, minority-related threatening enemy images.[11] Indeed, the writers' boundary encounters and dialogical attempts at actualizing the multiplicity of ethnicity and lifestyles that existed, and still exist, in Polish culture may be understood as the very basis for a literary project of modernization. This project entails, above all, the building – or rebuilding – of a democratic and tolerant state.

Notes

1. As indicated by Przemysław Czapliński (*Polska do wymiany. Późna nowoczesność i nasze wielkie narracje*, 2009), we should perhaps 'begin with brotherhood, because [Polish] literature after 1989 has treated freedom as something given, but brotherhood – as something problematic'.
2. For a bibliographical overview, see Stephen Corrsin's 'Works on Polish-Jewish relations published since 1990: A selective bibliography', *Antisemitism and Its Opponents in Modern Poland*. (ed.) R. Blobaum, 2005, London, 326–341.
3. I have borrowed this term from Ruth Gruber, who poses the following question in her book *Virtually Jewish: Reinventing Jewish Culture in Europe* (2002): How can there be a visible and perhaps even growing Jewish presence in post-totalitarian Poland without the significant presence of Jews? For some, Gruber explains, the process is a way of filling in communist blanks; for others, it is a means of coming to terms with the Nazi legacy or a key to building a democratic and tolerant state. Here sincere efforts to study or reintegrate what has been lost, destroyed or forgotten coexist with superficiality, slogans, lip service and show.
4. Consider Bakhtin (1986: 7) on how dialogic interrelations take place on the boundaries between cultures and are the sites of 'the most intense and productive life of culture'. A different, strange culture opens up in a fuller and more profound way when viewed through the eyes of another. Significantly, one meaning can reveal its depths when it comes into contact with another, alien meaning: It is as if a dialogue starts between them that overcomes the closed and one-sided nature of these meanings.
5. According to the *Jewish Virtual Library* (2006), there are only about 3200 self-described Jews living in Poland today, a country of 39 million – Online document: http://www.jewishvirtuallibrary.org/jsource/Judaism/jewpop.html.
6. For an explication of Bakhtin's concept of 'heterochrony' (*raznovremennost'*), see Morson and Emerson (1990: 48–49).
7. In Poland, this figure is deeply rooted not only in nationalist-rightist ideology, but also within the Catholic tradition. See, among others, Nowicka (1991) and Adamczuk and Zdaniewicz (1993).
8. In this connection, 'Uniate' denotes a member of the Uniate Church; that is, the Christian community in Eastern Europe that acknowledges papal supremacy but retains its own liturgy.
9. For various views on anti-Semitism in Poland before and after communism, see Meducki (1997), Machcewicz (1997), Steinlauf (1997) and Gross (2001, 2006).
10. Warlikowski and Krall have continued their joint exploration of the Polish-Jewish theme with the 2008 stage production of *(A)polonia*. Here, the director juxtaposes the writer's reportage about a Polish woman (Apollonia), who was killed by the Nazis for having hidden a large number of Jews, with a modern story about a Jewish woman who kills a Palestinian child in present-day Israel. Krall (2009) comments, 'Because Warlikowski bestows upon factual literature the status of art, there is a chance that people will treat life itself with more seriousness. That they will treat it with the same seriousness as they do with invention.'
11. Among other intellectuals and writers that promote a new mindset when it comes to respecting minority cultures and destabilizing old anti-Jewish prejudice, a learning process that includes the history of Poland's multi-religious and multinational past from before 1939, are Michał Czajkowski, Maria Janion, Leon Kieres, Tomasz Kitliński, Dorota Krawczyńska, Paweł

Leszkowicz, Eugenia Prokop-Janiec, Hanna Świda-Ziemba, Bronisław Świderski, and Joanna Tokarska-Bakir, as well as the late Stanisław Musiał and Jacek Kuroń.

References

Adamczuk, L. and Zdaniewicz, W. (eds) (1993) *Religiousness of the Polish People*. Warsaw: SAC.

Ansky, S. (2002) *The Dybbuk and Other Writings*. New Haven, CT: Yale University Press.

Bakhtin, M. (1986) Response to a question from the *Novyi Mir* editorial staff. In C. Emerson and M. Holquist (eds) *Speech Genres and Other Late Essays* (pp. 1–9). Austin, TX: University of Texas Press.

Błoński, J. (1990) The poor Poles look at the ghetto [1987]. In A. Polonsky (ed.) *"My Brother's Keeper?" Recent Polish Debates on the Holocaust* (pp. 34–52). Oxford: Routledge.

Bolecka, A. (1994) *Biały kamień*. Warsaw: Wydawnictwo Szpak.

Corrsin, S. (2005) Works on Polish-Jewish relations published since 1990: A selective bibliography. In R. Blobaum (ed.) *Antisemitism and Its Opponents in Modern Poland* (pp. 326–341). Ithaca, NY: Cornell University Press.

Czapliński, P. (2009) *Polska do wymiany. Późna nowoczesność i nasze wielkie narracje*. Warsaw: Wydawnictwo W.A.B.

Dąbrowski, M. (2006) Fantazmat żydowski w literaturze polskiej. In M. Dąbrowski and A. Molisak (eds) *Pisarze polsko-żydowscy XX wieku. Przybliżenie* (pp. 7–31). Warsaw: Elipsa.

Dunin, K. (2004) *Czytając Polskę. Literatura polska po roku 1989 wobec dylematów nowoczesności*. Warsaw: Wydawnictwo W.A.B.

Dunin, K. (2009) Sklep z Żydówkami. In Zespół KP (eds) *Polityka literatury. Przewodnik krytyki politycznej* (pp. 270–279). Warsaw: Wydawnictwo krytyki politycznej.

Głowiński, M. (2005) *The Black Seasons*. Evanston, IL: Northwestern University Press. (For the Polish original, see M. Głowiński (1998) *Czarne sezony*. Warsaw: Open.)

Gross, J.T. (2001) *Neighbours: The Destruction of the Jewish Community in Jedwabne, Poland*. Princeton, NJ: Princeton University Press.

Gross, J.T. (2006) *Fear: Anti-Semitism in Poland after Auschwitz: An Essay in Historical Interpretation*. Princeton, NJ: Princeton University Press.

Gruber, R. (2002) *Virtually Jewish: Reinventing Jewish Culture in Europe*. Berkeley, CA: University of California Press.

Grynberg, H. (2003) *Monolog polsko-żydowski*. Wołowiec: Wydawnictwo Czarne.

Grynberg, H. (2004) Wojna polsko-żydowska. In H. Grynberg (ed.) *Uchodźcy* (pp. 145–152). Warsaw: Świat Książki.

Krall, H. (2007) Dybbuk (excerpts). Transl. C. Garbowski – Online document: http://www.polishwriting.net/index.php?id=31. Accessed 24 July 2010. (For Polish original, see H. Krall (1995) Dybuk. In H. Krall (ed.) *Dowody na istnienie*. Poznań: Wydawnictwo a5).

Krall, H. (2009) Interview in *Gazeta Wyborcza* (Duży Format), 16 May – Online document: http://wyborcza.pl/1,99220,6614675,Krall_i_Warlikowski_o__A_polonii.html. Accessed 24 July 2010.

Lubkiewicz-Urbanowicz, T. (1997–1998) *Boża podszewka*, 1–2. Opole: Prószyński i S-ka SA.

Machcewicz, P. (1997) Antisemitism in Poland in 1956. In A. Polonsky *et al.* (eds) *Poles, Jews, Socialists: The Failure of an Ideal* (Polin 9) (pp. 170–183). London: The Littman Library of Jewish Civilization.

Meducki, S. (1997) The Pogrom of Kielce on 4 July 1946. In A. Polonsky *et al.* (eds) *Poles, Jews, Socialists: The Failure of an Ideal* (= *Polin 9*) (pp. 158–169). London: The Littman Library of Jewish Civilization.

Michlic, J.B. (2006) *Poland's Threatening Other: The Image of the Jew from 1880 to the Present*. Lincoln, NB: University of Nebraska Press.

Morson, G.S. and Emerson, C. (1990) *Mikhail Bakhtin: Creation of a Prosaics*. Stanford, CA: Stanford University Press.

Nowicka, E. (1991) Polak-Katolik: O związkach polskości z Katolicyzmem w społecznej świadomości Polaków. In E. Nowicka (ed.) *Religia a obcość* (pp. 117–123). Krakow: Wydawnictwo NOMOS.

Rymkiewicz, J.M. (1994) *The Final Station: Umschlagplatz*. New York: Farrar Straus and Giroux. (For Polish original, see J.M. Rymkiewicz (1988) *Umschlagplatz*. Paris: Instytut Literacki).

Segel, H. (1996) *Stranger in Our Midst: Images of the Jew in Polish Literature*. Ithaca, NY: Cornell University Press.

Steinlauf, M. (1997) *Bondage to the Dead: Poland and the Memory of Holocaust*. Syracuse, NY: Syracuse University Press.

Szewc, P. (1999) *Annihilation*. Normal, IL: Dalkey Archive Press. (For Polish original, see P. Szewc (1987) *Zagłada*, Warsaw: Czytelnik).

Tokarska-Bakir, J. (2003) O czymś, co zginęło i szuka imienia. In *Tygodnik Powszechny*, 36 – Online document: http://www.teatry.art.pl/!recenzje/dybuk_war/oczyms.htm. Accessed 24 July 2010.

Tokarska-Bakir, J. (2008) *Legenda o krwi. Antropologia przesądu*. Warsaw: W.A.B.

Ubertowska, A. (2007) *Świadectwo – trauma – głos. Literackie reprezentacje holokaustu*. Kraków: Universitas.

Warlikowski, K. (2003) Interview in *Tygodnik Powszechny*, 38 – Online document: http://www.teatry.art.pl/!rozmowy/dybukc.htm. Accessed 24 July 2010.

Conclusion
Discursive Negotiations of Cultural Identity and Europe's Eastern Rim

Ljiljana Šarić

The tradition of dividing Europe into several regions is centuries old. Such politically and culturally loaded 'zoning' has always demonstrated the drawing of mental maps and a hierarchy established among countries and their alliances. These tendencies have been reflected on and contested in the past: for example, one chapter of this volume (Hudabiunigg) examines the works of the Croatian author Miroslav Krleža, who presented an alternative view of the European continent that rejects defining a single center in the West and referring to other territories as the periphery. Krleža advocated representing Europe as a territory with two poles, which would help to evaluate the cultural achievements of Europe's eastern and southern countries on their own merits.

The notion of Europe's eastern rim proposed in this volume seeks to avoid the connotations inherent in the terms *Mitteleuropa*, *Central Europe* and *Eastern Europe*. In the impetuous flow of events that has saturated the political life of Eastern Europe for the past several decades, the cultural-identity construction of the Eastern European countries has been evolving at the same time as the changing relations among these countries, as well as the relations between them and the rest of Europe. Nations have been forced to find their place in the modern political environment and choose the message they broadcast to the world community, as well as the language of delivering this message. Today, the west-oriented vector of joining the European Union has proved to be the most attractive to the majority of countries on Europe's eastern rim. However, after the initial stage of nation-building in the 1990s, the countries of southeast Europe found themselves in different positions regarding the possibility of joining the European Union. Among all the former Yugoslav states, only Slovenia was included in the 2004 European Union enlargement. Other countries that have applied to join the European Union have remained (potential) candidates. All of these tendencies have seriously impacted the process of creating these countries' cultural identity, and in particular the images and value systems that dominate in their societies.

Public discourse is a challenging arena for illuminating the process of cultural-identity transformation within the societies of Europe's eastern

Conclusion

rim and, at the same time, for supplying it with a definite direction. Modes of identity construction such as deconstruction, reconstruction, reformulation and invention have acquired special characteristics under the political transformations that have been taking place in the countries considered in this book, and under the increasing political interaction between these countries and the European Union.

Because of the importance of this west-oriented vector for the countries of Europe's eastern rim, it is essential that the diverse perception of southeast European countries and the relations between insiders and outsiders in the European Union enlargement process be reflected in eastern and western European public discourse. This discourse is the topic of the research presented in this volume.

The relations between the countries conceptualized as insiders and outsiders in the European Union enlargement are related to certain discursive means, which in turn construct the linguistic and conceptual dimensions of shaping the vector for construction, reconstruction, invention and reinvention of national and cultural identities. This book has approached these issues with reference to such concepts as Conceptual Metaphor Theory, Conceptual Blending Theory and Discourse Metaphor Analysis. Critical Discourse Analysis (CDA) considers the bilateral impact of processes taking place in both a nation's public discourse and its social environment. Language is considered to be not only a means of reflecting the trends in forming a nation's cultural identity, but also a powerful tool to be able to influence this identity and to set and maintain its certain direction. Within CDA, grammatical and lexical choices are considered crucial for implementing these processes because they are a means of shaping discursive reality.

The first part of this book concentrates on models of formulating images of the Self and the Other in the old and new European Union member states and transformations of these images influenced by political and social processes. The second part focuses on discourse related to the former Yugoslav countries. These chapters analyze various media corpora and follow the discursive identity formulation practices related to the former Yugoslav countries in their own and foreign public spaces. The research primarily focuses on media discourses as expressions of current political debates and indicators of social and cultural changes. Several analyses have linked the discourse-analysis approach to social science research on public opinion and sociocultural stereotypes. The contributions in the third part of the book concentrate on literary texts that thematize contested national and cultural identities.

The analyses in this volume corroborate the appropriateness of focusing on the discursive variations taking place in the countries considered instead of perceiving public discourse as a stable phenomenon. The social environment is saturated with competing concepts, symbols and metaphors that evolve and replace one another over time.

This book has shown that the trends in public discourse concerning the countries of Europe's eastern rim differ not only in the historical dimension but also geographically. The manners of explaining events connected with these countries have distinctive features within and outside the region. For a long time, external public discourse on the Balkans has been saturated with numerous stereotypes perpetuated by foreign journalists and even scholars, which have had an impact on the attitude toward these countries and foreign policymaking. In addition, this has partially influenced public discourse within the region and thus nations' perception of each other and even of themselves, interspersed with numerous simplified and stereotypical notions (the chapter by Šarić). The text analyses in this volume show that several concepts of perceiving and representing the Self and the Other within Europe's eastern rim can be observed. The outline of the notion of 'the Balkans', which is contrasted to that of 'Europe' and other manifestations of the Self and the Other, are reflected in media, expressed by means of certain linguistic, literary and visual tools.

The analysis in this volume demonstrates the diversity of techniques used in media to reflect the identity concepts encountered in society and to encapsulate matters of subjective vision and attitude. It also shows the degree to which the media have the power to affect social opinion and promote various stances. The direction of this influence, however, is not so predictable. Within this volume, the case of relations between Poland and Germany is considered (the chapter by Manz): After Poland entered the EU, sore points appear to have been aggravated by the mass media, which has nourished mutual aversion.

Using metaphors has become the most popular tool among journalists: the concepts of LEADERS, MOTORS, SCHOOL and FAMILY in the French press (the chapter by Buch and Helfrich) are used to express dominance and hierarchy within the EU; the metaphors of LOCOMOTIVE, ENGINE and ADVOCATE appear in press coverage of Lithuania's and Germany's positions within the borders of the European Union. Lithuanian journalists have enriched public discourse with metaphors specific to their own culture (the chapter by Petraškaitė-Pabst), thus linking the notions of Lithuania and the European Union more closely in the perception of the population. This volume also provides research devoted to the rhetoric used by the Polish press to explain Poland's attitude to the Balkan countries joining the EU (the chapter by Bąk): The sources analyzed contain the metaphors CONTAINER, ROAD-MOVEMENT, HOME and FAMILY. Polish discourse views European Union candidate countries as equal participants instead of representing them as potential victims of EU expansion. Discussion of Turkey joining the European Union was also characterized by specific discursive devices: The chapter by Musolff shows that the media formulated three possible scenarios for the development of relations between Turkey and the European Union, and each of these was supplemented with the appropriate rhetoric; for example, presenting Turkey as an outsider was reinforced by means of FAMILY, HOUSE and CLUB metaphors, and the idea that Turkey should amend its performance in different fields was supported with the PROGRESS metaphor.

As a common feature of the social environment of all European countries, discursive identity construction has also been flourishing in the former Yugoslavia. Slovenia's position today as an insider in the European Union has drawn researchers' attention to the special features of internal and external public discourse on this situation. Researchers have claimed that for several years Slovenian media attention has been directed toward separating the country from the rest of its Yugoslav 'brothers' in the popular perception. In other former Yugoslav countries, cultural identity construction has been evolving rapidly, also reflected in and forced by means of public discourse. The countries have tried to define their new 'brothers' and 'enemies' in view of today's political environment, which developed through the conflicts of the 1990s and then into the discussion of the possibility of joining the European Union. This reorientation from glorifying the former Yugoslav 'brotherhood' to aspiring to join the European Union has produced corresponding trends in public discourse. Within this volume, the chapter by Šarić shows how the content of the term *the Balkans* has evolved together with political reorientation, in some cases becoming a negative label. The chapter by Kuna and Kuna examines how the naming strategies for the former 'brothers' reflect the political and social trends that use media to signal that the conflicts have not yet been settled, having changed from warfare to discourse confrontation.

The research shows that the mass media serve as a powerful tool in the struggle of local political elites: for example, Winland demonstrates how Bosnian Croats are influenced by anti-Muslim rhetoric 'ordered' by the local political forces. A set of tools for political manipulation is not limited by using the texts themselves; instead, it is executed through both tangible and intangible devices. The chapter by Radanović Felberg on Serbian and Montenegrin newspapers reveals the techniques used to support the governments of Serbia and Montenegro and to promote their ideological positions. Vezovnik's study shows that during the period when the opportunity for Slovenia to join the European Union was discussed actively in society the symbols used for representing Slovenia as a European country coincided to some extent with those used in nineteenth-century Krekist rhetoric.

The process of shaping a nation's cultural identity is also observable in modern literature. According to the research in the third part of this volume, contemporary literature in Poland, Montenegro and Croatia has been contributing to the evolution of the nations' cultural identity, providing fresh, uncommitted points of view. The analyses consider examples from modern Polish literature (Grimstad's chapter), in which the current trends in the nation's cultural identity are reflected, as well as traditionalism and modernism in Montenegrin society (the analysis by Jovanović Lauvstad) with regard to identity, and reflection of a new perception of East and West represented in the works of an outstanding Croatian author (the chapter by Hudabiunigg).

Thus, the forces of literature seem to be strong enough to designate the direction of these nations' perception of the Self and the Other and the formation of their identities in general. The focus of public discourse, and especially modern works of literature, extends beyond political issues, touching on gender, nationality and other aspects of self-presentation in modern society. The analyses in Part III refer to Balša Brković's book *Privatna Galerija* (Private Gallery), which reflects the transformations taking place in the Montenegrin society (see the chapter by Jovanović Lauvstad): The author has become a herald of the trends that were already spreading with the evolution of the nation's identity, although this was not reflected clearly enough in public discourse. Grimstad's analysis shows how 'the Jewish question' has been reflected in Polish public discourse and how the image of a Jewish enemy has been dealt with.

The research in this volume corroborates the bilateral influence of trends taking place in the evolution of nations' cultural identities and the public discourse through which they are expressed. By touching on current tendencies in public discourse on the countries and mental and linguistic maps of Europe's eastern rim, this volume outlines aspects that will foster further research. The evolution of public discourse in Europe remains a perpetual and dynamic process, and the discursive construction of cultural identity will continue to supply new issues that demand further research.